POLITICAL PHILOSOPHY NOW

Chief Editor of the Series:
Howard Williams, Aberystwyth University, Wales

Associate Editors:
Wolfgang Kersting, University of Kiel, Germany
Steven B. Smith, Yale University, USA
Peter Nicholson, University of York, England
Renato Cristi, Wilfrid Laurier University, Waterloo, Canada

Political Philosophy Now is a series which deals with authors, topics and periods in political philosophy from the perspective of their relevance to current debates. The series presents a spread of subjects and points of view from various traditions, which include European and New World debates in political philosophy.

POLITICAL PHILOSOPHY NOW

Kant on Sublimity and Morality

Joshua Rayman

UNIVERSITY OF WALES PRESS • CARDIFF • 2012

© Joshua Rayman, 2012

All rights reserved. No part of this book may be reproduced in any material form (including photocopying or storing it in any medium by electronic means and whether or not transiently or incidentally to some other use of this publication) without the written permission of the copyright owner except in accordance with the provisions of the Copyright, Designs and Patents Act 1988. Applications for the copyright owner's written permission to reproduce any part of this publication should be addressed to the University of Wales Press, 10 Columbus Walk, Brigantine Place, Cardiff, CF10 4UP.

www.uwp.co.uk

British Library Cataloguing-in-Publication Data
A catalogue record for this book is available from the British Library.

ISBN 978-0-7083-2125-6
eISBN 978-0-7083-2507-0

The right of Joshua Rayman to be identified as author of this work has been asserted in accordance with sections 77, 78 and 79 of the Copyright, Designs and Patents Act 1988.

Typeset by Mark Heslington Ltd, Scarborough, North Yorkshire
Printed in the UK by MPG Books Group Ltd

Contents

Acknowledgements vii
Abbreviations viii
Preface ix

Part I: Genealogy of the Kantian Sublime

1 Longinus and the Origins of the Sublimity–Morality Connection 3

2 Sublimity and Morality in Eighteenth-Century British Aesthetics 13

3 Kant's German Precursors 34

Part II: Kant on Sublimity and Morality

4 The Moral Functions of Sublimity in the Kantian System 51

5 Replies to Objections to Sublimity's Moral Functions 93

Part III: Sublimity and Morality in German Idealism and Recent Continental Philosophy

6 Post-Kantian Continental Work on Sublimity and Morality 143
   I Sublimity and Morality in German Idealism
   II Sublimity and Morality in Contemporary Continental Philosophy

Notes 191
Bibliography 201
Index 211

Acknowledgements

In recognizing both finite and infinite debts to those without whom this book could not exist, I only postpone the inevitable default. My debts to Allison Moore, Isolde Rayman, Bill Rayman and Abby Wasserman are infinite and unmeasurable. To Andrew Cutrofello, I owe the original impetus for the project, which was hatched in his graduate seminar on Kant and Continental aesthetics, as well as continued advice and support, and a critical eye in reading the excised précis of the 'Analytic of the Sublime'. I would also like to thank Craig Greenman and Erik Gardner for our many useful discussions of Kant, sublimity and morality. Finally, I would like to thank the series editor Howard Williams for suggesting that I expand an article submitted to *Kantian Review* into this book, the University of Wales Press commissioner Sarah Lewis for working with me to bring the book to press and anonymous reviewers at the University of Wales Press for helping me to sharpen my arguments, holding me to the original format of my proposal and assuring the accuracy of my translations and uses of secondary sources.

Abbreviations

Immanuel Kant:
CPR *Critique of Pure Reason*
CPrR *Critical of Practical Reason*
CJ *Critique of Judgment*
GMM *Grounding for the Metaphysics of Morals*
MM *Metaphysics of Morals*
OFBS *Observations on the Feeling of the Beautiful and Sublime*

Theodor Adorno:
AT *Ästhetische Theorie* (German pagination)
GS *Gesammelte Schriften*

G. W. F. Hegel:
H. Hegel, *Ästhetik* (German pagination)

Longinus:
L Longinus, *On the Sublime*

Preface

> How such a synthetic practical proposition is possible *a priori* and why it is necessary are tasks whose solution does not lie any longer within the bounds of a metaphysics of morals. (Immanuel Kant, *Grounding for the Metaphysics of Morals*, *Grundlegung zur Metaphysik der Sitten*, GMM: Ak.445)

One of the more interesting questions in Kant's famous moral and epistemological works is what boundary conditions or horizons enable his moral and epistemological claims. What struck me in my first reading of Immanuel Kant's 'Analytic of the Sublime' in 1997 was that it seemed to assign itself a crucial role in his morality. Yet, the extant scholarship either denied sublimity's positive role in morality or minimized it on grounds that the sublime is merely an aesthetic analogue of morality, and hence unable to serve any moral functions. The primary aim of this book is to argue against these readings of Kantian sublimity and morality by examining the work that morality does in the sublime and, conversely, the work the sublime does in morality. I show that the relationship between sublimity and morality is closer and more important than has been understood. The sublime fills an essential function in the moral project guiding Kant's critical works and it does so at times precisely in virtue of its being an aesthetic analogue to morality.

Historically, the sublime has been understood as the idea, concept or experience of what is great in magnitude, power, number, nobility or elevation. As I demonstrate in my genealogy of the sublime, moral readings of the sublime date back to the earliest extant text on the sublime, that of the second century CE writer Longinus. The European revival of Longinus in the late seventeenth and eighteenth centuries inspired work on the sublime by nearly every famous writer of the era. But Kant (1724–1804) is certainly the most systematic and influential of the thousands to have written on the sublime in the modern era. Kant broke the historical mold of rambling, unsystematic commentaries on the topic by offering a systematic framework for considering the sublime and, accordingly, his work is far more influential than that of any other writer on the sublime since Longinus. This is not to say that Kant was wholly or even largely original. Even in construing sublimity in moral terms, as he did in his main works on the sublime, *Observations on the Feeling of the Beautiful and Sublime* (*Beobachtungen über das Gefühl des Schönen und Erhabenen*, OFBS, 1764) and the 'Analytic of the Sublime' in the *Critique of Judgment* (*Kritik der Urteilskraft*, third *Critique*, CJ, 1790), Kant was only following a long line of similar writers. His examples and descriptions of sublimity and its relation to morality borrow heavily from the aesthetic tradition dating back to Longinus. However, James Kirwan exaggerates greatly in saying that, with one significant exception, Kant's 'description of the range of the sublime, and even his grounding of it, represent . . . no advance on the writings of his predecessors in the field' (Kirwan 2005: 53), that 'Kant's text inaugurates nothing' (Kirwan 2004: 4) and that Kant did much less to set subsequent debates on aesthetics, which, Kirwan alleges, are dominated by Hegelian, rather than Kantian readings, than to end eighteenth-century debates to which his work belongs (ibid.: 1–2). Against Kirwan, I will argue that Kantian sublimity differs from the tradition both formally and in its systematic moral functions, that no previous account of sublimity is associated with a morality of the Kantian style and that the Kantian sublime has been immensely influential. I agree with Paul Guyer that 'Kant's interpretation of both the beautiful and sublime differed from what was commonplace' (Guyer 1993: 254), but I would like to ascribe the main difference in Kant's interpretation of the sublime, and hence the source of his importance and originality, to his systematic framework and transcendental methodology, as in his epistemology, not to the details of his claims. By incorporating the sublime within the epistemological, ethical, aesthetic and teleological structures of his critical system, Kant adds something new and profound to empiricist and rationalist debates concerning sublimity. However, in associating the originality of Kantian sublimity with its moral functions, I do not accept Kirwan's thesis that Kantian sublimity's novelty consists in its substitution of 'a genuinely moral import [for] . . . the commonly *felt* moral import of the experience of sublimity', which Kirwan describes as 'of the greatest significance to the history not only of the sublime but also of aesthetics in general' (Kirwan 2005: 53). Kantian morality is in my view significantly more justifiable than the casual virtue ethics and utilitarianism of previous eighteenth-century accounts of sublimity, yet Kirwan begs the question as to what constitutes genuine moral import, feeling, as in these accounts, or reason, as in the Kantian account. For the former, what is commonly felt as morally significant *is eo ipso* morally significant. Kantian sublimity's moral innovation consists not in adding 'genuine' moral meaning, but in systematizing traditional accounts of the sublime by reference to transcendental reflective judgements and a synthetic a priori morality. This systematic turn transforms the debate in many ways, not the least of which are the introduction of justificatory and explanatory standards to a largely uncritical, descriptive set of discourses and the enforcement of greater consistency and interconnection with moral and epistemological questions.

Kant is by many criteria the most influential philosopher of the past three centuries, at least on other philosophers, as evidenced by the fact that as of April 2011 there are 17,166 references to Kant in the *Philosopher's Index*, four thousand more than Aristotle, six thousand more than Plato and seven thousand more than Hegel or Heidegger; and far more American Philosophical Association papers are on Kant than on any other philosopher. Within the smaller field of aesthetics, Kant is equally influential. Although Mary J. Gregor could write as late as 1987 of 'the long-standing neglect of the *Critique of Judgment* as a whole' (CJ: xvi), at present it is fair to say only that the *Critique of Judgment* has been neglected *relative to* Kant's epistemological and moral works and that the 'Analytic of the Sublime' has been neglected relative to the 'Analytic of the Beautiful', for the *Philosopher's Index* lists 1,324 citations on Kant and aesthetics, 517 on Kant and beauty or the beautiful, and roughly 300 citations of Kant and sublime or sublimity (depending on search order), nearly half of all references to the sublime and sublimity.

Of course, citations entail neither influence, nor accuracy. If genuine influence, defined as the effects of correct perceptions of Kantian sublimity on later developments, presupposes accuracy of reception, then it is indeed arguable that Kant's influence in the realm of sublimity, particularly in Continental philosophy, art history and comparative literature over the thirty years following the publication of Jacques Derrida's and Jean-François Lyotard's readings of the 'Analytic of the Sublime', is significantly weaker than it seems, because many readings of the Kantian sublime mischaracterize his views. But this standard is surely too stringent, particularly in philosophy, where interpretations are so contested. Thus, for instance, it would follow from this argument that Jean-François Lyotard's line by line *'explication de text'* of the 'Analytic of the Sublime', *Lessons on the Analytic of the Sublime*, was not genuinely influenced by Kant's 'Analytic of the Sublime', since it misconstrues the relation between Kantian sublimity and morality. But surely we can agree that work is influenced by Kant if its terms, concepts and arguments derive primarily from him. By this standard, the Kantian sublime is extremely influential, even in its derivative moments, for it is the central reference point and terminological/conceptual source for post-Kantian accounts of the sublime.

This book follows a tripartite, temporal plan. I begin with a genealogy of the sublimity–morality relationship prior to Kant in order to see in what respects his accounts both depend on and depart from those of the tradition. I then give a detailed argument for the role of sublimity in Kantian morality. Finally, I examine how post-Kantian Continental readings of sublimity and morality both build on and diverge from Kant. Given the great body of available texts, my genealogies of pre-Kantian and post-Kantian sublimity and morality are necessarily selective. In chapter 1, I discuss the ancient Greek critic Longinus; in chapter 2, I discuss Joseph Addison, the third earl of Shaftesbury, Frances Hutcheson, Edmund Burke and several other major figures in eighteenth-century British aesthetics; and in chapter 3, I discuss the eighteenth-century German aesthetic tradition of Alexander Baumgarten and Moses Mendelssohn. The purpose of this genealogy of pre-Kantian sublimity and morality is to show the philosophical context in which Kantian sublimity arose, to augment sparsely detailed views of Kant's highly derivative relations to his predecessors, to correct common misconceptions of Kant and the history of sublimity and to demonstrate that empiricist accounts of sublimity and morality lack the critical and evaluative dimensions necessary to transcend mere psychological description. More specifically, I attempt to restore Longinus' importance to the history of sublimity, to question claims to Kantian sublimity's reliance on Shaftesbury and Hutcheson, to deflate exaggerated accounts of Edmund Burke's importance, to introduce Alexander Baumgarten's accounts of sublimity to an Anglo-American audience for perhaps the first time, to detail many of Kant's debts to Longinus and eighteenth-century criticism and to trace the weakness of pre-Kantian sublimity to its failure not only to describe experience accurately, as Edmund Burke charges, but also to show why genuinely evaluative moral accounts, as opposed to descriptions of moral experience, require some reference to sublimity for their execution and justification.

In the middle section of the book, chapters 4 and 5, I examine in detail Kant's own accounts of the relationship of sublimity to morality, both within the 'Analytic of the Sublime' in the third *Critique* and outside the third *Critique*. Throughout the section, I distinguish my position from that of extant Kant scholarship. My account is heavily detailed in order to convey the significance and functions of morality in Kant's accounts of sublimity throughout his career. Failure to attend to the full range of Kant's remarks on sublimity is at the basis of deflationary accounts of Kantian sublimity as 'merely' analogous to morality. I develop and defend my claims to the systematic moral functions of Kantian sublimity, examine potential problems in sublimity's involvement with respect and moral feeling and refute a series of objections to sublimity's role in morality, including anthropomorphic and psychologistic criticisms of Kant.

The final section examines the legacy of Kantian sublimity and morality in post-Kantian German idealism and late twentieth-century Continental philosophy. I show that while the moral functions of Kantian sublimity were understood immediately by his successors, recent Continental philosophers, with the notable exceptions of Theodor W. Adorno and Jacques Derrida, have interpreted these functions in ways opposite to Kant. Without speculating on the psychological grounds for such misreadings, I argue that Continental readings of Kantian sublimity have opposed claims to its positive moral functions on the assumption that a moral role would subvert sublimity's ability to radically deconstruct the dichotomies between the limited and the unlimited, the bounded and the boundless and the rational and the irrational. But this assumption is unwarranted. As I demonstrate, Kant's close association of sublimity and morality merely extends the subversive effects of sublimity to morality. By showing that Kantian morality depends on the experience of sublimity, without thereby undermining their claim to universality, I show that there can be no absolute boundary between morality and aesthetics or subjectivity and objectivity in the Kantian critical system.

In making these arguments, I rely on primary sources. Where I use secondary sources, my primary concern is to treat the strongest arguments against my position. Considerations of space precluded my customary exhaustive treatment of secondary sources. All translations of Kant are my own, though I have consulted other translations, especially those of Pluhar and Guyer.[1] Not everyone will agree with the choices made in these translations. In general, they have been guided by the view that Kant's German should be discernible as much as possible in the English. Where Kant offers a gloss on the meaning of one of his technical terms, usually in Latin, I use the English correlate as much as possible. For instance, he glosses the term *Vorstellung* as '*repraesentatio*'. Hence, I translate *Vorstellung* as 'representation', rather than 'presentation', even though the term 'representation' seems to add distinct interpretations (repetition of some original presentation, for one) to the German. My second controversial application of the above principle is to try to replicate in English the natural associations of German words with the same root word. By retaining these etymological relations, I seek to make it clear to the English-speaking reader what is taking place in Kant's text. The consequence of ignoring these etymological relations is that the overriding ideas are lost; indeed, as I discuss in chapter 4, that is what has happened in the recent Cambridge translations of Kant because of their failure to associate the family of terms linked both to sublimity and to determination and determinability (*bestimmen, Bestimmung, Bestimmbarkeit*). One key example of my translation practice is to use the root 'sublim-' wherever possible in translating the various word forms related to the German term *erhaben*; when this practice is too awkward, I use a term related to the primary historical meaning of the Greek, French and German words for the sublime, elevation. Some will object that these word forms have different meanings in German. However, I believe that this move is justified by authorial intention and context, for Kant always uses *erhaben, das Erhabene, die Erhabenheit* and *erheben* in the context of the sublime, sublimity and acts of sublimation or elevation. He expresses this connection clearly in defining the sublime:

> Also heißt die Natur hier erhaben, bloß weil sie die Einbildungskraft zu Darstellung derjenigen Fälle erhebt, in welchen das Gemüth die eigene Erhabenheit seiner Bestimmung selbst über die Natur sich fühlbar machen kann.

Thus nature is called sublime [*erhaben*] here, merely because it elevates [raises, makes sublime, *erhebt*] the imagination to the exhibition of those cases in which the mind can make it possible to feel the proper elevation [sublimity, *Erhabenheit*] of its determination even over nature itself (CJ: 262).

A mixed German-English version of the sentence makes it plain that Kant uses the terms *erhaben/erheben/Erhabenheit* all in the sense of sublime elevation. Nature is *erhaben*, because it *erhebt* the imagination to exhibit cases in which the mind can feel the proper *Erhabenheit* of its determination beyond nature. The verb *erheben* means to raise or elevate, *erhaben* means raised, elevated or sublime and *das Erhabene* and *die Erhabenheit*, like their French and Greek correlates (*sublime*, ὕψος), mean the sublime. In CJ: 262, then, nature's label as sublime derives from its making sublime or 'sublimating' the imagination in order to experience the fact that its essential capacities of freedom transcend nature, even as they have effects in nature.[2] However, I avoid translating *erheben* and *Erhebung* as 'sublimate' or 'sublimation' because they have nothing to do with psychological transference or the unconscious, unlike the twentieth-century psychological term, used by Lacan to refer at times to the sublime. To articulate the systematic functions of sublimity in Kant, we need to recognize his very consistent use of the various forms of *erheben/erhaben/Erhabenheit/Erhaben* to mean sublimity, the sublime or the act of elevating consciousness to the sublime. I make no distinction between the terms 'sublimity' and 'the sublime', and I use the former term more often, primarily for stylistic reasons. However, I would argue that there is no thematic reason to prefer the one term to the other. Most Kant scholars, as Peter Warnek points out, use the term 'the sublime', since 'sublimity' seems to refer to a quality, whereas 'the sublime' refers to a substantive. Yet, Kant himself uses both terms, as well as a host of other terms cognate with '*erhaben*', interchangeably to refer to a subjective experience. *Erhabenheit* (sublimity) appears approximately seventeen times in CJ and *Erhaben/das Erhabene* about as often, with the exception of titles and section headings. The substantive *Erhaben* appears most frequently in the genitive form (usually in the phrase *das Gefühl des Erhabenen*, the feeling of the sublime, but sometimes in the phrases *der Begriff* or *die Idee des Erhabenen*, the concept or the idea of the sublime); verb forms of *erhaben* (uncapitalized: for example, 'I call sublime that which') are by far the most frequent variants of the root word. Nowhere does there appear to be a distinction in how Kant uses the different forms, except that the verb *erheben* refers to the action of raising or elevating the mind to a sublime experience, whereas *erhaben/ Erhabenheit/das Erhabene* all refer to the sublime experience. Hence, there is no good reason to follow other Kant scholars in preferring 'the sublime' to 'sublimity' in Kant.

I recognize that this approach to translation and terminology is imperfect. It sometimes differs from standard translations, it may obscure some distinct uses of cognate terms and it cannot extend to all cognates. Thus, for example, in translating *Stimmung* as attunement, I myself conceal the close relationship between *Stimmung* and *Bestimmung*, determination. But it is because of the indeterminacy of translation, in Quine's phrase, that I prefer literal translations and cognates. For all its flaws, this method both preserves many of the Kantian associations of root words and makes the translations sufficiently transparent to allow the reader minimally versed in Kant's German to know what it is that I am translating. Where the translation is particularly open to significantly different interpretations, I provide parenthetical references to the German words that I am translating.

Part I:
Genealogy of the Kantian Sublime

1 • Longinus and the Origins of the Sublimity–Morality Connection

Eighteenth-century debates on the sublime tell us much about the origins of Kantian sublimity and its connections to morality, for Kant relies heavily on these debates.[1] But many fail to see that eighteenth-century accounts of the sublime themselves rely on the ancient Greek author Longinus (long confused with the neo-Platonist Cassius Longinus c.220–73 CE, author of a rhetoric text (in Burke: 468)). No figure is more important to the history of sublimity. Longinus dictated the terms of all subsequent writing on sublimity and articulated positions that in some respects are more amenable to Kantian morality than any of the important eighteenth-century empiricist and rationalist accounts known to Kant. For this reason, a reading of Longinus serves the historical function of subverting attempts to derive Kantian sublimity from British empiricist aesthetics or to assert the originality of the latter. Reading Longinus also helps to show the origins of Kant's transformation of traditional associations of sublimity and virtue into a critical account of sublimity's functions in a universalistic morality. Longinus' account of the conditions and moral relevance of sublimity prepares the ground for the Kantian critical account in ways that exhibit the limitations of eighteenth-century empiricist aesthetics. Yet, the Longinian account shares many of the limitations of eighteenth-century aesthetics for Kantian morality. Longinus' acceptance of Aristotelian virtue ethics, his failure to warrant his assertions and his lack of a systematic critique of experience make it impossible for him to show how subjective experience might operate within a universal morality. As a result, his account of sublimity remains a mere collection of loosely associated, unargued claims. Hence, we will see that Kant's revisions of the Longinian tradition provide an explanation for sublimity and assign sublimity specific functions within his critical morality.

The sublimity craze in early modern Europe began with Nicolas Boileau's (1636–1711) phenomenally successful 1674 French translation of Longinus' work, περι ὕψους. The English and German translations of the text, following the French *Traité du sublime*, were *On the Sublime* and *Vom Erhabenen*, respectively, meaning 'on height' or 'on the elevated' (see Wood: 189). Although the tenth-century Parisinus manuscript of Longinus' text, missing about one thousand lines, had already appeared in three editions and been translated into Latin and Italian by the end of the sixteenth century, and into English by John Hall in 1652 (Grube: vii; Wood: 10), Boileau's translation 'produced a spectacular reaction'; for the next 150 years, Longinus was a 'household name' (Russell, introduction to Longinus 1964: xliii), so much so that Russell can claim that 'European literary criticism' owes its second-greatest debt, after Aristotle, to Longinus (Russell: ix).[2] Longinus' influence was particularly strong in England and within a few years the sublime began to appear in the writings of all the great English critics, from John Dryden in 1676 to John Dennis in 1701 and 1704, Alexander Pope in 1709, the third earl of Shaftesbury in 1711, Joseph Addison in 1711–12, Jonathan Swift in 1733 and Sir Joshua Reynolds in the 1760s (Russell: xlii). The sublime also became the focus of British, French and German philosophical work.[3] The most prominent were Edmund Burke's *A Philosophical Inquiry into the Sublime and Beautiful* (1757), Moses Mendelssohn's 'On the sublime and naive in the fine sciences' (1758) and Immanuel Kant's *Observations on the Feeling of the Beautiful and Sublime* (1764) and the 'Analytic of the Sublime' in the *Critique of Judgment* (1790).

From the perspective of modern aesthetics, which lacks access to any of his own ancient sources, Longinus did much more than merely inspire this torrent of writing. Indeed, he seems to have set forth the entire framework, subject matter, terminology, methods, definitions and examples used by eighteenth-century writers on the sublime, as well as the specific associations between sublimity and morality.

A partial list of ideas derived from Longinus includes:

- the mathematical and dynamical sublime,
- the methodological determination of the sublime (by reference to examples from classical authors),
- the description of sublimity as universal, elevated, noble, pleasing, boundless, heroic, grand, magnificent, formless, overpowering, a hybrid of nature and rule-governed *techne* and a moral, psychological ('subjective') experience.

(This psychological experience is linked closely to genius, enthusiasm, emotion – but not pity, grief or fear – affects, character, imagination, reason and other mental powers.)

In order to establish the relevance of Longinian sublimity to Kantian morality, it is necessary first to correct conventional accounts that place Longinus within an exclusively rhetorical, rather than psychological or aesthetic, tradition, concerned with identifying the essence of elevation, height or greatness in *speech and writing*, in words rather than images or vast, grand objects (Russell, introduction to Longinus 1964: x–xi; cf. Monk; Wood; Kirwan; Shaw: 5, 12, 71; etc.). The notion that rhetoric is exclusive of psychological and moral questions depends on a misreading of Aristotle. While Aristotelian rhetoric is indeed a linguistic art of rule-governed persuasion centred on proof, Aristotle argues that rhetoric, as a branch of ethics, may also work on character and emotions, and thus involve psychological *and moral* elements (Aristotle, *Rhetoric*: I.1–2). Nor can rhetoric be separated radically from aesthetics, for the persuasive, emotional and psychological elements of rhetoric engage the same mental powers as aesthetics, defined as the study of the images or representations experienced or considered by sensibility (Greek αἴσθησις, *aisthesis*), imagination, understanding and reason. Now if one turns away from the Aristotelian text and defines rhetoric differently as a non-psychological, non-aesthetic form of *techne*, as in Monk and others, then Longinus certainly does not offer a merely rhetorical reading of sublimity, for his account of sublimity as a *techne* contingent on mental activity recognizes the significance of practical questions of method and use in public speaking and, above all, 'the essentially moral and psychological basis of the problem . . . how can we develop our capacities to some degree of greatness?' (Russell: x). For Longinus, the moral and psychological task of self-development is simultaneously aesthetic, since words both originate in and conjure up mental representations or images and emotions. The moral function of aesthetic representation derives in part from the motivating, elevating power of these representations. Because ὕψος refers to words that evoke images associated with overpowering enthusiasm and passion, it operates by raising the passive reader violently beyond 'himself' through the affects, rather than by free and rational persuasion. By generating this self-transcendence, sublime experience situates the person in the virtuous position of a higher selflessness. Yet, the emotional force motivating this self-transcendence could be appropriated for all manner of actions, virtuous or otherwise. There is no clear control function regulating what actions sublimity may engender. Images or mental representations (*eidolopoiias*) not only make strong contributions in persuasiveness to 'dignity, elevation and power', but they apply to the mental ideas originative of all speech, and particularly sublime speech, speech 'carried away by enthusiasm [*enthousiasmos*] and passion' (L 1907: XV, 82–3). These affective, imagistic, ideational, rule-governed and linguistic understandings of the sublime demonstrate that Longinus conceives sublimity in moral, aesthetic and psychological terms transcending traditional 'rhetorical' readings of his work.

As befits its place in this Aristotelian 'rhetorical' tradition, the morality developed in Longinian sublimity is primarily the very same Aristotelian virtue ethics still dominant in virtually all eighteenth-century writings on the sublime, including Kant's early work and older elements of the 'Analytic of the Sublime'. Longinus describes sublimity in implicitly Aristotelian ethical terms, arguing that 'sublimity depends upon where [*pou*, the place] and how [*pos*, manner] and the circumstances and that for the sake of which [οὗ ἕνεκα, the motive]' (ibid.: XVI, 92–3). This reference to context, manner, circumstances and motive (final cause, that for the sake of which) could be drawn straight from Aristotle's account of right action (e.g. *Ethics*: II.1106b20, 1109a27, III.1110b33–11a6). Here we have no a priori guide to what context, manner, circumstances and motive are appropriate to sublimity, for the Longinian criteria for judging the sublime exhibit the Aristotelian concern to establish moral standards by reference not solely to reason or universal rules, but to practised moral judgement and the affects of the person as well. This reliance on moral exemplars, developed moral judgement and affects implies either an ideological reference to a foundational standard deemed moral in itself or an infinite regress, where each judgement or moral action is so considered by its reference to a prior, similarly 'justified' judgement. Hence, this reliance on an Aristotelian form of morality is inherently problematic. But if we ask what specific moral virtues sublimity involves, rather than speaking abstractly of moral foundations or virtue in general, we cannot easily associate the excess of Longinian sublimity with many of the moderate Aristotelian virtues. Where there is a clear link, from the very definition of the sublime, is to the Aristotelian virtues

THE SUBLIMITY–MORALITY CONNECTION 7

of greatness and magnanimity, yet this relationship directly connects the traditional account of sublimity to the transcendent form of Kantian sublimity and morality. Longinus argues that sublimity in literature is akin to the 'high-souled' disdain for 'riches, honours, distinctions, sovereignties and all other' external values to men of good sense (L 1907: VII, 54–5). The sublime collapses into admiration of the mortal, the lawless, the shameless, when softened by greed, as in peacetime, we become ignoble 'slaves of pleasure' (ibid.: XLIV, 156–61). Sublimity requires transcendence of mortal pleasures. This view, anticipating Kant, demonstrates that for Longinus, as for Kant, sublimity's relationship to pleasure and the affects consists in the drive to master them, and thereby to transcend the limits of human existence. In this respect, Longinus provides just the dominating, transcendent relationship to the affects called for by the Kantian critical account.

Indeed, Longinus already sets forth the elements of the moral 'transformation' of sublimity that Paul Guyer attributes first to Kant. In distinguishing two types of pre-Kantian eighteenth-century sublimity, the psychological and the theological-moral, Guyer argues that '[w]hat Kant did was to transmute the psychological account into an alternative moral account in which humanity is elevated rather than humbled' (Guyer 1993: 259). As we shall see, there were, in fact, numerous pre-Kantian readings of sublimity as moral elevation. But at least fifteen hundred years earlier, Longinus provided perhaps the first and most influential example of this particular moral reading in describing sublime height or elevation as *transcendence* of the merely human or mortal (a characteristic both of the sublime object and the spectator experiencing the sublime) in imagination's passing beyond the universe and all space to human purpose in this world (L 1907: XXXVI, 136–7; XXXV, 132–5), and in giving a moral reading of this form of transcendence.

The similarities to Kant's moral account of sublimity go much farther. In fact, it can be argued that Longinian categories, ranging from the association of sublimity with self-transcendence to the account of the power struggles of the faculties within the sublime, provide the framework for a Kantian moral reading of sublimity. Longinus and Kant agree that the tension between imagination and reason is definitive of sublimity, that reason and imagination are necessary to it (L 1907: XVI, 94–5), that morality depends on a power struggle between these two mental powers and that sublimity is incompatible with an excess or disorder of the passions, which Kant calls fanaticism (*Schwärmerei*) and Longinus calls παρενθυρσος or false enthusiasm (παθος ακαιρον και κενον), a hollow, untimely 'display of passion', immoderacy (L 1957: III, 6–7), or 'intoxication personal and independent of the subject matter' (L 1907: III, 48–9). Thus, the destruction of a certain unstable, temporary mean or balance between the powers of reason, imagination and the passions destroys the sublime. In allying beauty and sublimity in moral terms (ibid.: XXVII, 96–7), then, Longinus repeatedly describes them both as harmonic phenomena (ibid.: XXVIII, 114–15; XXXIX, 142–3). However, like Kant, he stresses the interplay of tension and release, disorder and order, imagination and reason, rather than simple harmony. If there are not two forms of sublimity at issue here, a simple or naive and a complex style, but only one (and Longinus does not answer this question), the harmony and dissonance described by Longinus might be combined into a single Kantian 'harmony' defined by the unification of contradictions or tensions, as in Sappho's desire to effect 'a concourse of the passions' (ibid.: X, 70–1). But it is certainly the case that for both Longinus and Kant, the tension definitive of sublimity, between sensibility or imagination and reason, is harmonious or morally productive in enabling the spectator's transcendence of sensibility. It might be asked whether the disharmony of sensibility or imagination with reason would always enable moral transcendence. In the Kantian case, the inclinations of sensibility must be negative, and negative inclinations covertly serve reason's moral ends by obstructing sensibility, but in the Longinian case inclinations often serve positively to reinforce rational commands, an effect that for Kant would occasion suspicion of the autonomy, purity or rational control of moral commands.

The most morally significant similarity between Longinus and Kant is the view that sublime height or elevation, both in the experiencing subject and the sublime object (ibid.: XXXVI, 134–7), constitutes an unrestricted transcendence of the merely human or mortal (ibid.: 136–7; cf. Weiskel: 3). Nature implants in humans, as spectators of the vast, mighty universe, 'the unconquerable love of whatever is elevated and more divine than we ... Wherefore not even the entire universe suffices for the thought and contemplation within the reach of the human mind, but our imaginations often pass beyond the bounds of space' to recognize the purpose of our existence in what is great in our life; humans 'reserve their admiration [*thaumaston*, wonder] for that which is astounding [*paradoxon*]' (L 1907: XXXV, 132–5). The sublime experience of what is transcendent frees the spectator's thought and imagination, prepared already by nature to admire what is elevated, to think and imagine freely what transcends spatio-temporal existence. Hence, sublimity serves to detach the spectator from earthly inclinations in favour of the universal. Longinus, like Baumgarten, Kant and many others, regards sublimity as a means of achieving virtue through the transcendence of earthly greed; as Philip Shaw argues, the sublime 'elevates man above the tawdry concern with wealth and status' (Shaw: 18). But this view is problematic in that it is unaccompanied in Longinus by a rational, universal system of non-natural morality reliant on transcendence and it fails to distinguish clearly between the capacities and functions of thought and imagination, neglecting the ancient philosophical tradition in which (visual) imagination is linked to finite material representations in the visual sphere.

In Longinus' account, the sublime exhibits for experience transcendent standards by reference to which the insignificance and baseness of all quotidian desires become evident. There is no cognitive judgement dismissing greed as wrong for particular reasons; the accepted rightness of virtue is, rather, given visceral demonstration and the person is motivated to live virtuously. Sublimity's role in preparing the virtuous person is clear. Virtue requires the transcendent greatness and nobility of the magnanimous man or the disengaged, purely theoretical life of the contemplative 'man', not, normally, the practically engaged man acting from the conventional midpoint between extremes of, say, passion and reason. The sublime is its own type of virtuous extreme. This association of virtue with sublime transcendence of nature enables the segregation of evaluative and factual realms, a step crucial to any conventionally successful morality. Yet, transcendence of nature remains dependent on our natural love for the supernatural. This move avoids the circularity of Aristotelian references to moral exemplars, although, as we have seen, Longinus elsewhere looks to the moral exemplar to establish standards for virtuous behaviour and to the exemplary author to exhibit the sublime. But, by conditioning virtue ultimately on natural functions, he undermines its claim to transcendence. The fact that we have some natural function cannot establish that it is morally good to possess that function or that the function is present in us for some transcendent purpose. While mere nature can explain the presence and pragmatic effectiveness of various functions, as in Darwinian natural selection, it cannot establish their transcendent value, and the mere love of transcendence, as a human emotion, is not thereby elevated beyond natural experience to this posited evaluative dimension.

However, for Longinus, the natural hierarchy of power somehow assumes moral significance. His stress on the mind's sublime transcendence of finitude, like Kant's, depends upon a model of sublimity and morality defined by the drive to mastery. For Longinus, power (*dynamis*) is a characteristic of sublimity. He writes that Demosthenes 'overpowers with thunder and with lightning' (L 1907: XXXIV, 132–3), and that Homer's sublimity is 'overpowering' (ibid.: IX, 62–3). These are externalized examples of the dynamical sublime. The external dimension suggests the fundamental incompatibility of sublimity with most conventional morality, in associating factual power with evaluative greatness. But Longinus anticipates Kant and many eighteenth-century writers on the sublime by also *internalizing* these power struggles, situating them within the mental powers. This internalizing move seems to attach moral significance to the mere fact of some particular, privileged, internal rank ordering of the mental powers. But there is here the kernel of a transcendental, evaluative argument, in that Longinus, like Kant, suggests that the highest mental powers are those that enable transcendence of nature. The naturally endowed mental powers somehow contain within themselves the possibility of going beyond nature.

Yet, Longinus at times defines this internalized sublimity in terms of sublimity's enslavement of the listener's reason and will by the emotions, whereas Kant argues that sublimity requires reason's dominance over sensibility. For Kant, reason is master, and sensibility is reduced to slavery. For Longinus, if enslavement to pleasure destroys sublimity, sublimity itself constitutes its own form of slavery. When vehemence and passion are infused in spoken words combined with argumentative passages, 'it not only persuades the hearer, but even makes him its slave [*douloutai*]' (ibid.: XV, 88–9); sublimity is defined as the struggle to convince by the *violence* of rhetorical force (Shaw: 4–5). Sublimity's combination of reasoning and imagination overpowers the spectator's will by circumventing the strictures of rational persuasion. As Longinus describes the battle between imagination and reason, power of its own nature (*physis*) determines conviction and arguments *concealed in images* motivate with much greater power than rational demonstration by itself (L 1907: XV, 90–1). Thus, for Longinus and Kant, reason is involved in sublimity, but the emotional forces of sublime experience motivate moral action far more strongly than reason alone. However, the effects of power differ significantly for Longinus and Kant in that, for the former, the power of sublimity enslaves the listener, undermining moral autonomy, whereas for the latter sublimity's negativity enables moral autonomy by clearing away any positive subjective inclinations obstructing rational power over nature.

If the psychologistic character of sublimity's affective function undermines its moral utility from a Kantian perspective, Longinus corrects for this problem by positing universal standards for the judgement of sublimity, and thus, grounding a normative connection of sublimity and morality. He argues that genuine ὕψος 'stands the test of repeated reading and reflection by experienced critics'; it is universal (Russell: xii, genuine examples of sublimity 'please all and always') (L 1907: VII, 56–7)). This universality is made possible by the universal psychological effects of genuine ὕψος, namely, that it 'pleases all conditions of men'. The experience of its judge, its quantity and its effects on the reader's affects provide a general basis for distinguishing true from false sublimity.

The conflict between Longinus' two singular, non-discursive, non-rule-governed criteria (judicial expertise and its effects on the reader) and the third universal, discursive, rule-governed criterion (its universality) exposes the inherent tensions within his account of the sublime. He first adopts the argument that the cultivation of expertise is necessary for the judgement of sublimity and then undermines any requirement of expertise by arguing that genuine ὕψος pleases men of *any* condition. Later critics objected to the claim to universal pleasure (Russell: xii), both on grounds that contingent affects such as pleasure are non-universalizable and that the sublime is characterized not merely by pleasure, but by displeasure or a combination of the two. Kant himself would have accepted the second criticism and added a third, namely, that the judge's requirements of reflective cultivation and long experience make it impossible for the sublime to please all conditions of men, although he also posits a certain degree of cultivation as the condition for the sublime in the *Critique of Judgment*. But Longinus and Kant would agree that the sublime is subjectively universal, and thus, independent of the reader's will, choice or activity.

We shall see many of the details of this brief account of Longinus repeated over and over in eighteenth-century accounts of the sublime. Addison, Shaftesbury, Hutcheson, Young, Gerard, Burke, Baumgarten and Mendelssohn offer views in large measure derivative of Longinus. But while Longinus already articulates the elements crucial to a Kantian moral account of sublimity, even if he weakens his account by omitting any systematic delineation of the functions of the mental powers in sublimity, Kant's eighteenth-century precursors offer few of the necessary conditions for a systematic treatment of sublimity's moral functions. However, this does not mean that we should ignore these accounts of the sublime, for it is important to examine their subtler disagreements, distinct emphases and more proximate influence on Kant in order to identify Kant's originality in his association of sublimity and morality.

2 • Sublimity and Morality in Eighteenth-Century British Aesthetics

Despite the many Longinian and German elements in Kantian sublimity, many Anglo-American scholars attribute the greatest influence on Kantian aesthetics to eighteenth-century British aesthetics. For instance, Edgar Carritt attributes the entirety of Kant's account of beauty, with the exception of systematic form, to British aesthetics; Lewis White Beck calls the 1763 Kant a disciple of the British critics Shaftesbury and Hutcheson (Beck: 332, in Zammito: 29); Paul Crowther, whose prehistory of the Kantian sublime refers only to the British critics Addison and Burke (Crowther: 7–8), argues that Kant relies 'very heavily' on Burke (ibid.: 12); Rachel Zuckert, ignoring other Kantian predecessors, similarly argues that Kant inherits many elements from Burke (Zuckert: 217); and John Zammito asserts that Kant tries to approximate his psychological accounts to those of Burke, whom Kant took 'as [providing] the exemplary psychological list of aesthetic states' (Zammito: 282). Moreover, a number of commentators have argued that the content of Kant's aesthetics remains derivable from the tradition of empiricist aesthetics throughout his career. The popularity of such one-sided genealogies of Kantian aesthetics stems from the fact that Kant scholars are rarely conversant with both British empiricist and German rationalist traditions.[1] Hence, they tend to exaggerate the significance of similarities between Kant and, say, Mendelssohn or Burke, failing to recognize that substantial methodological and doctrinal similarities run throughout eighteenth-century aesthetics and that certain features of Kant's work can be accounted for only by reference to the German tradition, while others must be traced to the British tradition.

Kant's empiricist influences should be assigned primarily to the period prior to the third *Critique* and viewed in conjunction not only with Longinus, but also with his German rationalist influences, as Zammito and Werner Pluhar argue. According to Pluhar, Kant's pre-critical *Observations On the Feeling of the Beautiful and Sublime*, his only aesthetics text other than the *Critique of Judgment*, is 'empirical . . . but not empiricist', 'consisting of amateur social psychology; it discusses beauty and sublimity in relation to the differences between people, ages, sexes, nationalities, temperaments', on the assumption that aesthetic theory is impossible (Pluhar, introduction to CJ: li); even as late as the first *Critique* (CJ: A21n/B35n), Kant rejects the German rationalist Alexander Baumgarten's idea of subsuming rules for judging the beautiful under rational principles, because rules are empirical (Pluhar, introduction to CJ: li). In the first *Critique*, 'reproductive imagination functions according to the "laws of association", i.e., in a "psychological" manner', as Burke argued (ibid.: lxix). But by the completion of the 'Analytic of the Sublime', Kant had abandoned his empirical explanation for sublimity, while retaining many descriptive features found in common in Longinian, British empiricist and German rationalist aesthetics, and we should view his turn from empiricism as a good thing, because a persistent 'empiricism' in the explanation of the Kantian sublime in the *Critique of Judgment* would destroy its originality and render it incompatible with his critical morality. However, it was not until the late 1780s that Kant recognized the possibility of synthetic a priori, universal aesthetic judgements about the beautiful and sublime (cf. ibid.: xxviii). Hence, empiricist influences persist in the form of Kant's aesthetics well into the critical period, and even the *Critique of Judgment* (1790) retains substantial similarities to British empiricist aesthetics (cf. Zammito: 30–1). But to say that Kant's aesthetics was empiricist is not to imply that it was ever purely empiricist in the sense often wrongly ascribed to the British empiricists of deriving claims entirely from sense experience without the imposition of reason or understanding.[2] Neither the early Kant, nor the British 'empiricists' did experiments to determine the nature of aesthetic experience or accepted a merely descriptive stance void of reason or understanding, opting instead to repeat claims about the psychological effects of (reading) classical and modern quotations about great power, magnitude and number. Nor was Kant's aesthetics purely empiricist in the sense of adhering only to the tenets of British empiricist writers, for, as Zammito and Pluhar argue, by the mid-1760s Kant, having abandoned certain tenets of his early rationalism, accepted both empiricist and rationalist tenets, tracing aesthetics and morality to feeling, as in empiricism, but tracing truth to intellection, as in rationalism (cf. ibid.: 29). Thus, for example, in a 1768 letter to J. G. Herder, Kant manages to praise both the empiricist David Hume and the rationalist Alexander Pope, even as he describes the early stages of his own critical *Metaphysics of Morals*, which would overthrow empiricist and rationalist moralities (Kant 1997: Kant to Herder, May 1768: no. 40, X.74). Kant developed his positions by reference to multiple sources within the European philosophical and aesthetic traditions. Hence, it is reasonable to examine both empiricist and rationalist traditions for their influence on Kantian aesthetics.

Indeed, Alfred Bäumler argues that scholars had accepted 'much too strong an influence of the English' on Kant, neglecting entirely not only Baumgarten's influence on Kant, but also the influence of the French on the foundations of German aesthetics (Bäumler: 149).[3] However, it is clear that, despite his lack of English, Kant also read, and was influenced by, English and Scottish critics via French and German translations and secondary sources. Kant's education in British aesthetics began in the late 1750s and continued through at least the mid-1770s. It is difficult to determine exactly which authors and texts Kant knew, since he refers only occasionally to other authors, and rarely to their texts, not being particularly concerned with writing a history of philosophy. Perhaps for this reason, different sources provide different Kantian reading lists, but the lists typically include the third earl of Shaftesbury (1671–1713), Joseph Addison (1672–1719), Frances Hutcheson (1694–1747), Edward Young (1683–1765), Henry Home (later Lord Kames (1696–1782)), David Hume (1711–76), Adam Smith (1723–90), Alexander Gerard (1728–95) and Edmund Burke (1729–97). I have seen explicit references in his writing to all of these thinkers, except for Gerard. Kant refers to Addison just once (*Anthropologie in pragmatischer Absicht*: VII139), but to Hutcheson, author of *Inquiry into the Original of Our Ideas of Beauty and Virtue* (1725, German translation 1762), in at least four works. In his 1762 prize essay, he writes of 'Hutcheson and others' as adherents of moral feeling (*Untersuchung über die Deutlichkeit der Grundsätze der natürlichen Theologie und der Moral*: II300); in his 1765 report on his 1765–6 lectures, he praises the 'incomplete and flawed' moralities of Shaftesbury, Hutcheson and Hume (*Nachricht von der Einrichtung seiner Vorlesungen in dem Winterhalbjahre von 1765–66*: II311); and in the critical period, he associates Hutcheson with the inner, subjective doctrine of moral feeling (CPrR: 40) identified with happiness (GMM: 442n). Kant refers to Shaftesbury in three other texts (*Metaphysics of Morals, Logic* and *Lectures on the Philosophy of Religion*); he read Hume's *Enquiry Concerning Human Understanding* in translation; and he was familiar with Burke's *Philosophical Enquiry into the Origin of Our Ideas of the Sublime and Beautiful* (1757), though possibly not before 1768. It is said that Kant was influenced by Shaftesbury's critique of the dangers of enthusiasm in religious fanaticism (*Letter on Enthusiasm*, 1708) (Zammito: 33), as well as Kames's *Elements of Criticism* (1762, German 1763; Zammito: 29–30) and Gerard's *An Essay on Taste* (1758) (Nahm 1970: 816). Kant refers critically to Young's poetry as overly uniform in its sublime tone (*Beobachtungen über das Gefühl des Schönen und Erhabenen*, 1764: II211n1); and he read Smith (cf. Kirwan: 53), though he does not refer to him in print until 1797 in his *Metaphysics of Morals* (*Die Metaphysik der Sitten*: VI289) and 1798 in his *Anthropology* (VII210), both of which were begun decades earlier. As we shall see, these authors provide increasingly 'empiricist' readings of sublimity, ranging from the early accounts of Addison, Shaftesbury and Hutcheson, in which reason and feeling both play roles in sublimity, to the later accounts of Young, Kames and Burke, in which feeling alone is key to the sublime; accordingly, the earlier accounts are in many ways more amenable to Kantian morality than the later.

The earliest and most important of these empiricists for Kant's moral reading of sublimity is Joseph Addison, who wrote a series of pseudonymous articles on sublimity in the *Spectator* from 1711–13. Addison is important for Kant because his account of sublimity, like that of Longinus, contains virtually all of the non-systematic elements crucial to Kant's moral reading of the sublime. For instance, Addison, Kant and Longinus all associate sublimity with elevation or height, the tension of opposites, the combination of pleasure and pain and the dismissal of superstitious imagination. Contra Zammito, who argues that Addison did not relate sublimity to morality and rationality (Zammito: 277), Addison, like Kant, not only connects sublimity to pain and gratification on similar aesthetic grounds, but also applies sublimity to moral and rational aims (e.g. Addison 1837: *Spectator*: nos 299, 555–6) and links sublimity closely to morality and freedom (ibid.: no. 309). Addison and Kant both argue that sublimity involves the tension between limited imagination and limitless reason (or understanding, which Addison, unlike Kant, fails to distinguish from reason), and that sublimity frees the soul from slavery to certain passions, turns it toward the divine and generates reverence. This reverence is linked to the humbling character of sublimity, which announces that 'my existence is of no concern to the universe, I am reduced to a kind of nothing and am less than the least of the works of God' (ibid.: no. 293). This view, in conjunction with Addison's psychological claims, corroborates Guyer's assertion that Addison offers both psychological and theological-moral accounts of the sublime (Guyer 1993: 259). However, Guyer is wrong to think that Addison, in contrast to Kant, regards the moral elements of sublimity as merely humbling ('as an occasion for reflection on our own finitude and for humility before the infinitely greater power, as well as goodness, of our creator') and not also elevating (ibid.: 258–9), since Addison regards the sublime as elevating and liberating the spectator, and thereby exercising moral functions. Thus, Guyer misses the positive side of this experience of our finitude. For Addison, as for Kant, the indeterminacy or infinitude approached in sublimity, the spacious horizon, constitutes an 'image of liberty' (Addison 1837: *Spectator*: no. 412); sublimity requires speculative or imaginative freedom from 'slavish fears and apprehensions hanging upon his mind' (ibid.: no. 287). Here Addison makes two distinctions key to Kantian sublimity's moral functions. First, he distinguishes between humbling and elevating effects of sublimity. Second, he distinguishes what is represented in sublimity from what makes sublimity possible and, therefore, what must exist in order for the experience of the sublime to occur. In its indeterminacy, sublimity represents liberty and presupposes the freedom of speculation or imagination from heteronomous fears. Hence, the immediately humbling effects of sublimity give way to a recognition of moral autonomy by attention to sublimity's indirectly revealed conditions. But Addisonian freedom is heteronomous from a Kantian perspective, because it lacks a purely rational basis and is associated in its origins with pleasure, as illustrated by Addison's account of imaginative power.

Although Addison associates beauty as well as sublimity with morality (no. 309), he shares Kant's alliance of sublimity to admiration, wonder and formlessness; he argues similarly that sublimity presupposes preparation in ideas; and he provides a virtually identical explanation for sublimity. The imagination discovers its limits in progressing through comparatively greater (or smaller) magnitudes via its free play of ideas (enlarging, compounding and varying, in Addison) almost to infinity, whereupon the mind's power of reason (and understanding, in Addison) furnishes perfect ideas greater even than nature; the sublime is generated by the tension of apprehension and comprehension. Hence, if, as Shaw claims, Addison heteronomously assigns the cause of sublimity externally to 'the naturally magnificent object' (Shaw: 35), he agrees with Kant in tracing sublimity to the internal tension between the powers of imagination and thinking. However, Addison parts with Kant in ascribing a positive affect to the imagination's recognition of its own incapacity. For Addison, the imagination experiences delight at the magnitude of objects too big for it, whereas Kant identifies this experience with pain, locating pleasure rather in the recognition of reason's ability to think of the infinite. The imagination's positive pleasure in Addison is incompatible with Kantian morality, in so far as the latter depends on reason's negative (dominating) relationship toward the imagination and sensibility, and the former results from the imagination's domination by external things, not reason.

Addison's division of sublimity into ruleless and rule-governed forms also limits its use in Kant's critical morality by disconnecting the sublime completely from either the rational order, on the one hand, or the motivating force of aesthetic experience, on the other. By choosing sides, the Addisonian account forecloses the mediating Kantian critical stance, which sustains relations to reason and sensibility at the same time. Whereas Kant and Longinus derive genius from the combination of nature and *techne*, enabling an account of sublimity amenable to rules, and thus, to their understandings of morality, Addison distinguishes between ruleless and rule-bound geniuses. The first class of 'nobly wild', extravagant, natural geniuses emerges from ruleless nature, 'never disciplin'd and broken by Rules of Art' (nos. 160, 315), whereas the second class, different, not inferior, though too often 'cramped by imitation', is 'formed by Rules and restrained by Art' (e.g. Plato, Aristotle, Virgil, Tully, Milton and Francis Bacon, no. 160). It is arguable that neither of these one-sided geniuses is amenable to the moral functions of Kantian sublimity, because the first class lacks the morally necessary relation to reason's indeterminate ideas, while the second class lacks the motivating force of aesthetic experience. The real problem, then, consists not in Addison's inability to provide a unifying account of sublimity's relationship to rule but, rather, in his failure to differentiate the powers of imagination, understanding and reason and to assign each a specific aesthetic function.

In contrast to Addison, his contemporary, Anthony Ashley Cooper, the third earl of Shaftesbury, has been assigned an exaggerated influence on eighteenth-century accounts of sublimity, without proper note being taken of his moral readings of the sublime. Stanley Grean, R. L. Brett and many others credit Shaftesbury with transforming sublimity from a rhetorical to an aesthetic concept, constructing an original account of sublimity and being the primary influence on subsequent writers, including Burke and Kant. However, Shaftesbury's aesthetic turn, if there is such a thing, is unoriginal; his specific account of sublimity introduces nothing new; and Addison's account of the sublime is far more detailed and supported by examples. Longinus had already understood sublimity in both aesthetic and 'rhetorical' senses, and Shaftesbury's own project is less an aesthetic turn than a fusion of aesthetic and rhetorical uses of sublimity in the simultaneously intellectual and emotional uses of rhetoric (cf. Grean: 25; Brett: 146; Cooper: v.III, 140).

However, if Shaftesbury's work has been considered striking for the wrong reasons, it remains interesting in exhibiting through its failure the inadequacy of empiricist moral readings of sublimity. Its importance today rests largely on its affinities to Kant and I would argue that these affinities are greatest in their common moral readings of sublimity. Shaftesbury anticipates Kant in rejecting a concept of morality as mere awe and terror of God or Hell (Cooper, *Characteristics of Men, Manners, Opinions, Times*: v.II, 119–20), while connecting sublimity to character (Cooper: v.I, 336), to free, disinterested, magnanimous virtue (as in Kant's early aesthetics) and to reason, in contrast to slavery to passion (Cooper: v.1, 101; v.II, 154). The sublimity of the act for Shaftesbury, as for Kant, depends on its disinterestedness, rational basis, connection to virtue and free choice of virtue. Moreover, Shaftesbury and Kant both argue that imagination's initial failure in grasping the sublime is followed by recognition of reason's superiority (Brett: 155). If this rational power is merely cognitive or intellectual like the power of estimation in Kant's mathematical sublime, Shaftesbury also anticipates Kant's dynamical sublime in imputing to sublimity a practical power of transcending inclinations, and thus elevating our moral power beyond pleasure, pain and the emotions (Cooper: v.II, 99–100).

Poetic transport or sublime oratory aims to raise 'the mind from its dependence on the sensual things of the world to a perception of underlying intellectual and moral harmony' (Shaw: 39), to see the ultimate goodness of the world (ibid.: 40). Within the realm of inclinations, Shaftesbury prefigures Kant, Young, Burke and Kames, among others, in arguing that the sublime provides a means of resolving a painful experience pleasurably by bringing contentment or satisfaction (Cooper: v.II, 101, 106). Shaftesbury thus agrees with Kant that sublimity successively includes opposite emotions, such as hatred and love, disturbance and disgust (ibid.: 111).

However, their explanations for this phenomenon differ, because of their distinct understandings of the role of reason in sublimity. Kant regards sublimity as a function of the relationship of imagination and reason, whereas Shaftesbury links sublimity to irrationality at some points, and to reason at others. Shaftesbury identifies reason itself as sublime (Cooper: v.I, 8) and argues that the proper attitude toward sublimity's excesses is Stoic manly calm (Shaw: 40–1). Yet, despite his rationalist, neoplatonic views that 'mind alone forms' and that beauty refers to mental ideas, Shaftesbury also holds that sublimity is non-rational and capricious, involving a nature that exceeds mental control (Cooper: v.1, 79). This latter view isolates the variable emotions from reason, asserting that sublimity's capricious, non-rational character entails its succession of opposites, in contrast to the Kantian view that sublimity includes emotional variability while still being defined by reason's simultaneous harmony and tension with imagination. Shaftesbury's belief in an innate moral sense (McReynolds, introduction to Hutcheson: ix) and his association of *beauty* with the sacrifice of pleasures also differ from Kant. The force of beauty for Shaftesbury is such that if we 'are ready to sacrifice our highest pleasure and ease' even to false magnificence and false beauty, becoming abject slaves, we are all the more ready to sacrifice our pleasures to genuine beauty, whose moral nature is identical to truth, for 'nothing affects the heart like that which is purely *from it-self*, and *of its own nature*; such as *the beauty of sentiments*' (Cooper: v.I, 139–40). In Shaftesbury, sublimity is not opposed to beauty, as in Dennis and partly in Addison, 'but rather works in concert with it to assist the mind in its ascent from corporeal distraction to visionary perception' (Shaw: 40). Had Kant relied on such a sacrificial conception of beauty, he might have included both beauty and sublimity in moral attunement.

Shaftesbury's disciple, Francis Hutcheson, further develops this association of sublimity with moral sense. Although heavily indebted to Shaftesbury, Hutcheson provides a 'less metaphysical, more empirical and more systematic' aesthetics (McReynolds: x). In *An Inquiry into the Original of Our Ideas of Beauty and Virtue* (1725), dedicated to Shaftesbury, and *An Essay on the Nature and Conduct of the Passions and Affections with Illustrations on the Moral Sense* (1728; 3rd edition, 1742), Hutcheson follows Shaftesbury in speaking of natural dispositions of mankind (McReynolds: vi) and defending the idea of an innate, universal, moral sense of beauty (Hutcheson 2004: 9, 61). McReynolds argues that Hutcheson prefers a variety of internal senses, defined by 'every determination of our Minds to receive Ideas independently on our Will, and to have Perceptions of Pleasure and Pain' (Hutcheson 1969: 4), to Shaftesbury's 'equation of the esthetic and moral senses' (McReynolds: x). However, Hutcheson also links the aesthetic and moral senses, connecting beauty to morality and divine goodness (Hutcheson, 2004: 196; cf. 164, 171, 175). For Hutcheson, morality is universal, despite its irrational, contingent basis (Hutcheson 1969: 324), as is our enjoyment of the noblest pleasures of internal senses, including the '*sensus communis*' used later by Kant, in contemplating natural works (Hutcheson 2004: 77; 1969: 5–6).

If these views, with the exception of the *sensus communis*, are antithetical to Kant, Hutcheson is much closer in the mechanisms by which he associates sublimity and morality. His passage on nonobjective horror articulates relations of reason and sensibility amenable to Kantian morality (Hutcheson 2004: 62). In linking sublimity to a horror independent of objective form, he identifies sublimity as subjective; in referring to reason's capacity to overcome fear in the experience of the object, he identifies a rational power over nature; and, in predicating the experience of the sublime on the spectator's successive pain of fear and rationally induced pleasure in safety, he articulates a mechanism by which sublimity might involve what for Kant are the morally requisite negative relation to sensibility and positive relation to reason. In sublimity we experience the 'Limitation of our Minds, which cannot admit an infinite Multitude of Singular Ideas or Judgments at once, yet this power [abstraction] gives us an Evidence of the Largeness of the human Capacity above our Imagination' (ibid.: 36). Hence, Hutcheson, like Kant, argues that sublimity's exhibition of the limits of imagination demonstrates our own transcendent power. Here we see again Guyer's error in arguing that Kant first transformed purely psychological or humbling, theological-moral accounts into an elevating moral account ('What Kant did was to transmute the psychological account into an alternative moral account, in which humanity is elevated rather than humbled' (Guyer 1993: 259)), since Hutcheson's psychological account is simultaneously (and without contradiction) an elevating moral account. If, for Kant and Hutcheson, sublimity's moral functions depend on revealing the capacities of our minds to exceed the limits of the imagination, false sublimity in both cases annuls sublimity's moral functions precisely in conveying the illusion of exceeding these mental capacities. By ignoring the limits of our minds, excessive honour and desire may 'run into *Enthusiasm* and pernicious *Madness*' (Hutcheson 1969: 99), while unbridled imagination and opinion necessarily lead the affections into useless, evil extravagance and folly (ibid.: 101). Thus, Hutcheson criticizes '*unnatural Enthusiasm*' in those inquiring into the passions, favouring instead '[*a*]*ttention to what passes in our own Hearts*' (McReynolds: v). If Kant differs in identifying enthusiasm, an evanescent madness (*Wahnsinn*), as sublime, he too excludes from sublimity an excess enthusiasm, which he calls fanaticism, a deranging mania (*Wahnwitz*, CJ: 275). Hutcheson also shares the view of Shaftesbury, Burke and Kant that there is no contradiction in the simultaneous experience of pleasure and pain (Hutcheson 1969: 101), which occurs in most of our violent desires (ibid.: 15), but never in beauty (Hutcheson 2004: 62). Finally, Hutcheson anticipates Kant in arguing that the experience of morality is itself sublime and that it motivates moral action in a way foreclosed to beauty. The contemplation of moral objects 'affects us more strongly and moves our Passions . . . in a more powerful manner than natural Beauty' (ibid.: 173).

However, Hutcheson differs from Kant in deriving morality from a non-rational moral sense, conditioning virtue on pleasure and limiting the role of sublimity in morality. Hutcheson restricts sublimity's moral role on the grounds that the sublime is destructive of moral universality and counterproductive in its movement of the passions. Interestingly, these are the very criticisms that Allison and others have incorrectly levelled at moral readings of Kantian sublimity, a misreading that might account for claims to Hutcheson's influence on Kant. For Hutcheson, sublime speculations on God cannot be the source of a virtuous mind without excluding 'the Bulk of Mankind' from any moral capacity (Hutcheson 1969: 338). The reason is that many lack the moral cultivation, the moral ideas, necessary for sublime feeling; moreover, sublime moral feelings produce a strong disincentive to moral action, because the combination of these ideas with desire is unpleasant. '[W]hen Ideas of *Dignity, Grandeur, Magnificence, Generosity*, or any other *moral Species*, are joined to the Objects of Appetites, they may furnish us with endless Labour, Vexation and Misery of every kind' (ibid.: 94). In this claim, Hutcheson anticipates Kant in associating sublimity closely with morality and displeasure. However, Hutcheson regards this displeasure as a hindrance to morality, because the latter is based on the feeling of pleasure, whereas Kant regards displeasure as *aiding* morality, because morality requires reason's *overcoming* of feeling. Like Shaftesbury, then, Hutcheson differs radically from Kant in deriving morality from a non-rational moral sense and conditioning virtue on pleasure. In the *Critique of Practical Reason* (second *Critique*, CPrR), Kant criticizes inner, subjective principles of moral feeling of the explicitly Hutchesonian type as 'empirical', and hence, inadequate to the 'universal principle of morality' (Kant, CPrR: V.40–1). In very un-Kantian language, Hutcheson lauds '[a]n instinct, or a Determination previous to Reason which make us pursue private Good' (Hutcheson, 2004: 133). He defines disinterested virtue in this non-rational way as agreeableness (McReynolds: xv) to our inherent moral sense (ibid.: ix) or as life according to nature (ibid.: xvii). Virtue is in our truest interest, *because* our greatest pleasures are those of virtue (ibid.: viii); our nature constitutes us to receive pleasure from moral virtue (Hutcheson, 2004: 110). Although this astonishingly unrealistic association of nature, virtue and pleasure is antithetical to the Kantian account, the early Kant, like many of Hutcheson's empiricist followers, shares Hutcheson's association of sublimity with virtue.

Similarly, Edward Young, like many other eighteenth-century critics, associates sublimity, virtue and divinity. He argues that Addison's virtuous last words are most sublime, for they 'spoke human nature not unrelated to the divine' (Young 1966: 108).[4] '[V]irtue assists Genius . . . the writer will be more able, when better is the man' (ibid.: 73). But virtue is not, as in the later Kant, a tacit means of reintroducing reason into subjective emotions. For Young, like the early Kant, virtue is a (somewhat vague) question of character, actions and feelings unimproved by education or rule. If virtue aids sublimity, reason only detracts from it. In contrast to Addison's acceptance of both natural and rule-governed geniuses, then, Young rejects any rational reduction of sublimity, deriving it from the inexplicable, invisible, creative, imaginative power of original geniuses, whom he compares to divine or cosmic forces (ibid.: 12, 26–7). Rules set 'rigid Bounds to that Liberty, to which Genius often owes its supreme Glory' (ibid.: 27). Thus, Young distinguishes the absolutely free, original imagination, crucial to the 'true sublime' (ibid.: 68), of 'the divinely-inspired Enthusiast' from the rule-governed scholar (ibid.: 55). Sublimity requires an absolute ruleless liberty, based not in reason but imagination. If the imagination is ultimately imitative, it takes its inspiration, knowledge and moral fervour from the book of nature (ibid.: 9, 81). Noble tragedy, 'like virtue, . . . demands the heart' (ibid.: 81). Hence, sublimity and morality in Young are derivable neither from an absolute, rational liberty, nor from objective nature. Feeling is its own law. Despite its natural derivation and general (objective) characteristics, then, sublimity depends on subjective emotions and produces subjective affects, such as admiration (ibid.: 13) and the combination of pleasure and pain. In this last regard, Young, like Hutcheson and others, anticipates Kant, asking '[b]ut whence . . . this odd generation of pleasure from pain? The movement of our melancholy passions is pleasant, when we ourselves are safe: We love to be, at once, miserable, and unhurt' (ibid.: 94–5). Sublime pleasure in Young, as in Kant, derives from an experience that is initially unpleasant and that requires safety. But Young differs from Kant in providing no explanation for this alliance, and Young's romantic account of virtue and genius, heavily influential on Goethe's *Sorrows of Young Werther*, is certainly irreconcilable with Kant's critical morality.

Henry Home, Lord Kames, one of many eighteenth-century critics to cite Longinus and Addison frequently (e.g. Home, *Elements of Criticism*: 150n, 154, 159, 161, 165–6), also rejects a rational identification of sublimity. For Kames, the universal association of elevation with grandeur (or sublimity) is founded not on rules or reason, but on feeling, and indeed, 'its universality proves it the offspring of a natural feeling' (ibid.: 158). Kames writes of 'refined and sublime pleasures' (ibid.: 13) and associates sublimity with terror (ibid.: 152) and enthusiasm (ibid.: 154). But he does not adhere to a merely subjective or psychological account, for he understands sublimity in terms of objects, as well as the emotions produced by them (ibid.: 151). If sublimity and grandeur are identifiable for Kames (ibid.: 83, 154), and beauty belongs to the same genus (the agreeable) as grandeur, beauty differs from grandeur in magnitude; regularity, proportion, order and colour contribute to grandeur, yet they do not *define* it, unlike beauty (ibid.: 152).

Kames's account of sublimity shares a variety of morally significant attributes with Kantian sublimity, such as the description of mental ascent, the mixture of pleasure and pain in sublimity and the attachment of respect to sublimity. Like Kant, Kames describes as pleasurable the mental ascent from great to comparably greater objects; the descent is not painful but increasingly less positively pleasurable until indifference emerges and pleasure may mix with pain (ibid.: 157). But here the ascent excludes the negative pleasure linked to Kantian sublimity. This negative pleasure is contained, rather, in the maximal Kamesian descent, from the greatest to the smallest objects. However, if this descent generates sufficient displeasure to resist natural inclinations, it remains mixed with pain, rather than attached to distinct elements of the process, as in Kant, and its affects depend on an experience of what Kant would consider contemptible and, hence, unworthy of respect or sublimity. Yet, Kames anticipates Kant in linking respect (attached to persons of 'more elevated character', including unjust emperors) to sublimity (ibid.: 177–8) and in regarding God as transcending sublimity, contra Longinus (ibid.: 172). As in Kant, in the presence of God, the emotion of grandeur quickly gives way to humility and veneration (ibid.: 172–3). In identifying sublimity with grandeur or elevation, used typically in a moral sense, and arguing that it is incompatible with the humbling presence of God, Kames presents a further counter-example to Guyer's claim that pre-Kantian accounts of sublimity lacked elevating moral forms. Kames, like Kant, identifies the sublime with what is great, but not without limits. '[C]arried to its due height and circumscribed within proper bounds [the sublime] enchants the mind, and raises the most delightful of all emotions', in contrast to the false sublime (ibid.: 175). The implication is that sublimity, like magnanimity, is a mean between extremes. The mean, in Aristotle, is set by the character of the moral actor. The mean with regard to the general notion of the sublime is set by human nature in general. Our sentiment for grand and lofty objects is constant and universal, in the sense that it is general to all humankind, and this universality can be explained only by its origin in human nature (ibid.: 165). As in Kant, sublimity's universality is neither cognitive, nor rational, nor objective, but rooted in a subjective, natural capacity shared by all persons (CJ: 265–6). To identify this view with the Kantian, however, would require that we identify Kamesian feeling with the Kantian harmony of reason and imagination, and the contingent *sensus communis* of Kames and Kant with the a priori subjective universality of Kantian sublimity and morality, which we cannot do.

Far better known than Kames within the same empiricist tradition of reading the sublime is Edmund Burke's *A Philosophical Enquiry Into the Sublime and Beautiful* (1757), which is widely and wrongly considered the second most important eighteenth-century text on sublimity, after Kant's 'Analytic of the Sublime'. The reputation of Burke's work rests on the strength of its 'sensationist' (Womersley, introduction to Burke 2004: x), empiricist, psychologistic account, as well as its alleged originality and influence on Kant. Kant himself attests to this influence, calling Burke 'the foremost author in this type of treatment', namely, an empirical exposition of the sublime (CJ: 277). Here I cannot examine these claims in detail. However, there is a good argument to be made that Burke's account is only nominally empiricist, and that it is neither original, nor influential. Burke describes his method of examining the nature of taste in empiricist terms as introspection of our own passions; aesthetics can be determined only from surveying 'the properties of things which we find by experience to influence those passions; and from a sober and attentive investigation of the laws of nature, by which those properties are capable of affecting the body, and thus of exciting our passions' (Burke 1998: 1st Preface). Although few if any precedents may exist for this physicalist account of sublimity's causation, Burke himself did not hold such a position consistently. This is not surprising, given the dubiousness of accounting for many sublime experiences via, say, ocular 'vibration'. Thus, even if Burke recasts sublimity in empiricist language as an object of 'scientific enquiry', he wavers in this view, recognizing that the clear ideas of sensibility, with their evident links to physical causation, are inferior in affect to the vague ideas of verbal description, which seem to function symbolically, rather than by physical causation (Shaw: 49–50). If Burke's method were empiricist, psychologistic description of natural phenomena, that would be of limited advantage, for psychologistic descriptions cannot support normative claims and, while Burkean psychologism suits his moral emphasis on feeling, a psychologistic account would be incompatible with Kantian morality. Yet, in fact, the great majority of his book involves the very same textual analysis of canonical authors as virtually every other writer on the sublime.

As we have seen, the claim to Burke's influence rests primarily on his alleged originality and his influence on Kant. Thus, for instance, Rachel Zuckert argues that Kant's 'account of the sublime in the *Critique of Judgment* ... inherits many elements from Burke's account' (Zuckert: 217), such as their association of pleasure and displeasure in the sublime, their choice of examples, their use of aesthetic judgement and their distinction between sublimity and beauty. But these similarities could be traced back to any of a dozen earlier figures, for Burke's own account of sublimity is as derivative of Longinus, Addison, Shaftesbury and others as that of any mid-eighteenth century critic. Hence, these similarities are no proof of influence. Philip Shaw's argument to Burke's originality is more detailed. He identifies this originality with Burke's subjective turn from nature to the mind of the spectator (Shaw: 71), his construction of sublimity as an idea internal to mental states, his secular account of sublimity, his assignment of its causation to physical states, such as the near pain caused by the eye's vibration (ibid.: 48–9), his attempt to lend sublimity a primarily negative valence, with the exception of positive associations of sublimity with the dignity of mental elevation (ibid.: 54–6), his focusing of British accounts of sublimity on pleasure and pain (ibid.: 5) and his argument 'that the sublime turns on the distinction between the raw immediacy of terror and its more pleasurable representation' (ibid.: 69). But what makes this reading problematic is that Burke's secular, psychologistic and ideational readings of sublimity, as well as his negative reading of sublimity and his identification of sublimity and terror, all have many pre-Burkean examples, ranging from Longinus, Addison and Shaftesbury to Hutcheson, Kames and Young.[5] Neither the methods nor the content of Burke's account of sublimity are at all original. Hence, his similarities to Kant can be traced to common sources. Moreover, Kant himself, in the 'Analytic of the Sublime', explicitly rejects Burke's avowedly empirical, psychologistic methods (what Kant would call Lockean 'physiology' (CJ: 277, incl.

Br. n51)), his empiricist de-emphasis on reason and his objectivist emphasis on the sublimity of nature and the arts. While Kant cites Burke (using a German translation: *Philosophical Investigations on the Origin of our Concepts of the Beautiful and Sublime*, Riga, with Hartknoch 1773) as the best of the authors on the physiological exposition of the sublime, Kant restricts the force of these claims on his own work, for he grants Burke's claims title only to psychological acuity, regarding them as rich material for examinations in empirical anthropology. In Kant's reading, Burke analyses mental phenomena acutely, but fails to provide the necessary transcendental exposition and deduction. Indeed, Kant seems not to have drawn even his earlier accounts from Burke, for he wrote his first work on sublimity, *Observations on the Feeling of the Beautiful and Sublime* (1764), prior to reading Burke. However, it is possible that Kant was already familiar with Burke's arguments second-hand via Moses Mendelssohn (1729–86), who had summarized Burke's arguments for a German audience in *Über die Mischung der Schönheiten* in 1758, well before Lessing's 1773 German translation (cf. Zammito: 25), or the French translation recommended by Herder in his November 1768 letter to Kant (Kant 1997: Herder to Kant, November 1768: no. 41, X77).

Nevertheless, there is indeed significant overlap between Kantian and Burkean sublimity, even in their moral dimensions. Although Kant and Burke certainly offer radically different moralities, the extensive similarities between Kant's and Burke's accounts of the sublime include many elements adaptable to Kantian morality. In CJ, Kant consciously derives from Burke the association of vigorous affects – delight, horror and pain – with sublimity, and languid affects – love and a dying delight – with beauty. Kant discusses Burke's derivation of the feeling of the sublime from the drive to self-preservation and fear. For both, speaking roughly, this feeling is a pain that produces movements purifying the soul against dangerous obstacles, thus exciting pleasant sensations. But these sensations, for both Kant and Burke, are not pleasure per se, but a thrill or tranquillity mixed with terror (in Burke's words, a 'delightful horror' (Burke 1757: IV.vii; cf. Pluhar, introduction to CJ: 138n50)). Kant also identifies his similarity to Burke in the latter's grounding the beautiful on the *passion* of love, independent of desire, and associating beauty with 'the relaxing, slackening and enervating of the body's fibres, and hence, to a softening, dissolution, exhaustion, a fainting, a dying and melting away with delight' (Burke 1757: IV.xix, in CJ: 277). As Shaw discusses, here and elsewhere there is obvious fodder in both Kant and Burke for sexualized, gendered Freudian readings of sublimity and beauty. On a broader level, Burke's characterization of the sublime is extremely close to Kant's. Like Kant, Burke allies sublimity to what is vast or large, to greatness of dimension (Burke 1757: II.vi, 113), to what is infinite, terrorizing (II.xi), grand (II.xv), immense, extreme (II.xv), magnificent (in great profusion 'of splendid, valuable things', uncountable in number and apparently disordered and confused, which increase grandeur (II.xiii)), amazing, of immense force and difficulty, for example, Stonehenge (II.xii, 118) and to the reconciliation of opposites (for example, light and darkness in sun-blinded eyes (II.xv)). Although Burke differs from Kant in accepting the sublimity of the infinitely small (like Addison; II.VII, 114), on grounds that it is terrorizing, he agrees with Kant that the *merely* small is not sublime, that a spectator in mortal danger cannot experience sublimity and that sublimity can be identified with the imagination's progression to infinity (sublimity 'amazes and confounds the imagination', staggers and hurries the mind (II.xvii)). Like Kant, Burke associates sublimity with a feeling of negative pleasure distinguished both from pain and positive pleasure (Crowther: 134; Zuckert: 217). Yet, Kant, Burke and Addison all list multiple causes of the sublime and equivocate in identifying its locus and definition, whether in nature, art, the subject or the object. Thus, Burke describes the 'feeling of delightful horror' as 'the most genuine effect and truest test of the sublime' (II.viii), as if sublimity were either a feeling or an object determinative of the feeling, only to refer elsewhere to a sublime image (II.xi) and to a sublime passion produced through sensation (II.xvii).

To this point, we have seen that many of the psychological elements that Kant uses in his moral reading of sublimity are present in Burke as well. However, we have not yet seen Burke explicitly associate sublimity with morality, and Paul Guyer argues that there is no such connection, for Burke's account is 'purely psychological', not moral (Guyer 1993: 259). Guyer distinguishes two types of pre-Kantian, eighteenth-century accounts of sublimity: psychological accounts like those of Addison (at times), Burke and others, with 'no obvious moral implications', and theological accounts like those of Addison (at other times), J. G. Sulzer (*Allgemeine Theorie der schönen Künste*, 1771–4) and others, who charge sublimity with the moral role of generating humility by exhibiting human finitude and divine goodness (Guyer 1993: 259). However, this is a false distinction. Burke, like every other eighteenth-century writer on the sublime that I have seen, associates sublimity with morality. Like Kant, Burke, at least in *A Philosophical Inquiry*, praises sublimity's fitness for morality, while minimizing and even disparaging beauty's moral adequacy.

> virtues which cause admiration, and are of the sublimer kind, produce terror rather than love; such as fortitude, justice, wisdom and the like . . . Those which engage our hearts, which impress us with a sense of loveliness, are the softer virtues; easiness of temper, compassion, kindness and liberality; though certainly those latter are of less immediate and momentous concern to society, and of less dignity . . . The great virtues turn principally on dangers, punishments and troubles, and are exercised rather in preventing the worst mischiefs, than in dispensing favours; and are therefore not lovely, though highly venerable. The subordinate turn on reliefs, gratifications and indulgences; and are therefore more lovely, though inferior in dignity. Those persons who creep into the hearts of most people, who are chosen as the companions of their softer hours, and their reliefs from care and anxiety, are never persons of shining qualities or strong virtues . . . In [Cato] we have much to admire, much to reverence and perhaps something to fear; we respect him, but we respect him at a distance. [Caesar] makes us familiar with him; we love him, and he leads us whither he pleases. (Burke 1757: III.x)

For Burke, then, the nobler, dignified virtues produce terror, admiration, respect, reverence, fear and dignity, never love or familiarity, and thus, are sublime, whereas the soft virtues are lovely but enervating, promoting identification with weakness (Shaw: 62). If beauty is here associated with virtue, it is certainly the weaker virtues dismissed by Burke. Indeed, in III.xi, Burke criticizes the association of beauty with virtue as misleading, confounding distinct qualities. 'The beautiful fails . . . as a support for ethical behaviour: "[the beautiful is] inferior in dignity"' (Shaw: 57, citing Burke). But, if Burke in 1757 anticipates Kant in emphasizing beauty's unsuitability to morality, Shaw argues that in 1790, in *Reflections on the Revolution in France*, Burke parts with Kant in stressing beauty's positive contribution in producing a necessary softening, and hence, civilizing, while dividing sublimity into the dangerous excesses of the French revolution and the 'awful gravity', noble reverence and dignity of the British people and constitution (Shaw: 65–71). However, it is arguable that here beauty simultaneously plays this softening, civilizing role and constitutes a third type of sublimity, distinct from both the horror of revolution and the reverence for constitution. Recalling his experience of the young Marie Antoinette, Burke calls her the most 'delightful vision' ever to grace this planet, almost floating above this world in her unearthly 'elevation', and assigns to her older self all the sublime, noble virtues proper to women, such as dignity, serene patience and lofty sentiments; in the failure to rescue her, there is effected the death of chivalry, that 'nurse of manly sentiment and heroic enterprise, . . . which ennobled whatever it touched' (Burke 1987 (1790), *Reflections on the Revolution in France*: 66–7). Chivalry, through no act of its own, engendered social flourishing, and 'noble equality'; '[w]ithout force or opposition, it subdued the fierceness of pride and power' and in all ways tamed humanity, 'harmonized the different shades of life, and . . . by a bland assimilation, incorporated into politics the sentiments which beautify and soften private society' (ibid.: 67). Revolution destroys both this beautiful sublimity and the awful sublime gravity of constitution. For Burke,

> the French revolution is the most astonishing that has hitherto happened in the world. The most wonderful things are brought about, in many instances by means the most absurd and ridiculous . . . Everything seems out of nature in this strange chaos of levity and ferocity, and of all sorts of crimes jumbled together with all sorts of follies. In viewing this monstrous tragicomic scene, the most opposite passions necessarily succeed and sometimes mix with each other in the mind: alternate contempt and indignation, alternate laughter and tears, alternate scorn and horror, . . . [while to others] it inspired no other sentiments than those of exultation and rapture . . . [seeing in France] a firm and temperate exertion of freedom, so consistent, on the whole, with morals and with piety as . . . to render it a fit theme for all the devout effusions of sacred eloquence. (Ibid.: 9–10)

Revolution involves no measured, pious, moral and, thus, positive, sublime exercise of freedom, for the terrible sublimity of the evil, unnatural, monstrous upheaval in the French revolution results precisely from uprooting those '*ancient*, indisputable laws and liberties' (ibid.: 27) that define a moral sublime linked to divinity (ibid.: 81); the very idea of this creation *ex nihilo* 'is enough to fill us with disgust and horror' (ibid.: 27). Burke's concern here is with the terrorizing destructiveness of a sublimity unrestrained by reverence for traditional values, and there is no internal corrective for Burkean sublimity that would ensure its retention of moral standards. It is utterly contingent whether sublimity is linked to divine moral standards. Hence, he proposes a dialectical reading of the relation between feminine beauty and masculine sublimity in a mature society, where the one is used as a corrective against the other (Shaw: 69). In the last chapter, we will again see this concern for the disconnection between sublimity and morality, in Lyotard and Žižek. But I would argue that this problem derives from the psychological character of the Burkean sublime. By setting forth non-psychological, transcendental conditions for sublimity consonant with morality, Kant is able to reject in advance the notion that sublimity might involve a terrorizing destructiveness transcending any moral limitations. The excessive forms of subjective experience belong to the non-sublime categories of fanaticism (*Schwärmerei*) and the monstrous. So, while Kant differed from Burke in viewing the idea of freedom excited by the French revolution in terms of a moral sublime, he also departed from Burke in denying that the monstrous or horrific can be included within the category of the sublime. Even war, for Kant, is sublime only in so far as it is waged with respect for civilizing rules (CJ: 263). Burkean sublimity cannot establish a necessary connection between sublimity and virtue, because its stress on feelings warrants claims to sublimity for any terrorizing feelings, irrespective of their accordance with virtue or their intensity, objects or effects.

Finally, while Kant and Burke both regard sublimity as universal, Burke differs in claiming its actual universal extension, despite its being out of the ordinary and distinct from the crowd (Burke 1757: II.xxii). Obviously, Burke's view involves a direct contradiction. Sublimity cannot be both actually universal in extension and out of the ordinary. However, if we set aside the view that sublimity is out of the ordinary, the assertion of actual universality makes the Burkean sublime readily assimilable to a morality defined by universal extension, such as a 'common sense' account based on moral feeling, whereas Kant still needs to explain how his more rarefied notion of sublimity, dependent on the possession of cultivated moral ideas, can play a role in a universalizable morality. The problem with pre-Kantian accounts of the sublimity–morality connection is that they lack standards for ensuring the moral character of sublime experience, given their inability to provide a non-psychological, universalizable account of sublimity and its role in moral motivation. The Aristotelian and empiricist moralities associated with sublimity prior to Kant's critical writings fail because they are anthropological and psychologistic, lacking universalizable standards for determining whether past practice or 'moral' exemplars are moral. Accordingly, they cannot tell us how to act in cases not covered by experience or exemplars. In place of justifiable prescription, they provide us only limited, partial, often questionable description and unwarranted commands to follow such practices, the basis for which is inherently arbitrary and variable. Setting aside consequentialist criticisms, the most powerful external charge against Kantian morality (the internal charge, levelled by J. S. Mill, among others, criticizes Kant's ability to rule out any conduct at all through the principle of universalizability) is that its rational, anti-psychological form rules out the motivational history necessary for its implementation. The dilemma is that our moral accounts seem both to require and to exclude anthropological and psychological considerations. Without an anthropological or psychologistic treatment of what might motivate moral action, we cannot understand why we should act morally or how we might eliminate all non-rational elements from our process of intentional action; yet, if we admit anthropological or psychological elements into a rational morality, we seem to destroy its universality. Pre-Kantian accounts of sublimity and morality have no means of avoiding these problems. What Kant does is to provide both a rational morality, addressing the anthropological and psychologistic (or physiological, in his term) problems that he identifies in previous moralities, and a non-psychologistic account of sublimity designed to provide the motivation necessary for a rational morality. In order to see how Kantian sublimity can provide this moral motivation without lapsing into the psychologism and anthropology characteristic of the eighteenth-century accounts of the sublime from which he borrows so heavily, we shall have to turn to previous German accounts of the sublime.

3 • Kant's German Precursors

If there is good reason to accept the common view that British empiricism strongly influenced Kantian aesthetics, it is important to recognize both that this influence waned after the 1760s and that the German rationalist tradition in which Kant was trained provided an intellectual framework for his early, non-systematic aesthetics as well as his later critical, systematic aesthetics. This intellectual framework is the basis for Kant's transformation of the experience of sublimity into something of real significance for a universalizable morality. The key German philosophical figures for Kant's aesthetic development were Gottfried Wilhelm Leibniz (1646–1716), Leibniz's disciple, Christian Wolff (1679–1754), Christian August Crusius (1715–75), Alexander Gottlieb Baumgarten (1714–62), Baumgarten's student and collaborator, Georg Friedrich Meier (1718–77) and Moses Mendelssohn (1729–86). Pluhar attributes Kant's early rejection of a science of aesthetics not to British empiricism, but rather to the Leibnizian-Wolffian problematic, according to which there were entirely distinct, higher and lower modes of cognition, clear thought and confused sense perception (Pluhar, introduction to CJ: xlviii). Because sense perception is nothing other than confused thought, it 'can have no perfection of its own, and hence no rules of its own to govern such perfection' (ibid.). Since beauty is merely pleasure in perceiving natural perfection or art's imitation of nature through the senses, there can be no rules for beauty and only a psychological aesthetics is appropriate. Thus, German psychological aesthetics arrives by different means at a similar position to British empiricism, except that the German version retains a robust view of the powers of reason *outside of aesthetics*. In the third *Critique*, Kant extends reason to this sphere as well, making possible a universal aesthetics, while maintaining the subjectivity of beauty and sublimity. As Pluhar argues, Kant charges empiricists with failing 'to account for the fact that judgements of taste demand everyone's assent and hence claim a universality and necessity (CJ237), which presupposes some necessary and hence a priori principle' that cannot be provided by '[s]couting about in empirical laws of mental changes' (CJ: 278) or 'gathering votes and asking other people what kind of sensation they are having' (CJ: 281), even if empirically many agree, since 'there is a contingent uniformity in the organization of [different] subjects' (CJ: 345-6); empiricist analysis cannot differentiate subjectively universal judgements of taste from merely subjective, agreeable (CJ: 346) judgements (Pluhar: liii). For these reasons, Kant's comparison of his transcendental exposition of aesthetic judgements with the physiological exposition of Burke and others in the 'General Remark' in CJ specifically delimits the use value of an empirical exposition of the sublime and beautiful. The key to the physiological reading lies in what Kant considers the correct claim that all representations in us, whether their object be sensuous or intellectual, can be linked to pleasure (*Vergnügen*) or pain, since they all affect the feeling of life, as a modification of the subject. Kant agrees explicitly with Epicurus that all pleasure and pain, whether originating in imagination or representations of understanding, are ultimately bodily. For Epicurus, the advancement or inhibition of the life forces depends on bodily feelings; otherwise, life would be mere consciousness of existence. The mind, by this argument, is the life principle itself and the promotion or inhibition of our vital forces is external to the mind, yet internal to the person, consisting in the body's connection to the mind (CJ: 277-8). The problem with the Epicurean argument, for Kant, is that it destroys the possibility of apodictic universal aesthetic judgements. If aesthetic judgements consisted solely in a liking for the object defined by its pleasing through charm or emotion, which involves only our private sense and rests on an immediate sense of well-being, then it would be impossible to criticize differences in taste between individuals, for even when there was chance agreement (*Übereinstimmung*) in judgements, these judgements could never command the approval of others. Because of the posited universality of the internal drives, in the Epicurean account, judgements of taste would be pluralistic, rather than egoistic, despite their internal location, but without relying on lists of favoured judgements compiled by others. Yet, this universality would fall short of Kantian apodictic universality, because it would depend upon the chance constitution of human beings according to these posited drives. In order to necessitate agreement, judgements must be grounded on a priori principles, whether objective or subjective, and such principles can never be found by 'scouting about in empirical laws of mental changes: because these reveal only how we do judge; they do not give us how something should be judged . . . [or] that the *command* is *unconditioned*' (CJ: 278). Hence, Burkean psychologism cannot generate unconditioned, universally valid judgements of taste that immediately bind liking with representations. However, the empirical exposition of aesthetic judgements may provide the basis for a higher, transcendental exposition, as in the critique of taste, which grounds affirmative and negative verdicts concerning the judgements of others on a priori principles. Aesthetics demands not contingent agreement but universal and necessary judgements, which are to be established in the Deduction, in the case of beauty, or in the Exposition, in the case of sublimity. Hence, these judgements cannot be derived from psychological feelings. For the same reason, a merely psychological aesthetics cannot play a role in a universalistic morality. A rational, non-psychological element is necessary to transcend empirical contingency.

The inheritors of the Leibnizian-Wolffian tradition first exhibit this flaw in empiricist aesthetics and provide a rational framework for correcting it, but they deny that reason can be extended to morality or to a merely subjective aesthetics. As a result, Baumgarten and Meier suggest a way out of empiricist aesthetics while remaining trapped within the same psychologistic understandings of sublimity and morality. Kant's contemporary, Moses Mendelssohn, prepares the ground for the Kantian position in differentiating three forms of sublimity, subjective, objective and hybrid subjective-objective forms, dividing between mathematical and dynamical sublimity and conceiving sublimity as universal. However, Mendelssohn too developed from the Leibnizian-Wolffian tradition and accordingly retains psychologistic elements in his accounts of sublimity and its relation to virtue.

In Kant's own time, the Leibnizian-Wolffian tradition engendered a series of critical German responses, inspired by a broad European tradition in which non-rationalist elements predominated. Chief among these responses for Kant's intellectual development, according to Zammito, was the Pietist religious tradition in which he was raised and educated. In opposition to the Leibnizian-Wolffian tradition, the Pietist thinker Christian August Crusius (1744) attended more, Giorgio Tonelli says, 'to English and French empiricism, sensationalism and common-sense philosophy than [did] orthodox Wolffian rationalists' (Tonelli: 269; cf. Zammito: 18–19).[1] But Crusius was hardly alone in this cosmopolitanism. In the 1750s and 1760s, the Berlin *Aufklärung* via Baumgarten, Meier and Mendelssohn, who, unlike Kant, could read English, brought into German discourse the British and French aesthetic notions of feeling, genius and the sublime; prior to Kant's *Observations*, Friedrich Resewitz (1755) and Johann Sulzer (1757) lectured in Berlin on genius, Mendelssohn (1758) summarized Burke's aesthetics (Zammito: 24–6), Meier published *Anfangsgründe aller schönen Wissenschaften* (1748–50) and Baumgarten published his *Aesthetica* (1750–8). Kant became acquainted with Mendelssohn from the 1761–3 Berlin Academy Prize Competition, which was won by Mendelssohn but also saw the publication of Kant's contribution, and they corresponded until Mendelssohn's death in 1786 (Zammito: 24), although it is disputed whether prior to his own *Observations* of 1764, Kant learned about Burke's account of the sublime and the beautiful (1757, German 1773) from Mendelssohn, as Theodore Gracyk argues (Gracyk 1986a: 207; cf. Zammito: 32). Kant read Mendelssohn's *Jerusalem or on Religious Power and Judaism* (1783) and Leonhard Meister (1700–81), whose *Über die Schwärmerei* (1775) linked passion to imagination as the source of visionary and poetic frenzy (Zammito: 41), in contradistinction to Kant's own separation of the emotion of sublime enthusiasm (*Enthusiasm*) from directed passion. For Kant, enthusiasm involves the association of an affect with the idea of the good (CJ: 271–2). Affects relate only to feeling and are blind, whether in the choice of ends or through rational production, and involve a mental agitation that restricts the mind's ability to establish free reflection on principles by which it can determine itself. For this reason, the affects generally undermine moral self-determination. However, affects of the vigorous sort, leading us to consciousness of our power to overcome any resistance, are aesthetically sublime, and the sublime in nature outside us and within (in our affects) is represented as the mind's power 'to swing itself beyond *certain* hindrances of sensibility through moral principles' (ibid.). Passions, by contrast, are inclinations belonging to the power of desire, which 'make it difficult or impossible for all determinability of the power of choice through principles' (CJ: 272). Passions would 'abolish' the determinability of choice by moral principles, whereas the sublime, aesthetic affect of enthusiasm, despite its impeding the mind's freedom, still functions as 'a tension of forces through ideas, which give to the mind an impetus [*Schwung*] that works far more powerfully and lastingly than the drive [*Antrieb*] through sense representations' (ibid.). But an affectless mind, a mind in the state of *apatheia*, that vigorously strives after unchangeable principles remains far more sublime, for it is noble and is liked by reason (ibid.).

As Zammito argues, for Kant in the early 1760s, the two poles of work on aesthetics, science and critique, were defined by Baumgarten and Henry Home (Lord Kames), rather than Mendelssohn and Burke (Kant 1800: IX15; cf. Zammito: 30). In a section of his *Logic* lectures, the text of which was based on class notes, Kant prefers Home's form of aesthetics, critique (*Kritik*), to Baumgarten's science of aesthetics on the grounds that aesthetics is a 'mere critique of taste', with no canon, law or a priori rules, but only empirical, a posteriori norms, patterns or standards of universal agreement (*Einstimmung*) for judging (Kant 1800: IX15).[2]

Although Kant, prior to the third *Critique*, defined aesthetics as a merely historical a posteriori discipline, a type of criticism rather than science, he prepared the ground for his future critical aesthetics by rejecting irrationalist approaches to aesthetics in early German romanticism. In Johann Gottfried von Herder (1744–1803), Johann Georg Hamann (1730–88) and Friedrich Gottlieb Klopstock (1724–1803), as well as Edward Young, he saw dangers of *Schwärmerei* or fanaticism, which he linked to genius in Herder's implicit substitution of intuitions for reflective understanding and reason (Zammito: 34, 37–8; *Reflection* 771).[3] At this point, Kant was advancing toward his critical aesthetics by rejecting both the scientific and the irrationalist positions. He argued in the *Observations* that 'genius had no place in science' (Zammito: 41); genius, judgement and aesthetic appreciation could not be taught (ibid.: 33). But he also rejected the intuitionist view, shifting genius from the irrational grounds of natural, sensual and material elements in human subjectivity to that natural, yet universal and rational element in the subject that cannot be subsumed under determinate rules or concepts. Thus, even though Kant continued to deny the possibility of subsuming aesthetics under determinate concepts, the indeterminate aesthetic-cognitive relations of his mature aesthetics owe much to Baumgarten's aesthetic interpretation of the Leibnizian-Wolffian science of cognition, as Alfred Bäumler argues.

Baumgarten was almost certainly fundamental to Kant's allowance of a rational account of beauty and sublimity. In 1742, Baumgarten became the first to lecture on 'aesthetics' (*aesthetica*), a term he coined in 1735's *Meditationes philosophicae de nonullis ad poema pertinentibus*, according to Kai Hammermeister. Departing from the Leibnizian-Wolffian view that beauty was unintelligible (Hammermeister: 6), Baumgarten defined aesthetics as a theory of sensibility regarded as a gnoseological, or knowledge-producing, faculty, enabling a cognitive examination of beauty and the fine arts (Zammito: 20). From Leibniz and Wolff, Baumgarten and Meier borrowed a model of cognition divided into the lower level of confused sense perception and the higher level of distinct thought; aesthetics involved the transition from unconscious and obscure cognition to distinct cognition (Hammermeister: 13).[4] However, Baumgarten and Meier differed from Leibniz and Wolff in denying that the perfection of sense perception transforms it into thought, for sense perception is not a stage on the way to thought. There are two kinds of cognition and, correspondingly, two kinds of theory or science of knowledge, logic and aesthetics. Aesthetics is the science of sense knowledge.

This is precisely Kant's use of the term in the first *Critique*'s 'Transcendental Aesthetic' (A19–49/B33–73). Thus, despite Kant's homogenization of sense perception, concepts, ideas and so forth under the general category of representations (*Vorstellungen*) (A320/B376–7), he argues in the 'Schematism of pure concepts of understanding' that pure concepts are 'quite heterogeneous from empirical intuitions, and indeed from all sensible intuitions', and thus require a *tertium quid*, a 'third thing' homogeneous with each, namely, a 'mediating representation' (A137/B176ff.). In the third *Critique* as well, according to Pluhar, 'Kant accepted and defended the major innovation offered by Baumgarten and Meier: . . . that sense perception is not the same as thought and can be perfected without turning it into thought', while objecting to Baumgarten and Meier's cognitive analysis (CJ:207–9) for transforming beauty into a conceptually expressed, purposive property or perfection (Pluhar, introduction to CJ: l–li). If judgements of beauty were conceptual, then they could be proved by rules, as in Baumgarten-Meier, but this is impossible (CJ: 284–5), according to Kant; therefore, there is no fine science but only fine art and no aesthetics as science of the beautiful 'but only critique' (Pluhar: li). However, we need to be careful about what is meant by critique here. It is true that Kant rejected Baumgarten's and Meier's notion of a science of aesthetics, both in CJ and prior to it. But, as we have seen, Kant's understanding of the alternative prior to CJ, Home's aesthetic *Kritik* (Home used the English word 'criticism'), admitted only empirical, a posteriori judgements, defined by universal agreement, whereas Kant's developed aesthetics accepted a third alternative of subjective, universal, synthetic a priori judgements. Hence, Kant's ultimate position accepted Baumgarten's view that there were a priori universal judgements in aesthetics, while still rejecting the dogmatic rationalist reading of aesthetics as a science governed by determinate concepts.

Aside from its terminological and systematic importance in the development of aesthetics, the first volume of Baumgarten's *Aesthetica* (1750) (the second volume appeared in 1758), which includes at least seventy pages on sublimity (§§281–334, §§394–422), more than Kant's 'Analytic of the Sublime', predates by eight years Moses Mendelssohn's *Über das Erhabene und das Naïve in den schönen Wissenschaften* (1758). Hence, Hammermeister is erroneous in calling Mendelssohn the first German philosopher 'to devote significant attention to the sublime' (Hammermeister: 17). Although there are approximately sixty references to Baumgarten in *The Philosopher's Index* and his *Aesthetica* is regarded as the founding text of aesthetics, his influence on subsequent philosophers is limited, for he wrote in a Latin that remains untranslated into English, and his work is almost indistinguishable from that of the more widely read G. F. Meier, his pupil and collaborator (ibid.: 6). However, Baumgarten's science of aesthetics is important in constituting an alternative to empiricist aesthetics, and he was very important to Kant, who used Baumgarten's texts as a basis for his own lecture courses on ethics and metaphysics (Heath and Schneewind, introduction to Kant 1997: xxiii–v; cf. Schmidt: 151), while using the logic texts of Baumgarten's closely affiliated student, G. F. Meier, for his logic lectures. Thus, according to Bäumler, despite Kant's criticism of Baumgarten's science of aesthetics, Baumgarten's influence on Kant was greater than he acknowledged (Bäumler: 261).

In referring typically to 'subjective' and 'objective' forms of sublimity, Baumgarten prepares the way for the subjective and objective moral roles that Mendelssohn envisions for sublimity. Baumgarten's references to the objective sublime support a moral reading, in so far as they include qualities, such as what is maximum or magnificent (Baumgarten 1750: §281; §283), great, and high (*altum, summam*), that are amenable to an Aristotelian, aristocratic, virtue ethics in constituting an inspiring model for human disposition. Baumgarten's many references to the subjective sublime in part validate this Aristotelian reading, but they also add qualities specific to the history of the sublime. Affects, such as tranquillity of soul (§284), horror/fear, the sacrilegious (§321), what moves most violently (§327, §403), Bacchantic raving and shrinking back from our senses with admiration and desire or longing rather than hatred (§301), may be sublime (§327) if they are not excessive, in which case they increase the baseness of swelling or the false sublime (§328). Sublime subjective qualities also include morality and heroic virtue (§281, §291, §315), rational thinking, elevated natural disposition (*ingeniique elevationem*, §288), magnanimity (e.g. §291, §§405–7)), the grand (ibid.), what is fullest in dignity (§291) and transcendence (§323). Contra Guyer, this association of sublimity with elevation and morality, like that of Kames, Addison and Longinus, predates the same Kantian association. Baumgarten's understanding of the subjective sublime, like his understanding of the objective sublime, links sublimity to an Aristotelian virtue ethics, in which transcendent, grand, magnanimous and moderate qualities, linked to rationality, somehow all count as sublime, along with their antipodes, the most violently moving affects and even raving madness.

Like Kant, then, Baumgarten repeatedly links sublimity to moral virtue. Aesthetic magnitude in general, and sublimity in particular, can evoke (maximum) virtue in so far as it represents it pictorially 'in all its majesty' (§397). But Baumgarten refers sublimity to a wide range of elements or types of virtue, including the 'twofold type of morals', the natural disposition or seat of reason (§289), heroic virtue (§291), ancient examples of virtue suggested for imitation and magnanimity (one of Aristotle's primary general virtues). Aristotelian moral and intellectual virtues are dispositions or states of character. Moral virtues derive from choice and habituation, while intellectual virtues derive from nature and training. The category of intellectual virtue might describe Baumgarten's sublime *ingenii*, if translated as natural dispositions, rather than genius (§404). In these links to Aristotelian virtue, Baumgarten's account is similar to Kant's early account of the sublime. Kant allies virtue to sublimity as early as the *Observations on the Feeling of the Beautiful and Sublime* (1764) and as late as the *Metaphysics of Morals* (1797). Kant's 1764 text asserts that '[i]n moral properties, true virtue is alone sublime'; 'as soon as this feeling [of universal goodwill] has climbed to its proper universality, it is sublime' (OFBS: 215–16; cf. 220; MM: 435). Yet, Baumgarten's moral reading of sublimity also frequently anticipates Kant's later morality in linking sublimity to freedom and arguing that natural desires destroy sublimity and morality. Baumgarten understands sublime liberty as freedom from external restraints (§414; §416), but he also speaks of internal moral slavery, supernatural liberty and internal psychological complements and supplements (§414). Conversely, intemperate external desires undermine sublime freedom, softening morals, costing masculine strength and requiring a grand quantum of courage to overcome (§420). Longinus is the explicit source for this view, which we also see in Kant. Baumgarten cites Longinus to the effect that desires are among the reasons that the power of small souls degenerates below the level of the sublime. Vices such as ambition, arrogance, lack of love of honour or truth, the tyranny of insanity and the mores of the many contribute to swelling, rather than sublimity (§421). Like Kant, Baumgarten also rejects the sublimity of the small in aesthetic magnitude (§321) and contrasts vile and abject things with the sublime dignity of others (§396). Hence, Baumgarten articulates significant elements of Kant's moral reading of the sublime.

However, he fails to provide a systematic explanation for sublimity and morality, to distinguish his morality firmly from Aristotle's, to divide sublimity from beauty or to set forth standards for judging sublimity and morality independently of exemplars. Baumgarten's non-systematic approach combines heterogeneous elements without resolving their incompatibility. Thus, while he links sublimity to morality, transcendence, rational thinking and heavily motivating affects, as in Kant, he differs from Kant in dissociating sublimity from any universal, law-bound, non-affective morality. Despite his view of unemotional, rational thinking as sublime, he holds the psychological view that feelings for life and quanta are more suited to sublimity than magnitude (§334) and he speaks generally of non-rational, psychological causes (§410) of sublimity. This psychological turn may explain why he, like Kant, seems to reject sublimity's universal *extension*, saying that 'not all sublime things shine for all' (§303 ('*sublimia non omnibus omnia lucent*' (§324)). Baumgarten's failure to make distinctions is also evident in his conflation of beauty and sublimity (§319; cf. §292, §422) and his accordant link of beauty to morality (§292, §302, §309), for he fails to see any salient distinction in the moral relevance of beauty and sublimity. This view is hard to defend if the great or absolute is defined by its transcendence of relative magnitude, its incomparability, for the moral force of what is absolute and cannot by definition be augmented is surely distinct from finite aesthetic functions such as beauty, which admit of relative values.

This terminological confusion, which, as we have seen, is characteristic of accounts of the sublime, undermines even Baumgarten's extension of sublimity beyond individual ethical concerns to political questions. His political turn is significant not because it is original to the discourses on the sublime or novel to Aristotelian virtue ethics but, rather, because its limits on the political uses of the sublime anticipate the concerns of post-Kantian commentators. Baumgarten's virtue ethics falls within an Aristotelian tradition in which ethics is understood as a branch of, or introduction to, the sublime enterprise of political science. The subject of politics for Aristotle is the good of the community, for securing this good 'is something finer and more sublime' than seeking merely the good of the individual, as in ethics (Aristotle 1967: I.ii, 1094a22–b12). Accordingly, the end of politics, which includes the arts of war, property management and public speaking (a form of rhetoric), is already regarded as sublime. Hence, a political reading of the sublime is hardly inappropriate or surprising. Moreover, many before and after Baumgarten refer to political elements of sublimity, particularly in connection with war and peace. Like Kant and Longinus, Baumgarten suggests that universal world peace is a cause of the poverty of natural sublime dispositions in his own time (§415). Yet, Baumgarten also differs from them in adopting a straightforward view of sublime harmony as tranquillity (§308), rather than strife. He identifies unending war's restraining of our desires as an additional cause of the poverty of natural sublime dispositions (§415) and links sublimity to the harmony of the faculties of high reason and lower acquaintance, and will with the lower faculty of desire. Baumgarten places peace in the tranquillity specific to ordinary states of excellent magnanimity (§416). Baumgarten opposes Kant's judgement that (a well-ordered) war is sublime and peace softening. War for Baumgarten is 'a state of bestiality', lacking quiet, tranquillity, a 'sleep of reason and affects, and of instincts' without harmony, an 'infinite war . . . most inimical to the magnanimity of the sublime' (§417), because it weakens the soul (§418). Here we have an immanent restraint on the political uses or expression of the sublime, anticipating the concerns of a Lyotard or Žižek. The sublime is incompatible with irrational, infinite war; hence, we need not worry about sublimity lending itself to the destructive actions of warlike states. However, Baumgarten's account of the sublime lacks the specificity necessary to determine these limits. Since he also describes violent affects as sublime, referring sublimity to all sorts of inherently obscure and violent feelings, including horror and fear (§321), he must regard factors over and above the simple harmony of the faculties as definitive of sublimity. To state these factors would be to provide the requisite limits on sublime warfare, Žižek's primary concern for sublimity's use. But such a statement certainly eludes Baumgarten's vague, confused and highly derivative writings on the sublime.

Although Baumgarten's work predates Moses Mendelssohn's, the latter's initially anonymous 1758 essay, 'On the sublime and naive in the fine sciences', is the most fully developed German account of sublimity prior to Kant. Zammito argues that Mendelssohn, influenced by the sensationalist and naturalist positions of French writers Jean Dubos and Charles Batteux, the French Enlightenment, Hume and Burke's *Enquiry*, which he placed in the context of German scholasticism, took a more psychological and empirical stance than Baumgarten's cognitive work (Zammito: 24–6). But, as I have noted, Baumgarten also includes psychological elements in his account of the sublime.[5] Mendelssohn and Baumgarten also shared the general project of applying the Leibnizian-Wolffian metaphysical framework to topics treated more often by English and French critics (Dahlstrom, in Mendelssohn: ix), rather than adopting English or French positions. Although Hammermeister contends that Mendelssohn's *Letters on Sensations*, modelled on Shaftesbury's *The Moralists or a Philosophical Rhapsody* (1709), dispenses with moralism in aesthetics (Hammermeister: 15), Mendelssohn associates virtue with sublimity in terms similar to Kant's first and last accounts of sublimity in 1764 and 1797. The naïve, which falls under the sublime, is a case where outer actions or omissions are regarded as signs of inner morality and dignity; simplicity is in the signs along with the dignity and importance of the signified (Mendelssohn: 226). '[T]he idea of innocence and moral simplicity is forever bound up with sublime grace' (ibid.: 226, 229–30). Hence, Mendelssohn associates sublimity with morality as much as any other eighteenth-century philosopher.

More significantly, however, in allowing for subjective, objective and hybrid forms of sublimity, like many other eighteenth-century writers on the sublime, Mendelssohn opens up three potential domains in which sublimity might execute moral functions. First, the subjective sublime might produce virtuous affects in the observer. These affects cannot be universal, for he agrees with Charles Perrault that the *subjective* sublime is non-universal, since it depends on education, culture, class and other differences. This position is akin to Kant's view that sublimity is subjective and non-universal in extension, since it presupposes social and individual cultivation. But Kant differs in restricting sublimity entirely to the subjective sphere, excluding objective and hybrid forms, and asserting that the judgement of the sublime is universally valid, though not universally extended in fact to all individuals. For Kant, this universal validity is key to sublimity's moral role. For Mendelssohn, sublimity's subjective particularity is not exclusive of morality; rather, it merely limits those capable of attaining it to the great-souled, since subjective sublimity transcends the capacity of common-thinking people (ibid.: 217–19). Thus, the subjective sublime is enabled by and evidences the Aristotelian virtue of magnanimity. For Mendelssohn, virtue is an example of the second type of sublimity, unextended or intensive magnitude; like genius and power, virtue produces a 'spine-tingling sentiment' without ending in satiation or disgust through 'tedious uniformity' as 'generally happens' with extended immensity (ibid.: 194). This use of virtue ethics is compatible with Kant's early work on the sublime. However, it is incompatible with Kant's critical morality, both in its connection to utility and its failure to subject virtue to universal reason. Hence, if Kant's requirement of cultivation in his critical account of sublimity similarly destroyed the possibility of any real universality in the sublime, then Henry Allison would be correct that sublimity could not play a foundational role in Kantian morality.

However, Mendelssohn's notion of the objective sublime allows for this mode of universal extension. The objective sublime has the universal character of being necessarily 'pleasing to everyone everywhere' (ibid.: 218). Hence, it could furnish a model for human comportment, constitute a morally requisite link among all human beings via a *sensus communis* or, like the subjective sublime, produce certain virtuous affects in the contemplating subject. The products, and perhaps even the practice, of the noble or elevated arts fall under the objective sublime. Architecture and ornamental arts are sublime by their noble simplicity; 'wise indifference to wealth and splendor elevates our soul and teaches it its own dignity' (ibid.: 197). Accordingly, Mendelssohn follows Longinus and Addison in excluding from sublimity 'riches, splendor, stature and undeserved power' (ibid.). More positively, sublimity is constituted by transcendence of such desires. In deciding to return to certain torture in Carthage (*c*.250 BCE), Marcus Atilius Regulus's virtuous transcendence of fear and physical pain 'is sublime and awe-inspiring because we would not have believed that duty, the duty to keep a promise even to an enemy, could have had so much power over a human heart' (ibid.: 195). But if Mendelssohn overtly moralizes sublimity in thus conditioning it on the ascetic transcendence of earthly pleasures, he arguably smuggles in a moral reading of the sublime even in his seemingly amoral account of sublimity as defined by the experience of sensible perfection in nature or art. The mixture and confluence of different sentiments engenders awe at this sensible perfection (ibid.). The moral harmonization of the artist's or spectator's subjective powers is at the basis of this form of the sublime, despite the notion that particular qualities and entities are sublime in and of themselves, for awe directed to the artist concerns his qualities of wit, genius, imagination; in perfect art, the soul's capacities harmonize 'for so worthy a final purpose', revealing the hidden essence in his work (ibid.: 197). Sensible perfection is hardly amoral, because it reveals the harmony and *telos* of nature, art and the soul. Mendelssohn considers sublime the perfection of spirit, intellect, sensibility, imagination and noble, passionate emotions that elevate the soul above itself (ibid.: 198). However, the fact that Mendelssohn provides limited detail on the objective sublime, accentuating instead the artistic object's effects on the subject, suggests that the arts might better be situated within the final category, the hybrid sublime.

The third form of sublimity in Mendelssohn is this hybrid sublime. This category is defined by the claim that 'subjective sublimity can in many cases be combined with objective sublimity' (ibid.: 216–17). The hybrid sublime can produce virtuous affects on the inner sense of the spectator by generating a harmonious attunement of the outer senses to the object (ibid.: 196). Unextended (intensive) magnitude or power exemplifies this hybrid mode, for it may involve natural objects as well as subjective elements of passion, understanding, imagination, invention, rhetoric and literature (ibid.: 216). This form of sublimity is subjective, yet dependent on objects, for the properties of the object are integral to the proper sublime attitude. The hybrid sublime derives its universality from the subjective feeling of pleasure produced by experiencing certain objects, despite the fact that the subjective sublime is non-universal and the objective sublime universal. Mendelssohn provides a sort of physiological explanation for the universality of this subjective feeling. The 'immensity arouses a sweet shudder that rushes through every fiber of our being and the *multiplicity* prevents all satiation, giving wings to the imagination to proceed incessantly further' (ibid.: 195). However, a moral reading of hybrid sublimity would involve the naturalistic fallacy, because the objective and subjective, physiological elements of the hybrid would treat facts about external objects or internal experience as the basis for universalizable moral norms.

Kant's later moral uses of sublimity, by contrast, avoid the naturalistic fallacy by acting merely as a propaedeutic to morality, distinguishing themselves from morality itself and relying on transcendental, rather than psychologistic or objective, arguments. But Kant takes from, or shares with, Mendelssohn the use of a subject–object framework, the mathematical–dynamical division in the sublime, sublimity's dependence on cultural presuppositions, its association with virtue and its affective dimensions in the observer. At the same time, Kant seems to have taken from Baumgarten the very impetus for his critical approach to aesthetics, the notion that there can be a rational treatment of aesthetics, and thus, a priori aesthetic judgements. In the moral sphere, Baumgarten, Mendelssohn and Kant all agree with many eighteenth-century British writers that the sublime enacts virtuous functions precisely in elevating, rather than humiliating the human spirit. But Kant's views on the relation of sublimity to morality are not merely the sum of his general agreements with previous writers on the question. To see how Kant appropriates and systematizes the accounts of his non-systematic precursors, with their Aristotelian virtue ethics, for the purposes of his rational morality, we will have to examine closely his 'Analytic of the Sublime' together with his key moral treatises from the critical period.

Part II:
Kant on Sublimity and Morality

4 • The Moral Functions of Sublimity in the Kantian System

In the history of the pre-Kantian association of sublimity and morality that I have provided in the first three chapters, I describe significant respects in which Kantian sublimity is derivative of earlier views, including its definitions, its connection to Aristotelian virtues, its association with an exemplary list of phenomena involving power, magnitude and number, its mathematical–dynamical distinction and its transcendence of human or natural forces. I also identify many differences between Kant's views and any single previous account. Kant's differences with *all* previous accounts form the basis for the following chapters, in which I argue that the Kantian sublime is historically and philosophically significant because of its role in the critical project, as the first attempt to connect the sublime to a universal, rational system of morality. Kant's 'Analytic of the Sublime' can be situated within the critical project in at least three ways: 1) it uses a transcendental argument to define sublimity as a subjectively universal judgement; 2) it explains the experience of sublimity in terms of mental powers delineated in the first and second *Critiques*; and 3) it assigns sublimity the critical function of grounding the determinability of the moral subject. In demonstrating the inadequacy of the beautiful as a means of completing morality, tracing the need for sublimity and aesthetic reflective judgement back to the moral writings, prior to the third *Critique*, and defending the view that Kant assigns important moral functions to the sublime, I identify the sublime as the necessary condition of moral determinability and establish Kant's substantial continuity on this issue throughout his career.

My argument diverges from previous Kant scholarship in articulating the systematic function of the sublime in the Kantian system and providing a full treatment of sublimity's role in morality. Previous scholarship may be divided usefully into three historical subsets: 1) that which accepts the relation of sublimity to morality without detailing this relation (Elizabeth Neill, Rudolf Makkreel, Richard Kuhns, Theodore A. Gracyk, Paul Beidler, Iris Murdoch and Robert Wicks); 2) that which relates beauty to morality, neglects or denies the significance of sublimity's relation to morality (Ted Cohen, Paul Guyer (1979), William Charlton and Jean-François Lyotard) or even aligns sublimity with evil (A. T. Nuyen, Joseph H. Kupfer, Richard Kearney, Charlton and Lyotard); and 3) that which accepts that sublimity is related non-trivially to morality and provides significant details of its moral functions or its aesthetic functions analogous to morality without identifying its role in moral determinability, situating it properly within the critical project or correctly characterizing the relations of sublimity, moral feeling and respect (Milton Nahm, post-1979 Guyer, Donald Crawford, Henry Allison, Werner Pluhar, Paul Crowther, John Zammito, Rachel Zuckert, Kirk Pillow, Birgit Recki and James Kirwan). Twentieth-century Kant scholars did not tend to treat the third *Critique* at all, let alone the 'Analytic of the Sublime', until the late 1970s and early 1980s. Among those to recognize a connection between Kantian sublimity and morality, many treat the issue cursorily (the first group), while others at various points in their career either conceive the connection as oppositional, regarding sublimity as evil and beauty as moral (the second group) or delimit the significance of the connection and neglect its systematic dimensions (the third group).[1] Of course, there can be no hard and fast distinction here between subsets of scholars, for some who describe sublimity as an aesthetic analogue to morality simultaneously relate beauty to morality and deny or minimize sublimity's moral functions, and some scholars run the gamut of positions during their careers. For instance, Paul Guyer initially neglected the 'Analytic of the Sublime' (Guyer 1979), following the analytical aesthetics of the 1970s, on the assumption that Kant's treatment of the sublime merely bowed to the fashions of his time (Guyer 1993: 2–3), then he diminished its moral significance (1982) and finally he rethought his earlier views, recognizing, roughly, that 'the real heart of Kant's aesthetic theory and the underlying motivation for its creation is the connection to his moral theory which appears in his discussion of the sublime, of aesthetic ideas as the content of works of aesthetic genius, and of beauty as a symbol of morality', or at least that Kant's 'ulterior motive' involved the connection between aesthetics and morality (Guyer 1993: 2–3). In the past decade, in particular, Kant scholars have come to recognize significant, non-systematic connections between sublimity and morality, primarily the notion of sublimity as an aesthetic analogue to morality, but also in some cases sublimity's specifically moral functions. In detailing the sublimity–morality connection, these readings at best approximate Friedrich Schiller's very early position. But no readings of Kantian sublimity, to my knowledge, provide a serious treatment of the connection of the sublime to the critical project either through its role in reflective judgement or its moral functions.

There are several good reasons for the absence of any such treatment. First, Kant provides no exhaustive, direct treatise on the systematic role of the sublime. Second, he implies that the sublime is irrelevant to the *Critique of Judgment* and presumably useless to the critical system by describing this late addition to the text (the 'Analytic of the sublime') as 'a mere appendix to the aesthetic judging of the purposiveness of nature' (CJ: 246), within a work that is itself attached like an appendix to the system of critical reason, lacking any proper domain of its own (CJ: 168) and supplementing a system whose moral *telos* had seemingly been achieved already in the *Critique of Practical Reason*.[2] Third, he sometimes describes the relationship between sublimity and morality as analogous and occasionally associates beauty, instead of sublimity, with morality. Fourth, scholars have read Kant as accepting the current conceptual distinction between aesthetics and morality, and thus as rejecting any significant moral role for aesthetics. But none of these reasons is sufficient to dispense with the significant textual evidence that Kant assigns to the sublime a significant systematic role for morality. The strict disciplinary separation between aesthetics and morality can be applied to Kant only anachronistically. In his own work, he makes no such fixed distinction. In fact, he continually articulates moral dimensions of aesthetics and aesthetic dimensions of morality. While he never wrote a direct treatise on the systematic role of the sublime, he makes a strong case for this role in remarks scattered throughout the 'Analytic of the Sublime'. His claim that the sublime is a mere appendix refers specifically to the fact that it concerns our own supersensible purposiveness, not the purposiveness of nature (CJ: 246). For this reason, this claim only supports the view that the sublime is crucial to Kantian morality. However, the notion that the 'Analytic of the Sublime' is a mere appendix might also explain why it was a late addition to the *Critique of Judgment*, unaccounted for by the majority of the text. The topic of the sublime did not speak to the text's major question of natural purposiveness, except within the (human) subject. Moreover, the late addition of this section to the text suggests that Kant was unaware of, or did not express, certain systematic features of sublimity prior to adding the 'Analytic of the Sublime', and thus that he did not make note of these features in any prior text, including the remainder of the *Critique of Judgment*. Nevertheless, he did express these systematic features within the 'Analytic of the Sublime' and I would agree with Henry Allison that Kant's inclusion of the 'Analytic of the Sublime' should have led to deep, and not merely occasional, revisions in the remainder of the *Critique of Judgment*. As Allison claims,

> anything approaching an adequate integration of the theory of the sublime into the *Critique of Judgment* would have required, among other things, an extensive revision of Kant's conceptions of a purely aesthetic judgement, reflection, and purposiveness. Consequently, it becomes understandable why Kant only included a discussion of the sublime at the last minute, and even then tended to downplay its significance ... he came to realize that the sublime is too closely connected with his concern to ground a transcendental function for judgement and to establish a connection between aesthetic judgement and morality to be omitted altogether. (Allison 2001: 307)

Hence, Kant's claim to the marginal character of the sublime only draws attention to a weakness in the remainder of the text, not in the 'Analytic of the Sublime'. Similarly, he undermines his own sparse remarks linking beauty to morality by his frequent dissociations of beauty and morality. Kant's claim that the sublime is analogous to morality has been misunderstood to exclude any real moral functions on grounds that it is something like a simulacrum or simulation of morality, utterly distinct from the moral sphere. But sublimity does not merely provide a picture or simulated experience of morality; it exercises specific moral functions in exhibiting our moral powers and functions. The distinct operations that Kant assigns to the overlapping moral and aesthetic domains enable sublimity's moral functions, for these functions are specific to reflective judgement, and cannot be enacted by practical reason. It is only as an aesthetic analogue to morality that sublimity can engender the feeling of respect, the awareness of our freedom, the motivation to act against natural inclinations and the transition from nature to freedom, none of which can be assigned either to theoretical or practical reason.

THE MORAL FUNCTIONS OF SUBLIMITY IN THE KANTIAN SYSTEM 55

I recognize that in synthesizing the many clues left by Kant as to this systematic moral role, my account retains the ambiguities and explanatory gaps of Kant's own texts. But to give this account the precision, justifiability and completeness desired by Kant scholars would require the alien introduction into Kant of numerous precising definitions and post-Kantian categories. Kant scholars do frequently engage in that kind of project, either openly, as in Paul Crowther's book on the sublime, or tacitly, and there is philosophical value in such projects. However, my concern here is only to demonstrate the significant moral functions that Kant himself assigns to the sublime, not to augment or perfect them by the addition of anachronistic categories.

Kant defines this role for the sublime in piecemeal fashion in a series of texts dating from the pre-critical period to the *Metaphysics of Morals* in 1797. But while his earlier critical and pre-critical accounts establish sublimity's essential significance to morality and his later works specify this role further, the 'Analytic of the Sublime' in the *Critique of Judgment* is his only detailed, systematic account of sublimity and its role in morality and the critical project. The sublime appears briefly at the end of §14 of the *Critique of Judgment*, but Kant's only mature extended treatment of sublimity, 'The Analytic of the Sublime', extends from §§23–9, plus the 'General Remark on the Exposition of Aesthetic Reflective Judgments'. In the *Critique of Judgment*, the 'Analytic of the Sublime' is the second book of division I, 'Analytic of Aesthetic Judgment', within part I, 'Critique of Aesthetic Judgment'. The first book of the 'Critique of Aesthetic Judgment', the 'Analytic of the Beautiful', is divided into the four categorial moments of quality, quantity, relation and modality, whereas the 'Analytic of the Sublime', which begins with two transitional sections comparing and contrasting the beautiful and the sublime (§§23–4), is divided into the mathematical and dynamical sublime. In the first *Critique*, the mathematical categories of quality and quantity concern the objects of intuition as such, whether pure or empirical, and the dynamical categories of relation and modality concern the existence of those objects in their relation to one another or to the understanding (B110). In the 'Analytic of the Sublime', the terms 'mathematical' and 'dynamical' are still broken down into quality, quantity, relation and modality, but the order of categories is altered and the mathematical sublime refers to magnitude and number, while the dynamical sublime refers to power. Part A on the mathematical sublime (§§25–7) begins with an explication of the term 'sublime', followed by sections on quantity and quality, reversing the order of the 'Analytic of the Beautiful', for reasons given in §24. Part B on the dynamical sublime in nature (§§28–9) includes sections implicitly on relation and explicitly on modality (cf. Clewis: 62). The sublime is developed further in the 'General Remark', but then is excluded from the 'Deduction of Aesthetic Judgments' about objects in nature (§§30–8 or 30–54), for reasons explained in §30.

My basic argument that the 'Analytic of the Sublime' establishes the sublime as the condition of the determinability of morality runs as follows. In order to recognize its moral functions, we cannot think about the sublime in terms of natural objects and forces or even as a reaction to them. The sublime is not an object but, rather, *'what even only to be able to think proves a power of the mind that surpasses every measure of the senses'*; '[c]onsequently, what is to be called sublime is the mental attunement [*Geistesstimmung*] through a certain representation employing reflective judgement, but not the object [*Object*]' (CJ: 250); 'the true sublimity must be sought only in the mind of the judging person, not in the natural object the judging of which induces this attunement' (CJ: 256). Even in sometimes describing sublimity erringly (by his own terms) as an object, Kant stresses its subjective mental functions. 'One can describe the sublime so: it is an object (of nature), *whose representation determines the mind to think of the unattainability of nature as an exhibition* [*Darstellung*] *of ideas*' (CJ: 268). Sublimity produces the disinterested, subjectively universal (CJ: 271), 'mental attunement [*Gemüthsstimmung*]' (CJ: 276, 250) of 'respect for our own determination' and this respect takes the moral form of the categorical imperative of treating 'the idea of humanity in our subject [*Subjekte*]' as in itself worthy of respect (CJ: 257). Sublimity enables moral action as an *emotion* produced by overcoming its limits, an initial inhibition followed by an outpouring or emptying of vital forces, and a force that, as a form of judgement, 'give[s] the rule to the feeling of pleasure and displeasure' (CJ: 168; cf. 178) and demonstrates our internal power to transcend nature (CJ: 264).[3] The feelings of repulsion, attraction and displeasure (*Unlust*) involved in the sublime 'arouse [*rege macht*] in us the feeling of our supersensible determination [*Bestimmung*]' (CJ: 258). This recognition of our supersensible power provides in a certain way what practical reason cannot, for morality 'is a second (supersensible) nature, of which we know only the laws, without being able to reach through intuition the supersensible power within ourselves that contains the ground of this legislating' (CJ: 275). We cannot demonstrate the existence of this supersensible ability. Therefore, we should not follow Zammito in transforming legitimate critical, moral functions into the *Schwärmerei* or fanaticism of claiming Kant's supersensible reconciliation of laws of nature and laws of freedom, 'the transcendent unity of nature and man' (Zammito: 266). But the experience of sublimity symbolizes and thus, exhibits aesthetically this supersensible power and constitutes the subjective conditions for its use. Hence, the aesthetic judgement of the sublime provides for morality what practical and theoretical reason cannot.

Determination and determinability

If, as I argue, the sublime is the condition of the determinability of the moral subject, then the meaning and systematic functions of the determination (*Bestimmung*) and determinability (*Bestimmbarkeit*) of the moral subject are crucial to the Kantian critical project. Little can be gleaned about these terms from many Kant translations, such as the recent Cambridge project, for they either silently and mistakenly dissolve the distinction between determination and determinability by translating both *Bestimmung* and *Bestimmbarkeit* as determination (e.g. *Religion within the boundaries of mere reason*, Kant 1996: VI138, 164), or, as in Pluhar and Guyer, obscure their etymological relation by translating *Bestimmung* (a harmonization with one's internal possibilities) sometimes as determination and sometimes as vocation (a calling), which suggests a distinct concept with distinct associations from the Kantian German. If Kant had intended 'vocation' or 'calling', he would have used *Beruf* or *Berufung*, not *Bestimmung*, and the context in the 'Analytic of the Sublime' never requires that the last term be translated as 'vocation'. Indeed, the loss in translating *Bestimmung* and/or *Bestimmbarkeit* as vocation is considerable, for it means missing their etymological connection or their difference from one another, and thereby missing the very essence of Kant's understanding of sublimity's relation to morality. In this section, I examine the meanings and systematic moral and aesthetic importance of the terms *bestimmen*, *Bestimmung* and *Bestimmbarkeit*.

These terms appear extremely frequently in the *Critique of Pure Reason*, the *Critique of Practical Reason*, *Grounding for the Metaphysics of Morals* and the *Critique of Judgment*.[4] They serve a wide range of functions, and they seem sometimes to act as logical primitives or Wittgensteinian atoms, in that they serve as fundamental building blocks of key systematic concepts without themselves being expressible (determinable) by reference to other Kantian terms. Kant's three *Critiques* can be understood as attempts to determine or condition the determinability of theoretical and practical reason. He divides the two forms of judgement, determinative and reflective, by reference to the distinction between determining and furnishing determinability. Judgement 'is not merely a power [*Vermögen*] to subsume the particular under the universal (whose concept is given) [i.e. determinative judgement], but also, conversely, a power to find the universal for the particular [i.e. reflective judgement]' (CJ: XX 209–10). Both determinative and reflective judgement may be regarded analytically (as logical principles resting on non-contradiction) and synthetically (as a priori or a posteriori links between universals and singulars not contained already within the universal). 'Determination' can refer to logical categorization, action, production or disposition. Determinative judgement subsumes objects of intuition under pre-given concepts (logical categorization: for example, 'this is a cat' or 'lying is wrong'; Cutrofello 2005: 2), whether on transcendental or singular, conceptual or intuitive, levels. Reflective judgement can make determinative judgement possible and, hence, serve as a condition of determinability, in furnishing an indeterminate concept under which we might subsume objects. Through theoretical determinative judgement, the first *Critique* determines the nature and limits of theoretical reason; through practical determinative judgement, the second *Critique* determines the nature and limits of practical reason; and through reflective judgement, the third *Critique* establishes the possibility of these determinations in conditioning the determinability of practical (the sublime) and theoretical reason (teleology). Thus, to the notions of logical categorization and action, the *Critique of Judgment* adds notions of determination associated with both production and the conditions of logical subsumption, action and production.

The practical notions of determination are most relevant to my project. In GMM, Kant uses the terms 'determinacy' and 'determination' to mean: 1) a certainty and precision, lacking in empirical counsels (GMM: 418), as exemplified by a more exact determination, and contrasted with happiness, which is indeterminate in the sense that it is not definitely and consistently known what action will promote it; 2) the act of producing this greater certainty and precision, such as a condition restricting our action (GMM: 449); 3) the selection from a variety of options of (a) proper means (the realization of a given object of will, rather than choice of end), as in imperatives of skill (GMM: 415), or of (b) characteristics (specific, distinguishing marks contained in the categorical imperative (its determinations) (GMM: 431–2)); 4) the act of establishing (a) the laws of nature in general, as object of experience (natural philosophy), (b) the laws of reason (GMM: 406; GMM: 431), or (c) the proper specific application of the laws of nature or reason in any particular case; and 5) the act of commanding the will to act according to laws of reason (autonomy) or nature (heteronomy).

In the fifth sense, which delimits the possible functions of the will's determinability, determination refers to the mode and action by which the will becomes determined or determinate, the source of this change or its causation. The source of the will's determination can be either reason or nature. For purely rational beings not subject to inclination, reason infallibly determines the will, since it lacks any other power of determination. For rational beings also subject to inclinations, such as human beings, both reason and inclinations may singly or in combination determine the will. This struggle between reason and nature for power over the will exhibits the synonymy between determination (in at least one sense of the term), domination, causation and subjection, for to determine the will is to dominate and subject reason or natural inclinations, as a free cause of events in the world of nature. Heteronomy consists in the determination of the will by non-rational forces; even for rational beings, then, their 'actions as determined by other appearances, namely, desires and inclinations, must be seen [eingesehen] as belonging to the world of sense' (GMM: 453). In another formulation, the will is heteronomous if its object is the source of its determination (GMM: 444), for 'all laws determined [by reference] to an object yield heteronomy, which can be found only in laws of nature and can apply only to the sense world' (GMM: 458). By contrast, the proper, autonomous determination of the will involves objective indeterminacy and formal, rational determination by the categorical imperative. 'The absolutely good will, whose principle must be a categorical imperative, indeterminate in regard to all objects, will thus contain merely the form of willing in general and indeed as autonomy' (GMM: 444). This composition of formal determinacy and objective indeterminacy constitutes the critical alternative to the consequentialist combination of objective determination (heteronomy) and formal indeterminacy.

Kant at various times suggests that the mechanism of the will's determination involves representation, natural causality or a non-natural form of causality. The causal explanation could take either natural or non-natural forms. In many sections of GMM, Kant argues that to determine the will is to constitute the principle by reference to which it acts or the power that causes its action. The sense world 'gives no laws to reason in determining the will, and is positive only in this single point, viz. that freedom as negative determination is bound simultaneously with a (positive) power and even a causality of reason' (GMM: 458). Eliminating all matter, all knowledge of objects, from reason's ideal,

> nothing remains to me to think other than the form, namely, the practical law of the universal validity of maxims and according to this law, reason in relation to a pure world of understanding [or intelligible world, as below] as a possible efficient cause [*wirkende . . . Ursache*], i.e. as determining the will . . . Here now is the supreme limit of all moral inquiry, but to determine this is even already of great importance. (GMM: 462)

In this section, Kant regards the spheres of nature and freedom as analogous. Yet, there is no reason to believe that the physical causality of nature is at all like the posited causality of freedom, since we have no experience of freedom and Kant defines freedom, as an original causative power, by its difference or independence from the determining causes of nature. In any case, he certainly cannot identify the causality of the will with natural causality, because this reading would destroy freedom and morality by subjecting the will itself to the natural order of causation.

Kant's description of moral determination as an issue of the will's relation to representations of the law, then, constitutes a welcome alternative to natural or non-natural causal accounts of the will's determination. He uses the representational sense of determination in his account of practical good as that 'which determines the will by means of representations of reason and hence not by subjective causes' (GMM: 413).

The will is thought of as a power to determine itself to action in accordance with the representation of certain laws. And such a power can be found only in rational beings. Now that which serves the will as the objective ground of its self-determination is an end, and if this end is given by reason alone, then it must be equally valid for all rational beings ... the ground of the possibility of the action, whose effect is an end, is called the means. (GMM: 427)

The will is regarded as a power possessed only by rational beings to determine itself by reference internally to representations of the law (autonomy), if the will's objective ground of self-determination is an end given by reason alone, or externally to natural representations, if the will's objective ground of self-determination is an end not given by reason alone (heteronomy). Because both autonomy and heteronomy are predicated of the will's relation to representations, Kant is concerned here with the source by reference to which the will acts, not with how it acts or where it stands in relation to natural causes. The will is itself the cause or source of its own action and representation's role consists merely in providing a conscious guide by which the will determines its own action. But this account still fails to explain the transition from conscious representations of action and motivation to the actions of rational beings in the sphere of natural causality, and thus it fails to explain the mechanism by which the will determines actions.

There can be no theoretical resolution of this question. Because experience obeys objective laws of nature, the idea of freedom admits of no possible example in experience. Moreover, since we can have no intuition of the will as a thing in itself, we cannot shed light on its means of engendering action. Hence, Kant sets aside the question of the metaphysical reality of freedom in favour of the view that the idea of freedom

> applies only as a necessary presupposition of reason in a being who believes himself to be conscious of a will, i.e., of a power distinct from mere power of desire (namely, a power of determining himself to action as intelligence and hence according to laws of reason independently of natural instincts). But where determination according to laws of nature ceases, there likewise ceases all explanation and nothing remains but defense. (GMM: 459)

This account of the will's autonomous determination to action, then, can specify its mechanism only by stipulation, relying heavily on the view that rational beings necessarily presuppose the idea of their own freedom, regardless of its metaphysical existence or explanation. Indeed, the 'determinate concept of morality' itself derives from the idea of freedom as a power of self-determination by reference to its own idea. Thus, Kant argues that 'we must attribute to every being endowed with reason and a will this property of determining itself to action under the idea of its own freedom' (GMM: 448–9), where freedom is

> independence from the determining causes of the sense world (an independence which reason must always attribute to itself) ... the concept of autonomy is bound inseparably with the idea of freedom ... [and] the universal principle of morality, which ideally even lies at the ground of all actions of a rational being, just as natural law [lies at the ground] of all appearances. (GMM: 452–3; cf. GMM: 454–5)

Here, despite Kant's need to reject the notion that the will possesses a power of natural causality or that it can be situated within the sphere of natural causes, he describes morality again by analogy to laws of nature and argues that we must conceive ourselves in terms of both natural causality and freedom. All rational-natural beings subject to an 'ought', rather than a 'would', must regard themselves in two ways simultaneously, as sensible beings or appearances subject to natural causes, and as intelligible beings or things in themselves subject to nothing other than the laws of freedom that they give themselves.

> The concept of a world of understanding is thus only a standpoint which reason sees itself compelled to take outside of appearances in order to think of itself as practical, which would not be possible if the influences of sensibility were determining for human beings, but which still is necessary if the human is not to be denied the consciousness of himself as intelligence and hence as a rational cause that is active through reason, i.e., a free, efficient cause [*frei wirkende*] ... it makes not the slightest claim to anything more than to think of such a world merely according to its formal condition – i.e., the universality of the will's maxims as law and thus the will's autonomy, which alone can exist with its freedom. (GMM: 458)[5]

The ability to accept this twofold mode of determination without asserting its noumenal truth is the key to the sublimity–morality relation. Morality requires this consciousness of the self in the intelligible sphere as free rational cause with the power to dominate sensible influences. Thus, the role of conditioning the determinability of the moral subject is laid out in advance in GMM.

> The just claim of common human reason to freedom of the will grounds itself on the consciousness and the admitted presupposition of the independence of reason from merely subjectively determining causes which together make up what belongs merely to sensation, therefore, [belongs] under the universal designation of sensibility. The human being ... posits himself in another order of things and in a relationship to determining grounds of another type if he thinks of himself as an intelligence endowed with a will, consequently with causality, rather than if he perceives himself as a phenomenon in the sense world (which he actually is also) and subjects his causality to external determination according to laws of nature ... For that a thing in appearance (which belongs to the sense world) is subjected to certain laws, from which it is independent as a thing or being in itself, contains not the least contradiction; but that the human being must represent and think of himself in this twofold way rests on the consciousness of himself in the former case as object affected by the senses, and in the latter, as intelligence, i.e. as independent of sensible impressions in the use of reason (accordingly as belonging to the world of understanding). (GMM: 457)

The determinability of the moral subject, then, requires not only the necessary presupposition of freedom but also a consciousness of ourselves as both sensible beings determined by causal forces and rational beings independent from natural and subjectively determining causes. But, as we shall see, only the sublime exhibits this free power aesthetically, generates the feeling of respect for the moral law and moves us to act against all natural inclinations and solely according to this rational law. In this sense, the sublime makes the will of the moral subject determinable or capable of determination.[6]

In the first *Critique*, Kant calls the principle (*Grundsatz*) of determinability a merely formal or abstract logical principle resting on the law of non-contradiction (B599). Yet, the term 'determinability' is appropriate to these particular moral functions of generating consciousness of freedom and our moral powers, for Kant uses the term to refer to the act of making conscious the conditions of experience or morality. Thus, he argues that the determinability of my existence in time entails *consciousness* of this existence in time (CPR: Preface to 2nd Edition, BXL). In order to determine my existence in time, to prove that it is and what it is, I must first be conscious of this existence in time. Consciousness enables this determinability by identifying the immanent conditions belonging to a concept, and thus linking the universal to one or more singulars, in this case, connecting concepts to intuitions or the form of intuitions. Hence, the transcendental and synthetic a priori moves constitute a species of determinability. My thinking establishes the possibility of determining my existence by reference to temporal representations, because it is the empirical evidence for this existence, and determinations of contingent or necessary cognition depend on the existence of some empirical intuition (B420). Similarly, the determinability of the moral subject logically entails (or presupposes) consciousness of morality and the conditions of acting morally (the condition of the possibility of morality). Kant writes that the determinability of the moral good is moral feeling (CJ: 267), which in CJ is respect, the consciousness of the will's subordination to law, and this identifies moral determinability with consciousness of our moral conditions. He also writes of 'the will's property of being determinable [*bestimmt werden zu können*] *a priori* by reason' (CJ: 296) and asserts that 'freedom is a property that becomes known [*kund*] for the human being from the determinability of his faculty of choice [*Willkür*] by the unconditioned moral law, . . . because its cognition can be communicated to everyone', although the unexamined ground of freedom, whether in nature or the supersensible, remains secret, 'because it is not given to us for cognition' (Kant 1960: VI138).

If consciousness of freedom *derived* from the will's determinability, as in this late text, then it would be uncertain how determinability itself became possible. The function of enabling consciousness of freedom would be termed a derivative, singular function, an effect of determinability, whereas the function of enabling determinability itself would be transcendental. This dilemma can be resolved by recognizing that sublimity executes both transcendental and derivative, singular functions in moral determinability and that the determinability of morality depends more on conscious functions than existential powers. It would seem that the determinability of morality, the ability to enact the moral subject's determination (its disposition or capacity to act freely according to the moral law, for example, CJ: 258), to determine the moral law, is always already present for a rational being, in so far as the ability to determine the moral law depends on reason and freedom. Hence, sublimity's functions of exhibiting our rational power, generating respect and subjecting the inclinations to the rational law would seem to be derivative functions parasitic on an already extant moral determinability. If consciousness were itself only an effect of determinability in morality, in contrast to theoretical determinability, then the power of reason and the will's property of freedom, as necessary conditions of morality, would be stronger candidates for the will's moral determinability. Reason's power (the power of desire, '*Begehrungsvermögen* – – – *Vernunft*' (CJ: 1st Introduction, XX244'–5')) would be the ground of the determination of the rational concept of freedom, as Kant argues (CJ: 1st Introduction, XX206'–7'). But because freedom is taken as a necessary presupposition, instead of a really existing power, the conditions of determinability consist, rather, in the moral subject's stance toward the conditions of acting morally. Hence, sublimity can exercise the transcendental functions establishing the determinability of the moral subject without presupposing the moral subject's reason and power of freedom. The cognition and universal communication of the will's property of freedom are not *effects* of the possibility of determining the *Willkür* or power of choice by the moral law but, rather, conditions of this determinability. Moral determinability, like theoretical determinability, requires such an experience, for the will cannot be determined unless we think that we are free and rational, feel respect for the moral law and act independently of inclinations, for the sake of the moral law alone. This requirement enables a role for sublimity in moral determinability, because sublimity makes us conscious of our moral power, our freedom, produces respect and subjects our inclinations to the moral law.[7]

Reflective judgement in the critical project

With this account of determinability in hand, we may now examine its conditions, showing first that aesthetic reflective judgement is necessary to establish the determinability of the moral subject and second that the aesthetic reflective judgement of beauty cannot satisfy this function. Kant argues in the 'Analytic of the Sublime' and the second Introduction to CJ that sublimity's function is to constitute the determinability of the moral subject. This does not mean that sublimity is *identical* to morality or that it is the condition of the determination of morality. Rather, it means that sublimity is the necessary and sufficient condition for the *determinability* of the moral subject. While practical reason determines the identity of the moral law, determinative judgement identifies the law's proper application and the autonomous will enacts the law, the experience of the sublime enlightens us to our supersensible moral power or determination, engenders in us the proper attunement to the moral law and moves the subject to act with the consciousness of the sublimity of this moral power, to determine our will by reference to the moral law. Understanding gives a priori laws to nature and points to the supersensible substrate of nature without determining it or providing for the possibility of its determination, whereas judgement, 'through its a priori principle of judging nature in terms of possible particular laws of nature, provides nature's supersensible substrate (within as well as outside us) with *determinability* by *the intellectual power*', and reason 'through its a priori practical law, gives this same substrate *determination*' (CJ: 196). Judgement provides the determinability of nature's supersensible substrate internally and externally, on the basis of which reason may then determine the possibilities and entailments of this supersensible substrate in action. Thus, practical reason's determination of the moral law through the supersensible substrate of freedom is made possible by judgement's provision of the determinability of this substrate.

> [T]his power provides us with the concept that mediates between the concepts of nature and the concept of freedom: the concept of a *purposiveness* of nature, which makes possible the transition from pure theoretical to pure practical lawfulness, from lawfulness in terms of nature to the final purpose set by the concept of freedom. For it is through this concept that we cognize the possibility of [achieving] the final purpose, which can be actualized only in nature and in accordance with its laws. (ibid.)

Judgement's concept of natural purposiveness has a moral function in that it makes possible this mediation between nature and freedom, moving from theoretical to practical universality by allowing us to recognize and enact our power (reason) to determine nature's supersensible substrate (ibid.). Judgement presupposes a priori the condition or power that makes it possible to effect nature's final purpose, especially in the nature of the human subject. The concept of freedom aims at a final purpose which ought to exist, or whose appearance ought to exist in the sense world. Judgement must presuppose a priori the condition of the possibility of achieving this final purpose in nature (that of the human subject as a being of sense) independently of the practical. The type of judgement conditioning the power of morality a priori is sublime reflective judgement.

While the function of determinability might, then, be read to apply solely to teleological, rather than aesthetic, judgement, in so far as it concerns nature, Kant applies the determinability of the supersensible to inner *and* outer nature: teleological judgement provides outer nature with determinability for theoretical reason; aesthetic judgement provides practical reason 'within' with determinability. This interpretation allows us to assign the following tasks to the critical powers of theoretical reason (first *Critique*), practical reason (second *Critique*) and judgement (third *Critique*): the understanding, or theoretical reason, determines nature with respect to its laws, while leaving the supersensible substrate of nature completely undetermined; practical reason determines the supersensible (laws of freedom) through the moral law; reflective judgement grounds the determinability of the subject's enacting scientific laws in (external) nature *in concreto*, on the one hand, and enacting moral laws in the supersensible (laws of freedom, inner nature), on the other. Hence, Kant argues, with regard to the first two claims, that

> [t]he understanding legislates a priori for nature, as object of sense, in order to give rise to theoretical cognition of nature in a possible experience. Reason legislates a priori for freedom and for freedom's own causality, in other words, for the supersensible in the subject, in order to give rise to unconditioned practical cognition. (CJ: 195)

Determinability in general is a function of judgement. But the determinability of aesthetic, as opposed to teleological, judgement specifically involves morality, for it concerns the possibility of determining the idea or concept of our supersensible power of freedom; 'judgement will effect [*bewirken*] a transition from the pure cognitive power, i.e., from the domain of the concepts of nature, to the domain of the concept of freedom, just as in its logical use it makes possible the transition from understanding to reason' (CJ: 179). Effecting this transition involves enabling our moral determinability. In relating sensibility to understanding and reason, judgement brings about the transition from concepts of nature to concepts of freedom, and thus, morality. For Kant, 'our ability to judge [provides] a transition from sense enjoyment to moral feeling ... [judgement is] a mediating link in the chain of man's a priori powers, the powers on which all legislation must depend' (CJ: 297–8). However, this operation cannot occur through all forms of judgement. The function of transferring the subject from the cognitive power to the domain of freedom is a task for reflective judgement, for, while determinative judgement, the form of judgement operative in the second *Critique*, moves from the universal to the singular, assuming the universal, reflective judgement in the third *Critique* moves from the singular to the universal: reflective judgement generates the universal by giving itself the law (CJ: 179–80). But teleological 'reflective' (CJ: 360) judgement is not a candidate to generate moral determinability, because it involves natural purposes, rather than the concept of freedom. Whereas practical reason ascertains what it means to determine what is the universal law for morality, establishing the source and 'correct determination' of moral principles (GMM: 405), aesthetic reflective judgement establishes the determinability of the moral subject by exhibiting the supersensible power and subjecting itself to the moral law.

Since the power of reflective judgement grounds the determinability of the supersensible sphere by the intellectual power and effects the transition from concepts of nature to concepts of freedom, it follows that the determinability of the moral subject depends on reflective judgement in the third *Critique*. It is then easy to reduce the candidates for moral determinability to the two modes of aesthetic reflective judgement, beauty and sublimity, for Kant argues explicitly that determinability is a task for reflective judgement and that aesthetic, rather than teleological, reflective judgement grounds the determinability of the subject's moral determination. On the face of it, sublimity seems ill-suited for this task, for, while the a priori conceptual necessity of the good is attributed to freedom, the intellect and determinative judgement, sublimity is referred to nature, the aesthetic and reflective judgement.

> But the *determinability of the subject* by this idea [the absolute good], the determinability, indeed, of a subject who can sense within himself in sensibility *obstacles*, but at the same time his superiority to sensibility through the overcoming of these obstacles as a *modification of his condition*, i.e. moral feeling, is yet akin [related, *verwandt*] to aesthetic

judgement and its *formal conditions* in so far as it also can serve to make aesthetically representable the lawfulness of action from duty, i.e., as sublime or even as beautiful, without forfeiting the feeling's purity. (CJ: 267)

The possibility of the subject's determination by the moral idea, then, either depends on or is akin to transcendental aesthetic reflective judgement in referring to the 'formal conditions' of aesthetic judgement, namely, sublimity, but beauty as well, rather than individual judgements. The reason that Kant does not here exclude beauty from this function is that, as an aesthetic reflective judgement, it satisfies the first condition for moral determinability. But Kant associates moral determinability primarily with the sublime, rather than the agreeable or the beautiful, and he elsewhere excludes beauty from the role of moral determinability. Sublimity is the sole form of reflective judgement that contributes to the transition between nature and freedom (Wilson: 221, 223; Allison 2001: 307; Crawford 1985: 164), or the theoretical and the practical (Recki: 212). In providing for this transition, sublimity constitutes the determinability of the moral subject.

This association of the sublime with moral determinability is already clear in Kant's moral writings. In GMM, Kant anticipates morality's need for judgement and, specifically, reflective judgement by implicitly dividing the moral task between determinative and reflective judgement. He argues that the a priori laws of morality

> demand, furthermore, judgement sharpened by experience, partly in order to distinguish in what cases they have their application [i.e. determinative judgement], and partly to obtain for them access to the human will as well as influence [*Nachdruck*] on their practice [i.e. reflective judgement], for the will, affected by so many inclinations, is capable admittedly of the idea of a practical, pure reason, but is not so easily able to make this idea effective *in concreto* in the conduct of his life. (GMM: 389)

In order to act morally, human beings must not only conceive the idea of pure practical reason, they must also determine the will by subjecting it to the a priori moral laws and liberating themselves from the effects of inclinations. But these tasks require reflective judgement, which puts the will in the position of a universal moral legislator by giving a priori laws access to and power over the will, leading human beings to cognizance of practical reason and freeing them from dependence on inclinations. Although Kant does not argue explicitly here that the reflective judgement of sublimity, rather than beauty, is necessary for the determinability of the moral subject, he ties this determinability closely to sublimity and articulates originating conditions for morality that could be fulfilled only by sublimity, as described in the third *Critique*.

An account of the conditions of morality in GMM makes this connection clear. Kant defines morality as the will's self-determination according to laws: 'the will is thought as a power to determine itself to action *according to the representation* [*Vorstellung*] *of certain laws*' (GMM: 427). But this moral subjection to law is sublime:

> although under the concept of duty we think of subjection under the law, yet at the same time we thereby represent [*vorstellen*] to ourselves a certain sublimity [*Erhabenheit*] and worth to the person who fulfils all his duties. For not insofar as he is subject to the moral law does he have sublimity, but rather only insofar as in regard to this very same law he is at the same time legislative, and only thereby is he subordinated to the law. We have also shown above [Ak.400–2] how neither fear nor inclination, but solely respect for the law, is the incentive [drive, *Triebfeder*] which can give an action moral worth. (GMM: 439–40)

The moral actor is presented as sublime in so far as 'he' is legislative with regard to the moral law, and recognition of this power is both the essential attunement of sublimity and a condition for the possibility of acting morally. It is unsurprising, then, that Kant links the destruction of the sublimity of morality with the destruction of morality per se, as occurs when the drives to happiness subject the person to natural laws without also elevating 'him' above these laws (GMM: 442). Thus, the moral law in general and all of its particular instantiations are necessarily sublime, although sublime experience need not lead to any action, moral or otherwise. This connection can be explained transcendentally on the same lines as the notion that all objects are beautiful (CJ: 219, 292–3). Just as the harmony of the faculties, and thus, it is said, beauty, is the condition of the possibility of experiencing objects, so the condition of the possibility of the determinability of the moral subject is sublimity's chromatic harmony of imagination and reason, the attunement in which the self is considered simultaneously subject and sovereign. In GMM, sublimity is the only candidate to establish moral determinability, because it is the only form of reflective judgement capable of leading us to overthrow the rule of natural inclinations, to 'divorce [*trennen*] ourselves from all empirical interests by the idea of freedom' (the task of morality (GMM: 450)), to cognize our supersensible power and determination (*Bestimmung*) and to attune ourselves respectfully to the moral law.

In the conclusion to the second *Critique*, Kant again allies sublimity to the conditions of moral determinability in his famous comparison between the experience of the moral law and the (implicitly) mathematical sublimity (CJ: 270) of the starry sky (the 'unbounded magnitude of worlds beyond worlds and systems of systems and into the limitless times of their periodic motion, their beginning and their duration' (CPrR: 161–2). The process of leading the subject to the condition in which the moral law can be determined or enacted occurs through the existential attunement of sublimity. In order for humans to determine their action by means of the moral idea, they must

> feel the pain which only the morally good heart can very deeply feel . . . [and thereby] the young listener [can be led] step by step from mere approval to admiration, and from admiration to marveling, and finally to the greatest veneration . . . virtue is here worth so much only because it costs so much, not because it brings any advantage . . . [it is in suffering that the law of morals and the image of holiness and virtue] most notably show themselves. (CPrR: 156)

This articulation of the conditions of moral action expresses sublimity's functions. In the experience of the sublime, violent suffering leads us through admiration and marvelling to respect for the moral law in its purity, for it indicates that we have overcome the leading influence of natural inclinations.[8] The attunement necessary for morality involves this alternating repulsion from nature and attraction to our supersensible determination. The 'admiration and reverence' or 'admiration and respect' produced by the experience of the starry sky and the moral law within is sublime (CPrR: 162; cf. CJ: 245). These experiences produce opposite effects, but the simultaneous combination of these effects defines the operation of sublimity and the condition of the determinability of the moral subject. The experience of the starry sky in its unbounded magnitude and time destroys my importance 'as an *animal creature*', whereas the experience of the moral law infinitely elevates [*erhebt*] my worth as that of an *intelligence* by my personality, in that the moral law reveals to me a life independent of all animality and even of the whole world of sense, at least so far as it may be inferred from the purposive determination [*zweckmäßigen Bestimmung*] assigned to my existence [*Daseins*] by this law, a determination that is not restricted to the conditions and boundaries of this life but goes on into the infinite. (CPrR: 162)

This twofold movement describes the functions of sublimity. The destruction of the material, natural animality of human beings (the effect of experiencing the starry sky) elevates them or makes them sublime above all nature (the requirement of the moral law) by exhibiting their supersensible determination and producing respect for the worth of human being as such (CPrR: 87). Thus, moral determinations in the second *Critique* already presuppose sublimity; sublimity is not a product of an already existent moral state, for the determinability of the moral subject depends on sublimity.

Sublimity's transcendental functions

Sublimity's role in moral determinability rightly comes into question, because of its alleged dependence on moral feeling and its apparent status as an analogue to morality. But these problems can be avoided entirely by showing that sublimity carries out transcendental, rather than derivative, singular, functions in the determinability of the moral subject. That sublimity has this transcendental role is not always clear, for Kant often speaks of the sublime as a singular effect of morality, as if an antecedent experience of the moral law generated the experience of the sublime. Along these lines, Theodore Gracyk argues that sublimity depends on our moral awareness and 'often results from an appeal to moral ideas' (Gracyk 1986b: 52). Moreover, the notion that sublimity merely counterfeits moral feeling or produces a feeling and attunement akin to it or compatible with it suggests that moral feeling can be produced in other ways, and thus that sublimity is not the condition or unique condition of moral feeling. Kant writes that sublimity's conflictual harmonization of imagination and reason 'produce[s] a mental attunement that is in accord with [reason's ideas] and compatible with that [*welche derjenigen gemäß und mit ihr verträglich ist*] which the influence of determinate (practical) ideas would effect on feeling' (CJ: 256). Here the sublime seems to lack an essential function in the moral subject's determinability, for determinate practical ideas might attune the subject independently to morality through their separate influence on feeling. Indeed, the sublimity of the moral law does not entail that sublimity is the condition of the moral law or its determinability, for morality might produce sublimity without deriving any force from it. But Kant does not accept that sublimity is merely derivative of moral feeling.

By articulating two distinct types of sublimity, an active, transcendental, productive sublimity, determinative of respect, and a merely passive, singular product of our subjection to the moral law, he is able to argue both that sublimity is produced by the experience of the moral law and that it is the condition of the possibility of moral determinability. The recognition that sublimity presupposes moral sense means that the experience of sublimity proves the existence of our supersensible determination, and the existence of two types of sublimity, singular and transcendental, allows sublimity to play simultaneous derivative and transcendental roles in morality. Regarded as an effect of the moral law grounded by moral feeling, singular sublimity plays no part in conditioning morality; regarded as that which exhibits the subject's supersensible powers and is grounded on this supersensible determination, not merely on a singular version of moral feeling (CJ: 267), transcendental sublimity conditions the determinability of the moral subject. Subjection to the moral laws is sublime, but this subjection presupposes respect for the law, which is the product of sublimity. Thus, sublimity is both a product of experiencing the moral law and a transcendental condition of acting morally.

Beauty and sublimity

The many similarities between beauty and sublimity obscure the fact that their differences precisely enable sublimity's transcendental moral functions in establishing the determinability of the moral subject and exclude beauty from any such moral role. Yet, scholars who stress the differences between beauty and sublimity have typically regarded beauty as a good candidate for a moral role, given its status as a disinterested, harmonious symbol of the moral good (Zammito: 278; Cohen, in Cohen and Guyer: 222), and regarded sublimity either as merely analogous to morality or as a symbol of evil, disqualified from any positive moral role by its violent contrapurposiveness (e.g. Lyotard 1991: 229/189; Nuyen, 'The sublimity of evil'; Žižek). Among those who stress the similarities of beauty and sublimity, Robert Wicks and Paul Guyer both assign sublimity and beauty some moral roles (Wicks 1995: 193; Guyer 1993: 253–4). What is clear is that Kant identifies ten similarities between beauty and sublimity at the beginning of the 'Analytic of the Sublime'. Judgements of beauty (§§1–22) and sublimity alike fall under the aesthetic reflective power of judgement. The reflective judgement of the sublime follows the general principles of judgements of taste: the liking for the sublime, like that of the beautiful, can be represented as universally valid in quantity, devoid of interest in quality, subjective purposiveness in relation and necessary subjective purposiveness in modality (CJ: 247).[9] The beautiful and the sublime are singular (*einzelne*, they refer to an individual experience) judgements, liked for their own sake by reference to indeterminate concepts, rather than sensations or determinate concepts and constituted by the imagination's harmony with understanding or reason. Their liking is tied to exhibition (*Darstellung*) or the power (*Vermögen*) of exhibition, namely, imagination, for it is the effect of regarding imagination as harmonizing with the power of concepts of understanding (beauty) or reason (sublimity); 'in a given intuition, the power of exhibition or the imagination is observed in harmony [*Einstimmung*] with the *power of concepts* of understanding or reason as promoting the latter' (CJ: 244).[10] The universal, subjective validity of beauty and sublimity applies even though they stake claims only to the feeling of pleasure, not to the cognition of an object. Sublimity and beauty are ontologically indeterminate mental attunements (which is the insufficiently comprehensive basis for Kirwan's argument that sublimity is indistinguishable, except in its grounding, from dependent beauty (Kirwan 2004: 68–74)); they are neither objective, nor noumenal, nor a hybrid of the two, such as the transcendental object=x, and they are bounded by neither the objective sphere, nor the limits of any single mental faculty (CJ: 247).[11] While Kant erringly refers to beauty and sublimity (CJ: 244, 258, 268, etc.) as objective, he expressly defines both as subjective (CJ: 245, 258), as relations of internal powers occasioned by an internal or external object.[12] This subjectivity is both consonant with universality and requisite for morality. It makes possible an autonomous, non-natural connection to our moral powers, since the intrinsic liking for the beautiful and sublime does not entail or involve any interest, ulterior motive, sensation or determinate concept. Although we refer sublimity and beauty to indeterminate concepts, with 'the exhibition or power of exhibition, i.e., the imagination', we maintain their universal 'valid[ity] for all subjects' (CJ: 244), which makes them capable of dispute, entails the possibility of everyone's agreement and adapts them to moral purposes. The harmony, disinterestedness and universal validity of Kantian beauty suggest that it could be the basis of an accord with the law of understanding. At times, Kant even suggests that the sublime can, but does not necessarily, agree with beauty according to some of the very criteria by which he differentiates them, such as determinability (CJ: 267) and the form of the object (CJ: 244). But, if beauty and sublimity share so many important characteristics, then it seems rational for scholars to regard many of the distinctions between beauty and sublimity as merely contingent, rather than necessary or structural.

Thus, Guyer (1982) argues that the difference between the beautiful and the sublime is merely phenomenological and psychological, not logical or epistemic, although the psychological distinction entails some epistemological distinctions within identical categorical moments, such as between form and formlessness within the same relational subjective purposiveness or finality (Guyer 1982: 766, 774).[13] Guyer writes that Kant 'is describing an empirical difference in the specific phenomenologies and psychologies of the beautiful and the sublime, and not a fundamental difference in their logical or epistemological status. For he insists that in both cases the sources of response are equally necessary to human nature' (ibid.: 782). Beauty and sublimity differ phenomenologically, in that they involve qualitative differences in feeling; they differ psychologically, in that they involve different mental faculties (imagination and understanding versus imagination and reason) (ibid.: 757–8). However, they are identical from a logical or epistemic standpoint, because they fall under identical categories (ibid.: 778).

> From an epistemic point of view, judgements on the beautiful and the sublime are equally capable of satisfying aesthetic judgement's generic criterion of universal and necessary agreement even though differences in the psychological processes which underlie these agreements can only be expected to produce differences in the empirical circumstances in which

this requirement is satisfied. Once again the beautiful and the sublime both satisfy the generic requirements of aesthetic judgement but do so in specifically different ways. (Ibid.: 782)

Guyer's later treatment of this issue is essentially a refinement (a revised version) of his 1982 paper, not a rejection of its tenets, for, in both cases, beauty and sublimity satisfy the same logical/epistemological requirements in a variety of ways and differ only phenomenologically and psychologically, rather than logically and epistemologically. In 1993's *Kant and the Claims of Freedom*, which includes a significantly revised version of the 1982 article and a 1987 article consonant with these revisions, he continues to question whether any differences are possible between categorically identical aesthetic judgements whose four moments equally apply to the feeling of delight. He argues that Kant can hardly suppose 'that the different meanings of judgements of beauty and sublimity and the predicates they contain must lie in qualitative or phenomenological differences between the feelings of pleasure to which they give expression' (Guyer 1993: 194), because for Kant there can be no qualitative differences within pleasure (ibid.: 195). But Kant cannot differentiate beauty and sublimity 'by the purely logical and/or epistemological aspects of their form' either, because if the identity of the four categorical moments in beauty and sublimity ('universality, disinterestedness, subjective finality and necessity') exhausts the logical/epistemological aspects of their form, 'there seems to be no basis for attaching distinct senses to the predicates "beautiful" and "sublime"' (ibid.: 195). Neither the qualitative/phenomenological nor the logical/epistemological route alone seems to differentiate beauty from sublimity. Hence, Guyer's final 1993 alternative again invokes a combination: 'a variety of related but phenomenologically distinct forms of feeling and the related but distinct psychological processes which explain their occurrence satisfy a single but abstract set of requirements of logical and epistemological status in a variety of specifically distinct ways' (ibid.: 196). According to both early and late Guyer, the differences between beauty and sublimity consist in the distinct ways in which they fit the same logical and epistemological categories, and the multiple, distinct variations of the complex, rather than simple, pleasures involved in delight; thus, phenomenological distinctions can play a role in distinguishing between aesthetic judgements (ibid.: 197).

However, I would argue that Kant distinguishes sublimity and beauty in structural terms that exclude the latter from any moral role. Guyer places too much stress on the categorical moments under which beauty and sublimity are alike subsumed, for they play a limited role in constituting Kantian sublimity, and even these common moments turn out to conceal key structural differences, as we shall see in examining the differences between beauty and sublimity. Thus, for instance, the universality and necessity in beauty and sublimity (the second and fourth moments of the categories, their quantity and modality, respectively) rest on different bases, on the harmony of imagination and understanding as universal conditions for possible cognition, in the beautiful (CJ: 290, 292; cf. CJ: 217–18), and on the purposive harmony through tension of imagination and reason as universal conditions for the power of purposes, the will (CJ: 280), or for human nature's capacity for moral feeling, in the sublime (CJ: 265–6). Similarly, the identification of subjective purposiveness in beauty and sublimity (the third categorical moment of relation) overstates their categorical unity, for it reduces sublimity from a complex feeling incorporating both subjective purposiveness (with respect to reason) and contrapurposiveness (with respect to imagination) to a simple feeling containing only the former; pleasure (purposiveness) in beauty (CJ: 290) is identified with the complex alternating or successive positive and negative pleasure in the sublime. The undue focus on pleasure in the analytic literature also distorts the comparison, for· neither beauty, nor sublimity can be defined merely by reference to the far broader direction of pleasure or displeasure at some object. Sublimity is not distinguished from beauty merely phenomenologically or psychologically because the former is associated with both negative and positive pleasure, but also because its experience is distinct in origin, intention, explanation, function, effects and associations. Sublimity is aroused by, and thus involves, different objects, events and characteristics than beauty; it is explained by reference to different powers; and it differs in its association with moral ideas, its production of respect, its entailment of sacrifice, its revelation of our supersensible intellectual and practical powers and its function in moral determinability. Even if sublimity *felt* the same *and* involved the same mental powers, which it does not, its source, nature and effects would remain different. Thus, Guyer's argument that beauty and sublimity differ only phenomenologically and psychologically, in terms of the empirical circumstances satisfying the same categorical moments (Guyer 1982: 782), overlooks or underplays significant structural and functional distinctions. His failure to distinguish between either the phenomenological and the qualitative or the psychological and the mental powers enabling aesthetic judgements is also problematic. The phenomenological involves the totality of experience or its conditions, not merely one of Kant's four categorical moments (quality), while the universal mental powers enabling aesthetic judgement condition the particular or singular psychological events in consciousness and the unconscious. More broadly, Guyer's general account neglects numerous differences specified by Kant, and thereby fails to explain the moral distinctions between beauty and sublimity.

In §23 alone, Kant describes ten differences between beauty and sublimity.[14] These differences are complex and relatively neglected in the literature, for many philosophers, including Arthur Schopenhauer in 1819, Jared S. Moore in 1948 and Paul Guyer in recent years, have emphasized the similarities of beauty and sublimity, overstating the significance of their common subsumption under aesthetic judgements (Guyer 1993: 201; 1982: 782) under the spell of the view that sublimity is a category within beauty (Moore: 42), a 'limit case of the beautiful' (Lyotard 1991: 97 / English trans. 1994: 75) or 'distinguished from ... the beautiful only by the addition, namely the exaltation beyond the known hostile relation of the contemplated object to the will in general' (Schopenhauer: v.1, 202).

1. Natural beauty 'concerns' objective form or limitation, whereas the sublime 'on the contrary, is also [or even, *auch*] to be found in a formless object', represented as unlimited in its totality (CJ: 244). This ambiguous formulation has been interpreted to mean that sublimity's object is formless. But when Kant says again later that in the sublime 'the object can be formless', rather than that it must be or necessarily is formless (CJ: 249), it becomes clear that he means that sublimity's formlessness is contingent; beauty and sublimity can both involve objective form. The real difference consists in sublimity's independence from form, not its formlessness. The sublime is merely occasioned by some formless, unpurposive object; it does not involve a judgement in terms of form at all (CJ: 280). This autonomy from objective form, which includes the freedom to relate to objective form, is a necessary condition for sublimity's role

in moral determinability, for the determination or fixing of our moral determination cannot itself be grounded in objective limitation, as in natural beauty, since such an external ground would be heteronomous. Because sublimity's object can be formless, its liking is for the extension of the imagination, not for the heteronomous object as in the beautiful, where reflective judgement is determined as purposive in relation to cognition in general (CJ: 249).

2. We regard the beautiful as the exhibition of an indeterminate concept of understanding, and the sublime as the exhibition of an indeterminate concept of reason.[15] This relation to reason is critical to sublimity's moral functions.

3. Beauty and sublimity differ in a host of major and minor ways in their logical/epistemological categories, despite their nominal categorical unity. Because beauty concerns objective form, its liking and, hence, its first moment, is connected with the representation of quality, while sublimity's independence from objective form in its liking means that its first moment is quantity. Later, in the General Remark, in identifying the four moments in the table of judgements with the agreeable (quantity), the beautiful (quality), the sublime (relation) and the good (modality), Kant reassigns sublimity to relation, instead of quantity, while continuing to identify beauty with quality (CJ: 266). But, in either case, the distinction curiously assigns only one moment to an aesthetic judgement with all four moments, ignores the mathematical–dynamical distinction in sublimity and omits the fact that in §27 Kant assigns the quality of pleasure/displeasure to the sublime. If sublimity applies only to relation, then it should not itself have four moments, as Kant elsewhere argues, there should be no mathematical (the categories of quantity and quality), and perhaps even no dynamical (relation and modality) sublimity, since sublimity would apply only to one of the two moments of the dynamical, and no distinction between mathematical and dynamical sublimity would be possible. But Kant sets up two parallel discussions of the categories in relation to aesthetics without explanation or justification. In the schematic or general discussion, the agreeable, the beautiful, the sublime and the good each occupies one of the four categories, according to its dominant feature with respect to pleasure, whereas in the specific discussion, sublimity is considered under all four categories. At times Kant also considers both mathematical and dynamical sublimity according to all four first *Critique* categories, despite his limitation of the

mathematical to quantity and quality, and the dynamical to relation and modality. And, despite applying the mathematical–dynamical distinction only to the sublime, Kant assigns the categories definitive of the mathematical and dynamical to both beauty and sublimity. However, in claiming that the mathematical–dynamical distinction applies only to sublimity, Kant distinguishes beauty and sublimity on grounds that the judgements of the latter involve two distinct referents, the cognitive power, in the mathematical sublime, and the power of desire, in the dynamical sublime (CJ: 247). In the mathematical and dynamical sublime, 'the purposiveness of the given representation is judged only with regard to this *power* (without end or interest)' (ibid.). The distinct referents of the mathematical and dynamical sublime are internal, for they depend on different mental powers, cognition and desire; they are prompted by different sources, greatness and power; and they produce different feelings, all of which privilege sublimity's relation to morality over that of beauty. Thus, despite their identical logical/epistemological moments, beauty and sublimity are structurally heterogeneous both in the substance of their moment of relation and in the order and organization of their logical/epistemological moments.

4. The liking of beauty and sublimity differs in kind in such a way as to exclude beauty's moral possibilities, for the beautiful carries with itself 'directly a feeling of the promotion of life', unifiable with charms and imagination at play, whereas the feeling of the sublime is a pleasure (*Lust*) generated indirectly 'by the feeling of a momentary inhibition of life-forces followed immediately by an outpouring of them that is all the stronger', an emotion.[16] In the sublime, there is no play in the business of the imagination but, rather, a seriousness that cannot be unified with charms (CJ: 244–5). The free play of beauty is incompatible with the law-governed task of morality, whereas sublimity represents this moral task in exhibiting reason's law-governed dominance or violence over sensibility. 'In fact a feeling for the sublime cannot even be thought [*denken*] without connecting to it an attunement of the mind that is similar to the moral' (CJ: 268).[17] The same cannot be said for beauty, despite its connotations of liberality and independence.

> [A]lthough the immediate pleasure [*Lust*] in the beautiful in nature likewise presupposes and cultivates a certain *liberality* of the mode of thinking, i.e. independence of liking [*Wohlgefallen*] from mere sense enjoyment, . . . freedom is thereby represented more as *play* rather than

under a lawful *task*; which task is the genuine property of human morality, where reason must exert its violence [or dominance, *Gewalt*] over sensibility, only that in aesthetic judgement about the sublime, this violence is represented as exercised by imagination itself as a tool of reason. (CJ: 268-9)

5. The beautiful is connected with positive pleasure, the sublime with negative pleasure, as admiration and respect; in sublimity, the mind is alternately attracted and repelled by the object (CJ: 245). Kant says in the General Remark that '[t]he liking for the sublime in nature is therefore also only *negative* (whereas the liking for the beautiful is *positive*), namely, a feeling of the imagination's depriving itself of freedom, in that the imagination is determined as purposive according to a law other than that of its empirical use' (CJ: 269). Yet, the sublime is defined both by negative pleasure deriving from the imagination's loss of freedom and positive pleasure from its non-empirical purposiveness. 'Thereby the imagination acquires an extension and power, which are greater than what it sacrifices, but whose ground is concealed from itself; instead [of feeling this extension and power], it *feels* the sacrifice or the deprivation and at the same time the cause to which it is subjected' (ibid.). Hence, as in §27, the sublime involves feelings of both pleasure and displeasure. The agreement or harmony (*Übereinstimmung*) of reason with sublimity's judgement of the sense power's incommensurability with rational ideas brings pleasure, because this striving to commensurability with reason's ideas is commanded by reason's law and belongs to our determination (*Bestimmung*), namely, to estimate natural sense objects that are great for us as small in comparison to ideas of reason. Therefore, the source of this feeling of our supersensible determination harmonizes (*zusammenstimmt*) with rational law. This harmony consists in the fact that the imagination's utmost striving to exhibit unity for estimating magnitude provides a relation to the absolutely great, which is to say, to reason's law that only the absolutely great may constitute the highest measure of magnitude. The internal perception (*Wahrnehmung*) of the incommensurability of sensible measures with rational estimations of magnitude is both a displeasure and a pleasurable agreement or harmony (*Übereinstimmung*) with reason's laws. Displeasure from sense's incommensurability with rational ideas awakens the feeling of our supersensible determination, which harmonizes with reason's ideas. This harmony is purposive for our supersensible powers, and

consequently pleasurable, without thereby undermining the purity of reason's moral laws because of the independence of the conditions of sublimity from pleasure.

6. The most important or intrinsic distinction of (natural) sublimity from (natural) beauty is that beauty is purposive, as if the object were 'predetermined . . . for our judgement', and hence, likeable in its form, whereas whatever in us 'excites' sublimity in apprehension without reasoning may seem formally 'contrapurposive for our judgement, incommensurate [*unangemessen*] with our power of exhibition and as it were violent to imagination, but nevertheless is judged to be all the more sublime' (CJ: 245). This contrapurposiveness is morally purposive because it is detached from heteronomous objects and natural inclinations, and related instead to the suppression of inclinations and the reference to ideas of reason. If Kant here attributes the excitation of sublimity to an unreasoning internal power, he, nonetheless, links sublimity to ideas of reason, rather than to objects and their sensuous observation, on grounds of sublimity's contrapurposiveness, formlessness and violence to the imagination.

> We can say no more than that the object may be fit for the exhibition [*Darstellung*]¹⁸ of a sublimity that can be found in the mind; because the proper [*eigentliche*] sublime can be contained in no sensuous form, but rather concerns only ideas of reason, which, though no exhibition commensurate [*angemessen*] with them is possible, are aroused and called to mind even by this incommensurability [*Unangemessenheit*], which can be exhibited sensuously. (ibid.)

Later, in closing §28, Kant repeats that sublimity is contained not in things of nature, but in our mind, to the extent that we are conscious that we are superior to nature within and outside us, which is to say, to the extent that sublimity influences us internally, rather than externally through objects improperly called sublime (CJ: 264).

> Everything that arouses this feeling in us, including the *might* of nature, which summons our forces, is then (although improperly) called sublime; and only under the presupposition of this idea in us and in relation to it are we capable [*fähig*] of attaining to the idea of the sublimity of that being, which effects inner respect in us not merely through its might, which it proves in nature, but rather still more through the power [*Vermögen*] that is placed in us to judge nature without fear and to think our determination as sublime beyond that same nature. (ibid.)

Here Kant explicitly excludes this language of an 'objective' sublime as improper in substituting an external object for an internal mental attunement aroused by the object.

7. Because the sublime is negative, contrapurposive and independent of form, referring to ideas of reason to which no commensurate exhibition is possible, natural objects can be called beautiful but not sublime; we can say only that the 'object is suitable for exhibiting a sublimity that can be found in the mind' (CJ: 245). The sublime is aroused and called to mind by its very incommensurability, which paradoxically can be exhibited sensuously (ibid.). Kant has just referred sublimity to indeterminate concepts of reason, but now he refers it to *ideas* of reason, terms he often alternates in accordance with his first *Critique* definition of ideas as concepts of reason.[19] Preparation in ideas distinguishes sublimity from horror in experiencing nature. As a horrible view, the wide ocean raised by storms is not in itself sublime. The experience of the stormy sea becomes sublime only when the mind is already filled with many types of ideas; ideas are necessary 'if [the mind] should be attuned [*gestimmt*] through such an intuition to a feeling, which is itself sublime, in that the mind is incited to abandon sensibility and to occupy itself with ideas that contain higher purposiveness' (CJ: 245–6). The ideas involved in sublimity, then, are moral ideas concerned with our higher purposiveness beyond the sensible.

8. Whereas '[i]ndependent natural beauty uncovers for us a technic of nature', permitting representation of nature as a system of laws whose principle is absent from our understanding, namely, purposiveness directed to use of judgement with respect to appearances, the natural sublime leads to no 'particular objective principles' or accordant natural forms, given its excitation from nature in chaos, wildness, ruleless disorder and devastation, if they display magnitude and might (CJ: 246). Here Kant seems to position natural beauty, rather than natural teleology, as the condition of the possibility of determining nature as a system of laws via understanding, as described in the first *Critique*, and he argues that pleasure in the beautiful, its subjective purposiveness, may be required of everyone because it rests on the universally applicable conditions for the possibility of cognition as such (this is why one could ascribe to Kant the view that all objects are beautiful (CJ: 292–3)). However, natural beauty might be regarded either as a propaedeutic to, or a special case of, natural teleology, and Kant goes on to reverse himself

in subsuming natural to art beauty, for he regards appearances in nature *by analogy to art*, as in Aristotle's *Physics*, and accordingly attributes artistic intention to the creator of nature, as if natural things were art objects. Beauty expands only our concepts of nature, from mechanism to art, not our cognition of natural objects.

9. In contrast to beauty's order and natural purposiveness, sublimity's chaos limits its importance and implications. Sublimity 'indicates nothing purposive in nature itself, but only in the possible *use* of its [nature's] intuitions in order to make it possible to feel [*fühlbar*] a purposiveness in us entirely independent of nature'; thus, Kant says that the theory of the sublime becomes 'a mere appendix to the aesthetic judging of the purposiveness of nature', only 'develop[ing] [the] purposive use that the imagination makes of the representation of nature' (CJ: 246). Many scholars stress this poor-mouthing of the sublime, yet Kant here assigns to sublimity the role of discovering to us our non-natural purposiveness. Hence, this remark, far from constituting a legitimate basis for the dismissal of the sublime, clears the way for sublimity's moral use. This reading is supported further in the tenth point below and again later in the text, where Kant argues that '[t]he *sublime* consists merely in the *relation* wherein the sensuous (*Sinnliche*) in the representation of nature is judged as fit for a possible supersensible use' (CJ: 266–7), namely, a moral use.

10. For beauty we seek an external basis in what is purposive in nature, whereas the sublime involves an internal basis, a way of thinking concerning representations of nature (CJ: 246).[20] This internal purposiveness provides for sublimity's deduction, its necessity and its moral power. Sublimity applies subjectively to our practical application of a non-natural (moral) purposiveness. In §30, Kant argues that the exposition of aesthetic judgements involving liking or disliking of the form of objects, such as judgements of taste concerning the beautiful in nature, is inadequate to establish their deduction, which is to say, to legitimate their pretence to universal validity for every subject by grounding them on a priori principles (CJ: 279). Taste requires a deduction, despite the fact that the purposiveness of such objects is non-conceptual and unrelated to other objects by any determinate concept, because this purposiveness depends on the object and its shape in apprehension. Hence, there are significant debates concerning the purposiveness or beauty of natural forms, such as those at the bottom of the sea hidden from

the human eye and its judgement of purposiveness. This heteronomous, external relationship in what is still defined internally as a subjective harmony of imagination and understanding undermines beauty's ability to play a moral role. But the natural sublime falls into a different category. Pure aesthetic judgements about the sublime in nature, so long as they are not confused with teleological judgements involving the objective purposiveness of concepts of perfection, may be of what is formless or unformed (*ungestalt*) and yet involve objects of pure liking and subjectively purposive representations. Hence, in the case of the natural sublime, the deduction's formal requirement is absent. There is no need, then, to deduce a subjective a priori principle for the sublime, in addition to its foregoing exposition (ibid.). In fact, it is improper even to speak of the sublime in nature, for the sublime can be attributed properly only 'to our mode of thinking, or much more to its foundation in human nature' (CJ: 280). This internal basis for the sublime thus provides it an essential link to the moral powers. Although the sublime often involves apprehending 'an otherwise formless and unpurposive object', this apprehension merely arouses consciousness of sublimity, and thus, makes the *use* of the object subjectively purposive; the object itself or its form is not judged as subjectively purposive (ibid.). 'Therefore our exposition of judgements on the sublime in nature was at the same time their deduction' (ibid.). In other words, by showing that the apprehension of an unpurposive object arouses consciousness of the sublime's foundation in human nature, Kant claims to have legitimated the sublime's claim to universal validity for every subject merely through analyzing or making explicit what is contained in this representation (see Kant's discussion of the meaning of 'exposition' in the first *Critique* (A23/B38; A727/B755 ff.)). This foundation in human nature is the source of moral powers, for analysis of sublime aesthetic judgements reveals

> a purposive relation of the power of cognition, which must be laid a priori at the ground of the power of ends (the will) and therefore is itself purposive a priori: which then at once contains the deduction, i.e. the justification of the claim of a judgement of the cognitive powers to universally necessary validity. (CJ: 280)

The will, as the power of ends or purposes, is purposive a priori, since it makes possible all ends or purposes. The sublime reveals the purposiveness of the cognitive power as the basis of the will's a priori moral power. Hence, the exposition of the sublime exhibits the subjective a priori principle governing its existence, and thereby provides its deduction. Aesthetic purposiveness here means 'the lawfulness of judgement in its *freedom*. The liking for the object depends on the relation in which we want to set the imagination: [this requires] that the imagination entertain [*unterhalte*] the mind for itself in free activity [*Beschäftigung*]' (CJ: 270). Judgements determined by sense perception or concepts of the understanding, while possibly lawful, do not derive from a *free* power of judgement (CJ: 270–1). In this relationship between sublime purposiveness and freedom, we see again that sublimity's internal basis obviates the deduction because it entails its necessary connection to the moral power.

This extensive set of structural distinctions between beauty and sublimity simultaneously makes the case for a moral role for sublimity and undermines the case for beauty. The most obvious structural obstacles to beauty's moral role lie in its connections to understanding and pleasure. Whereas sublimity relates imagination to the desiderative power of reason and, thus, our moral power of practical reason, beauty relates imagination to the cognitive power of understanding, which plays no role in morality.[21] It is still possible to assign some moral force to beauty, for Kant concedes that 'to take an *immediate interest* in the beauty of *nature* [formally, not in terms of empirical charms] . . . is always a mark of a good soul', and if this interest is habitual and readily associated 'with the *contemplation of nature*, it at least indicates an attunement of the mind favourable to moral feeling' (CJ: 298–9). But, while the pleasure characteristic of beauty might not undermine morality if it is merely an effect of reason's determination of the will (ibid.), such an inclination cannot be a motivating ground of the will or a necessary consequence of its action, because the former would destroy morality and the latter would imply wrongly that contingent experiences of sensible beings could be determined in advance by a priori laws. Whereas action under the influence of sublimity awakens the morally necessary attunement of respect, action in accordance with duty but under the influence of beauty and its concomitant pleasure lacks any moral content, for it is driven by the heteronomous inclination of pleasure, rather than autonomous reason and, therefore, accords with the moral law only accidentally. Beauty's association with positive pleasure destroys the autonomy and universalizability definitive of

Kantian morality by subjecting action to non-universalizable, natural incentives, substituting pleasure (GMM: 413/413n) and natural incentives for respect. Hence, a beauty-based morality models Kant's third case of non-moral action in GMM, in which an action only accidentally 'accords with duty and the subject has in addition an immediate inclination to do the action', to act according to the moral law (for example, the desire for self-preservation in 'everyone' not stricken by adversity (GMM: 397–8)).[22] In contrast to the practical good, which determines the will by reason, 'the pleasant ... influences the will only by means of sensation from merely subjective causes' (GMM: 413). No such problem exists for a morality associated with sublimity, for it models the fourth case in GMM, in which an action accords necessarily with duty, since it is performed against or independently of all inclinations, solely for the sake of duty (where one is conscious of the demands of the moral law). Moreover, beauty pleases in judgement, rather than 'in perception of sense according to a concept of understanding', and, therefore, pleases without interest, whereas sublimity 'pleases immediately through its resistance [*Widerstand*] to the interest of the senses' (CJ: 267), which accords with the fourth case, because its pleasure derives from its resistance to sense interests; for Kant, it is licit for pleasure to arise from moral action so long as the action is not *based* or conditioned on this pleasure. This distinction in part explains Kant's privileging of sublimity over beauty in the aesthetic representation of the lawfulness of morality. Sublimity's relation to determinability or moral feeling would not be pure if it connected naturally with the feeling of the agreeable (*angenehm*).

Therefore, pleasure and hence, beauty, cannot serve any transcendental moral function. A beauty-based morality would be a variant of moralities reducible to more or less refined self-love, where reason is used 'only to look after the interest of inclinations, whether singly or, at most, in their greatest compatibility [*Verträglichkeit*] with one another' (GMM: 406). Morality cannot incorporate such sensuous inclinations as pleasure, for '[t]o catch sight of virtue in her proper form is nothing other than to exhibit morality stripped of all admixture of the sensuous and of every spurious adornment of reward or self-love. How much she then eclipses all else that appears attractive to the inclinations' (GMM: 426n19). Anything that accords with taste and is unrelated to need, such as 'a liking [*Wohlgefallen*] in the mere purposeless play of our mental forces, has an affective price', rather than a market price or incomparable worth, and hence is unsuited to morality (GMM: 435). This criticism applies specifically to beauty, rather than sublimity, since beauty is an unpurposive play of our mental powers, accompanied by delight, with an affective price, whereas sublimity is contrapurposive (in relation to the senses), opposes the inclinations and has a dignity or incomparable worth. Beauty lacks a moral basis, because its pleasure is neither enjoyment, lawful activity, nor reasoning contemplation according to ideas, but mere reflection (CJ: 292).

If there is a long list of reasons from various texts militating against beauty's moral role, the counter-argument in favour of beauty's moral significance derives primarily from a single claim in CJ §59 that beauty is the symbol of the moral good. Virtually every third *Critique* scholar regards this claim as testifying to an important relationship between beauty and morality (e.g. Zammito: 278; Cohen, in Cohen and Guyer: 222; Kirwan 2004: 68–74). Yet, as Wilson argues, the significance of this claim has been greatly overstated (Wilson: 223), for it is an isolated point, undermined significantly by comments within the section itself, and it is not immediately clear that it means what scholars have taken it to mean. Ted Cohen says that it means that beauty is analogous to morality. Kant, like Aristotle, seeks to identify a non-reductive relation of beauty to morality by speaking of 'the idea of the analogy of beauty to morality' (Cohen, in Cohen and Guyer: 221–2).

> When one thing symbolizes another, there is no way to prove that the one thing fits or instantiates the other. That is precisely the point, Kant's point. If a beautiful object is an indirect presentation of the concept of good will – which is what I have asserted Kant must mean by calling beauty a symbol of morality – then the beautiful object does not fit under the concept in the sense of being subsumed; it rather indicates the concept in some indirect way, metaphorically or analogically. (Ibid.: 235)

Still, this claim leaves undetermined what it means for the beautiful object to indicate the concept of morality or to indirectly present the concept of good will. Guyer argues that what it means is that the experience of beauty feels like the experience of freedom. 'Kant claims that the beautiful is the symbol of the morally good because the experience of beauty is felt to be an experience of freedom' (Guyer 1993: 252). Here it is obviously problematic for Guyer to identify the morally good with the experience of freedom, since freedom is only a condition of action, rather than the highest moral standard. What Kant says is, rather, that this experience refers to the unity of theoretical and practical powers connected neither to nature, nor freedom, but to the supersensible *ground* of freedom (CJ: 353). But there is an additional difficulty here, as Guyer claims, for the association of beauty with morality in §59 seems at odds with Kant's earlier exclusion of beauty from moral representation, in favour of sublimity (citing General Remark, CJ: 271, Guyer 1993: 253), and Kant elsewhere 'awards the symbolic plum of representing the morally good to the sublime, in explicit comparison with the beautiful' (Guyer 1993: 252). To resolve this problem, Guyer argues 'that the beautiful and sublime symbolize different aspects of human autonomy', the human potential for liberation from sensuous impulses, in the case of beauty, and the need to submit impulse to strict duty, in the case of sublimity in the General Remark (ibid.: 253–4). However, I believe that this is a misreading, for Kantian sublimity symbolizes both of these aspects, the submission of impulse to duty and the human potential for liberation from sensuous impulses. Moreover, at CJ: 271 in the General Remark, to which Guyer refers (ibid.: 253), Kant writes about the *representation* of the sublime, not its *symbolic* representation. Kant is not arguing there that the sublime is analogous to the moral good, but that the good is sublime *and* that it is represented as sublime, not beautiful. Thus, we have here three ways of understanding the sublime, first, as symbolizing the key moral elements of freedom and submission to duty, second, as a characteristic of the moral good and, third, as representing the moral good.

Kant never reconciles these different understandings of the sublime. But, in each use, he links the sublime, rather than the beautiful, to the moral good. Indeed, in several other passages putatively linking the beautiful to the good, Kant ultimately links sublimity to the good instead. He argues that beauty appears to point to our rational power for morality, despite its connection to pleasure, since the rational prescription of an ought for sensuously affected, rational beings entails the existence of a rational power to determine sensibility to feel pleasure or satisfaction in fulfilling duty (GMM: 460). But the rational prescription of pleasure from duty necessarily follows duty, rather than enabling it, and, in any case, sublimity, not beauty, is connected to reason. The experience at issue is again sublimity, rather than beauty, when Kant argues that like sublimity, natural beauty refers us indirectly to our highest moral purposiveness.

> Add to this the admiration [*Bewunderung*] of nature, which in its beautiful products shows [*zeigt*] itself as art, [i.e., as acting] not merely by chance but, as it were, intentionally, according to a lawful arrangement and as purposiveness without purpose [*Zweckmäßigkeit ohne Zweck*]; which latter, because we meet with it nowhere outside of us, we naturally seek in ourselves and indeed in that which forms the final purpose [end, *Zweck*] of our existence [*Daseins*], namely our moral determination. (CJ: 301)

This remark, like the passage on the beautiful as the symbol of the moral good, suggests an important moral role for natural beauty in leading us to turn inward to our moral powers.[23] However, Kant is, in fact, attributing this inward turning moral function to sublimity, for as he argues in the *Critique of Practical Reason*, the admiration or wonder at nature (the starry sky) is itself sublime and leads us to look inward toward our sublime, internal moral determination.

Similarly, then, in arguing that beauty is a symbol for the moral good in CJ §59, Kant describes the moral good as sublime and suggests that beauty can play no role in the determinability of the moral subject (CJ: 353–4). Hence, §59 on beauty as the symbol of the moral good in fact distances beauty from an actual role in Kantian morality, while providing further warrant for sublimity's moral significance, in sharp contrast to the popular scholarly reading of the section. An analysis of Kant's reading of beauty and sublimity as symbols of the moral good also allows us to understand how the sublime could still exercise key moral functions as analogous to the moral good.

In §59 he specifies how beauty might represent the lawfulness of an action from duty definitive of the moral good. Hypotyposes or exhibitions (*Darstellungen*, *exhibitiones* (CJ: 352)) make a concept sensible by subjecting something to inspection (*subiectio ad adspectum*); however, there can be no schematic hypotyposis of rational ideas such as the moral good. The objective reality of rational concepts or ideas cannot be manifested, since no absolutely adequate intuition (*Anschauung*) can be given for reason's ideas (CJ: 351). There is only symbolic exhibition of rational ideas. When no sensuous intuition can be given that is adequate to a concept thinkable only by reason, the ideas are exhibited *through intuition* only by analogy to the schematizing process, so that the process agrees only with the rule of judgement, the form of reflection, rather than its content (ibid.). Symbolic exhibition is analogical, served by empirical intuitions. 'Judgement executes a double task, first to apply the concept to the object of a sensuous intuition and then second to apply the mere rule of reflection on that intuition to an entirely other object of which the former is only the symbol' (CJ: 352). Language is replete with examples of symbolic hypotyposis, to which 'perhaps no intuition can ever directly correspond' (CJ: 352–3). The view that beauty exhibits the good through symbolic hypotyposis implies, first, that the good cannot be exhibited directly in intuition, second, that there is a similarity between 'the rules for reflecting on both [beauty and the good] and their causality' and, third, that the universal, natural analogy of beauty to the good warrants the claim of our liking for the beautiful to universal agreement (CJ: 352). But this very experience of a moral basis for the universal claim to beauty, which grounds associations of Kantian morality with beauty, is itself *sublime*. In recognizing the moral basis of beauty, the mind is conscious simultaneously of 'a certain ennoblement and elevation [*Erhebung*, sublimation, in a non-psychological sense] beyond the mere receptivity of pleasure [*Lust*] through sense impressions and evaluates the worth of others also according to a similar maxim of their judgement' (CJ: 353). Hence, from beauty, the subject rises to morality via sublimity (ennoblement, elevation). Taste indicates the subject's inner possibility to judge autonomously from empirical laws, though this judgement may still harmonize with external nature; this inner possibility is neither nature, nor freedom, yet 'is bound with the ground of freedom, namely, the supersensible, in which the theoretical power is unified [literally, bound to unity] with the practical in a common [*gemeinschaftliche*] and unknown way' (ibid.). For this reason, Kant concludes earlier in the General Remark that 'the intellectual (the moral-) good that is purposive in itself, judged aesthetically, must be represented not so much as beautiful but much more as sublime, so that it may awaken more the feeling of respect (which disdains charm) than that of love and intimate affection [or inclination, *Zuneigung*]' (CJ: 271). The good cannot be exhibited adequately in intuition; nor can we have any such intuition of our moral freedom. Hence, the elements of the good can be represented only indirectly or analogously through symbolic hypotyposis. In this process, the sublime applies the idea of the moral good or freedom to the object of a sensuous intuition through a certain subreption or wrongful exchange of an idea of respect for an object in nature (CJ: 257). To the extent that beauty provides for this movement, it is only as a process that is itself sublime, ennobling and elevating the subject through this attempt to exhibit the good.[24] Sublimity is suited for a moral role, then, because it can occasion respect, its liking is negative, exclusive of charms (CJ: 245), internal or external images, representations or incentives; and it is determined by the moral, law-governed freedom of reason's violence to the forces of sensibility (CJ: 268–9). By contrast, beauty may exhibit the idea of the good only analogically or symbolically, but it cannot serve a moral role, because its play and its association with pleasure destroy respect and heteronomously undermine the freedom of the will.

5 • Replies to Objections to Sublimity's Moral Functions

In this chapter, I address the strongest objections against this reading of the moral functions of Kantian sublimity. (1) I argue against the view that sublimity's functions can only be analogous to morality because there is a barrier between aesthetics or sublimity and morality. I show that Kant's moral and aesthetic projects are always mixed and that there is considerable continuity between the moral and aesthetic works. (2) I argue that respect in the 'moral' works is identical to respect in the 'Analytic of the Sublime'. (3) I argue that moral feeling, by contrast, is distinct from respect in the moral works, but identical to it in CJ. (4) I refute dismissals of sublimity's moral role based on its negativity and contrapurposiveness. (5) I address objections that sublimity is anthropological and/or psychologistic and, hence, inimical to Kantian morality, by showing that sublimity is no more anthropological than Kantian morality. Indeed, I argue that certain conditions of Kantian morality and sublimity are identical, for both involve conditions universal to the class of rational beings to whom moral *oughts* apply. (6) I refute attempts to restrict sublimity's moral functions to the dynamical sublime, arguing that the mathematical sublime also effects moral functions and, indeed, that these moral functions elucidate Kant's odd rejection of the sublimity of the infinitely small.

Despite Kant's detailed accounts linking sublimity to morality, scholars have readily dismissed claims that sublimity exercises nonanalogous moral functions.[1] What stands in the way of stronger readings of sublimity's moral functions is the underlying assumption, both in positive readings of beauty's moral functions and in most restrictive readings of the relation of sublimity to morality, that there are fixed disciplinary walls separating *sublime* aesthetics from morality, but no disciplinary walls separating the aesthetics of beauty from morality, or sublimity from epistemology (Lyotard 1991/1994: 98–9/76; Rush: 353–4; Crowther: 132–3; Allison: 343;

Guyer 1979: 359; 1993: 23–4). We have seen other reasons that beauty cannot exercise moral functions. But the claim to a barrier between sublime aesthetics and morality underwrites both the limitation of sublimity to an aesthetic analogue to morality (Recki: 209; Banham: 91; Crowther: 134–5; Allison 2001: 343; Kirwan 2004: 4) and the distinction between sublime and moral feeling or respect (Lyotard 1991/1994: 99/76, 157–8/127, 230–1/190–1; Crowther: 132–3). Even among the strongest moral readings of sublimity, as in Robert Clewis and the later Guyer, we see this disciplinary separation between sublimity and morality at work. Thus, Clewis writes that 'Kant ... clearly wishes to preserve the distinctness of and difference between aesthetic and moral judging' (Clewis: 126) and Guyer asserts that, although Kant's formalistic theory of moral motivation developed in the 1780s 'may have needed to be supplemented by the moral aesthetics he developed in the 1790s, we will never be well served by blurring the lines between aesthetics, ethics, and politics' (Guyer 1993: 23–4). On this assumption, scholars argue that there can at best be only an *affinity* or proximity between aesthetic (sublime) and moral feeling (Banham: 92–3; Recki: 209) or moral respect (Banham: 91; Pillow 2000: 106; Zammito: 282–3), because sublimity is radically distinct from morality. The most prominent scholars of Kantian sublimity have accepted only indirect or analogous moral roles for sublimity on just these grounds, while somehow accepting stronger moral roles for beauty. For instance, in his proposed moral resolution of the deduction of taste, the early Paul Guyer refuses to separate an aesthetics of *beauty* from morality. He suggests that if beauty 'assists in the development of a disposition suitable for moral action, then aesthetic response may be a means to an end legitimately required by practical reason', grounding universal claims to beauty (Guyer 1979: 359). Lyotard also refuses to separate morality and an aesthetics of beauty, even as he asserts that the aesthetic character of *sublimity* entails its absolute separation from morality. Like Crowther and Allison, he distinguishes between sublime and moral feeling or respect (Lyotard 1991/1994: 99/76, 157–8/127, 230–1/190–1; Crowther: 132–3), claiming that

> as something aesthetic, taste cannot be confused with moral feeling – strictly speaking, respect – nor can it be confused with the obligation of putting the law into action ... Thus the term to compare, in the order of

the aesthetic, with the feeling provided by the ethical maxim is not sublime feeling but the feeling of the beautiful. (Lyotard 1991/1994: 284/237)

Hence, for Lyotard, beauty is comparable to morality, whereas sublimity is comparable to evil. This is not to say that for other authors the view of sublimity as merely an aesthetic analogue to morality forecloses any moral role for sublimity. Indeed, Allison argues that

> the sublime is morally significant because it provides us with an aesthetic awareness of precisely what morality requires of us with respect to *all* duties, and of what is *sufficient* for the perfect duties that constitute the veritable foundation of the moral life for Kant. Otherwise expressed, the sublime puts us in touch (albeit merely aesthetically) with our 'higher self'; and, as such, it may help to clear the ground, as it were, for genuine moral feeling and, therefore, like the sensitivity to natural beauty, though in a very different way, function as a moral facilitator. (Allison 2001: 343)

Thus, even as he accepts the absolute distinction between morality and aesthetics, Allison recognizes a moral role for sublimity in providing aesthetic awareness of the requirements of moral duty, aesthetically linking us to our 'higher self' and clearing a path for 'genuine moral feeling'. However, he, nonetheless, greatly delimits sublimity's moral role by arguing that

> the purposiveness of nature with respect to this feeling is at best indirect, since it consists in nothing more than throwing us back upon ourselves and our 'higher purposiveness' as autonomous moral agents. And this again is why, in spite of its significance for Kant's moral theory, the doctrine of the sublime remains 'a mere appendix to our aesthetic judging of the purposiveness of nature'. (Allison 2001: 344)

As a mere appendix to aesthetic judgement, the sublime can play no essential, non-analogous moral role for Allison, because an aesthetic judgement of sublimity does not connote a judgement of moral approval (ibid.: 331–2). In my account, there is no need for sublimity to imply moral approval, because it need not play a role in assigning moral praise or blame in order to constitute important functions in moral determinability. Allison may have in mind the notion that there is no standard immanent within the sublime for preventing its association with evil, but while this is certainly the case for many other philosophers of the sublime, it is not the case for Kant. However, the basis of Allison's claim is the view that there is a strict separation between aesthetics and morality. 'Since . . . [the sublime] is a merely aesthetic feeling, without any direct motivating force, an attunement to the sublime obviously does not itself enable one to make the sacrifices that morality, particularly perfect duties, may require' (ibid.: 341–3).

However, this argument is highly problematic. First, as I will show, Kant explicitly lends sublimity a general significance in judgement that transcends any narrow construction of aesthetics. Second, Kant attaches to sublimity the *moral* feeling of respect. Third, sublimity involves an *emotion* and, hence, carries motivating force. Fourth, sublimity, through its 'negative pleasure', directly motivates the violent sacrifice of sensible inclinations. While Kant certainly played a role in the formation of the distinction between aesthetics and morality by dividing the critical project into primarily epistemological (e.g. first *Critique*), moral (second *Critique*) and aesthetic texts (third *Critique*), there was no such final distinction in his own time and his own work. As Kirwan writes, aesthetics was 'incorporated into "moral philosophy" in the eighteenth century' (Kirwan 2004: 1). Eighteenth-century accounts of sublimity were rife with moral associations, as we have seen, and Kant himself assigned crucial moral functions to the sublime in both his aesthetics and his moral writings. Indeed, Kirwan and Crowther acknowledge the falsity of the distinction as applied to Kant by accusing him of insufficiently distinguishing his aesthetics from morality (ibid.: 4; Crowther: 132–3). Moreover, despite his criticism of Crowther, Pillow and Kant for appropriating the purely 'aesthetic' concept of sublimity for the enhancement of life, ethics or cognition (Kirwan 2005: 155–6), Kirwan rightly speaks of 'Kant's attempt not merely to reconcile but actually to unite the interests of reason and morality with the experience of the sublime' (ibid.: 18). Kant refuses to alienate sublimity from domains of reason and morality, for 'the observation of human beings proves . . . that [the principle of 'the sublimity of the [human] disposition over nature itself'] can lie at the ground of the most common judgements, although one is not always conscious of this' (CJ: 262). But if the sublimity of the human moral disposition and, thus, sublime aesthetic judgement can ground many judgements that seem disconnected from the aesthetic, then the sublime can stand as the condition of moral and epistemic judgements, as well as aesthetic ones. Hence, the strong distinction between the 'aesthetic' or the sublime and the 'moral' exists only in the desiderata of critics, not in Kant's texts.

Now the objection might be raised that at the time of writing his main ethical works, Kant had not yet allowed for a critical role for aesthetics, let alone sublimity, and, hence, that it is anachronistic either to assign general moral functions to aesthetics or to invoke *Grounding for the Metaphysics of Morals* (GMM, 1785) or the *Critique of Practical Reason* (CPrR, 1788) specifically in support of sublimity's moral functions. Indeed, in GMM, he explicitly dismisses both the relevance of pleasure to morality and the possibility of a critique of judgement. Morality concerns

> objectively practical laws: we have no need to inquire into the grounds as to why something pleases or displeases, how the pleasure of mere sensation differs from taste and whether taste differs from a general liking of reason, or upon what the feeling of pleasure and displeasure [*Lust und Unlust*] rests ... for all of this belongs to an empirical psychology [*Seelenlehre*]. (GMM: 427)

However, in GMM and the second *Critique*, Kant already clears a place for the sublime in morality. He asserts that practical reason cannot complete morality. Moreover, he maintains sublimity's connection to morality throughout the critical period prior to the third *Critique*. Kant not only argues that the (third *Critique*) power of reflective judgement is necessary for morality (GMM: 389–90), but he also describes the worth of the purely good will (GMM: 426) and the experiential presuppositions of morality in terms of sublimity. A critique of practical reason cannot complete the grounding of morality, because it cannot ground the subject's moral determinability. Since it involves the transition between the spheres of freedom and nature, determinability is a task for reflective judgement, not practical reason. Practical reason is limited to exposing and deducing the determination of the moral power. Therefore, it would make no sense to argue that Kant only retrospectively constructs the need for the sublime in morality in the third *Critique*, by positing a lack in GMM or the second *Critique* that he had not recognized at the time. Kant did not just invent the connection between morality and sublimity in the third *Critique*, as Zammito suggests in referring to an 'ethical turn' in the final stages of Kant's composition of CJ in 1789–90 (Zammito: 276). In fact, Kant had already carved out a specific moral role for sublimity both in GMM and the second *Critique* and he explicitly identifies the conditions of morality as sublime in both pre-critical and late texts.

Hence, while it is certainly the case that moral feeling in GMM and the second *Critique* cannot be identified with respect or moral feeling in CJ, the relation of the sublime to morality and respect in the former texts is consonant with that in the later text. Kant had associated sublimity with morality long before writing the 'Analytic of the Sublime', and he continued to make this association in his late writings. Only four years after his pre-critical *Observations on the Feeling of the Beautiful and Sublime*, in which he links sublimity to virtue, in a 1768 letter to Herder describing the writing of his *Metaphysics of Morals*, which he hoped to finish that year, and not thirty years later, Kant speaks of 'direct[ing] [his] attention chiefly to the proper [or actual, *eigentliche*] determination [*Bestimmung*] and limits of human capacities and inclinations' (Kant 1997: Kant to Herder, May 1768: no. 40, X.74). In the long-overdue *Metaphysics of Morals*, this focus on the moral determination of human capacities and the connection between sublimity and morality persists, but it is explained in greater detail, prepared by the intervening texts, for now sublimity conditions moral determinability. Thus, Kant describes respect, the moral formula of persons as ends in themselves and the proper moral disposition all in terms of sublimity.

> Human being alone, observed as a person, that is, as a subject of a moral-practical reason, is elevated [sublimated, *erhaben*] beyond any price; because as such a one (*homo noumenon*) he is not to be valued merely as a means to others, or even to his own ends, but rather as an end in himself. (MM: 434–5)

Here again there is no indication that sublimity is limited in its moral significance because it is analogous to morality. Elevation or rising to the level of the sublime is the condition for the determinability of a moral subject, not merely a property of morality, for it generates the position of a morally practical subject. Thus, it is only in being elevated or made sublime that one becomes capable of acting morally. The *homo noumenon* is elevated beyond any price, raised above all standards of sense or relative worth, as an end in himself, through his subjection to a moral-practical reason. To be the subject of moral practical-reason (as opposed to technical-practical reason, the second form of Aristotelian practical knowledge in *Nicomachean Ethics*: book VI) is to be raised or made sublime beyond the realm of nature; the failure to be thus elevated to the sublime would make the subject heteronomous, governed by natural, not rational, law. Thus, the *Metaphysics of Morals* maintains GMM's notion that what 'is elevated [sublimated] beyond any price' is a worth (*Würde*) that has no equivalent (GMM: 434). The moral subject's elevation to the sublime establishes the attunement necessary to enact the formula of persons as ends in themselves, since in being elevated beyond any price, '[t]he humanity in his person is the object of respect' (MM: 435). In then describing the moral disposition as sublime, in terms similar to his 1764 characterization of virtue, Kant suggests that sublimity is an essential precondition of morality. '[H]e should always apply himself... with the consciousness of the sublimity of his moral disposition [*Anlage*] (which is already contained in the concept of virtue)' (ibid.). Virtue implies a moral disposition, and moral actions require consciousness of the sublimity or pricelessness of this disposition. Hence, Kant ties moral respect to the sublime and gives to sublimity a positive, constitutive role in morality in texts throughout his career, not merely in the third *Critique*. There is, then, in a very specific sense, no fixed boundary between Kant's moral and aesthetic works, for he not only insinuates aesthetic functions within his morality, but maintains a continuous account of the role of aesthetics in morality from his 'ethical' to his 'aesthetic' works, despite changes in his understanding of the critical possibilities of aesthetics.

Sublimity and respect

The primary reason that sublimity can execute moral functions is that it is defined by the identical relation of human powers determinative of Kantian morality. For Allison, though, the proximity of this relation indicates only that sublimity constitutes a mere analogue to morality, lacking any real moral functions. He argues that the feeling of respect relevant to sublimity is 'both causally and phenomenologically distinct from respect for the moral law' (Allison 2001: 341–3). Similarly, Paul Crowther identifies two distinct notions of respect in the second *Critique* and CJ.[2] In CJ, respect (2) is '[t]he feeling of our capacity to attain to an idea that is a law for us', whereas in the second *Critique*, respect (1) is a feeling produced by our awareness that the moral law is binding upon us. This recognition that our will is necessarily subject to the moral law thwarts our sensuous inclinations and humiliates our self-conceit. In turn, this effect akin to pain clears away obstacles to morality and renews our sense of its superiority, and is thus the ground of a further positive feeling. Now clearly the analogy between respect (2) and (1) is not exact. The former is a process that involves an *inexplicit* awareness of the superiority of our rational being only at the second stage. The latter, in contrast, transpires entirely at the level of conscious awareness and involves knowledge of the superiority of our rational self (in the form of our recognition that the moral law is binding upon us) as both its premiss and, in an enhanced form, its conclusion. Nevertheless, there is still some element of affinity between the two in so far as both involve a mental movement from a state of negative to positive feeling, and the ultimate ground, indeed, of this positive feeling is the superiority of reason over sensibility. (Crowther: 125)[3]

Yet, the twofold reading of respect is patently false. As Beidler notes, moral and 'aesthetic' respect are the same (Beidler: 180). Indeed, Crowther fails even to distinguish adequately between his two kinds of respect, for his two definitions are convertible. Our awareness of the binding character of the moral law (respect (1)) means that we are aware of, or feel our capacity to act on or attain, a moral idea, which is a law for us (respect (2)), because to understand that the moral law is binding on us is to be aware that we have the power of acting on moral law. For Kant, ought implies can. Moreover, the functions of respect (2) are precisely those negative relations toward inclinations characteristic of respect (1). The sublime, and hence, the form of allegedly non-moral respect (2) associated with the sublime, directly involves the functions of moral respect (1) listed by Crowther, namely, thwarting our inclinations, humiliating our self-conceit and clearing the way for our sense that morality and our moral powers transcend natural obstacles. Nor do I see any textual basis for Crowther's explicit–implicit distinction. Kant is quite explicit that the sublime 'uncovers consciousness of an unlimited power in us' (CJ: 250) and that it 'makes intuitable for us the superiority of the rational determination of our power of cognition over the greatest power of sensibility' (CJ: 257). There is nothing unconscious about the functions of the sublime in moral respect.

Notice that neither Allison, nor Crowther disputes that sublimity is connected with respect. The question is only whether this form of respect is in some unspecified sense parallel yet non-identical to respect for the moral law. Prima facie, it is implausible that Kant would construct two distinct notions of such an important term for him as respect, without noting the difference, in critical-era texts separated by only a few years. However, this point is merely suggestive, since it is possible for him to do so and I will argue that he *has* used two distinct notions of the more general term *moral feeling* in GMM and CJ. But Kant links sublimity to respect *and* morality in GMM, CPrR and CJ, accounts ignored by Allison in this context, though recognized by Crowther. Hence, I will show that 1) moral feeling differs from respect in GMM and the second *Critique*; 2) moral feeling in CJ is identical to respect in CJ; 3) sublime feeling is associated with respect in GMM, the second *Critique* and CJ; 4) respect is identical in GMM, the second *Critique* and CJ; and, finally, 5) the relation of the sublime to morality in GMM and the second *Critique* is consonant with CJ, despite the fact that in the earlier texts Kant had disputed the possibility of a critique of judgement.

To prove directly that Kant's accounts of respect are univocal, we need to examine Kant's definitions of respect in his 'moral' and 'aesthetic' writings. In GMM, Kant defines (moral) respect as 'the consciousness of the subordination of my will under a law without the mediation of other influences upon my sense' (GMM: 401n) and 'the representation [*Vorstellung*] of a worth that thwarts [*Abbruch thut*] my self-love' (ibid.); respect for the moral law must be 'bound [*verknüpft*] with my will as ground, but never as effect[;] what does not serve my inclination but outweighs it' is worthy of respect (GMM: 400). Respect concerns the will's activity, not the effect as such. There can be no respect for inclination as such, whether mine or someone else's, for the ground of the will, namely, the law itself, is the only possible object of respect, excluding or outweighing any inclinations (ibid.),

> [R]espect is an estimation of a worth that far outweighs any worth of what is recommended by inclination, and . . . the necessity of my actions from pure respect for the practical law is what constitutes duty . . . duty is the condition of a will good in itself, whose worth transcends all else. (GMM: 403)

What has dignity in the kingdom of ends is beyond any price, non-fungible and without equivalence (GMM: 434). The moral law and the end in itself share with sublimity their incomparability or irreducibility to external standards. And, like sublimity, 'respect is something that is observed as an object of neither inclination nor fear, although it has something analogous to both at the same time. The *object* of respect is, therefore, nothing but the *law*' (GMM: 401n14). The thought of the law alone, independently of any effects and ungrounded by 'any law determined for certain actions', must determine the will to action if the will is to be called absolutely good (GMM: 402). Thus, the law determines the will to action without determining particular actions; the law is causally determinative or effective but there is no law beneath the general conformity to law limiting the will to any particular actions. After excluding all inclinations and objects of the will, 'nothing remains left for the will that can determine it other than objectively the law and subjectively pure respect for this practical law, thus the maxim to carry out such a law even with the consequence of breaking off all my inclinations' (GMM: 400–1). The representation of the law is the moral good and, consequently, must be the determining ground of the will, in the sense that the will must act solely for the sake of this representation (GMM: 401). Hence, respect concerns the will's proper relation to the law.

However, Kant identifies respect both with the law's *determination* of the will and *consciousness* of the law's determination of the will. According to the latter account, 'respect is a feeling ... [not] received through any [outside] influence, but [rather] a feeling self-produced by a rational concept', defined by consciousness of the law's determination of the will (GMM: 401n14). Respect is a feeling produced autonomously by the rational concept of morality, rather than heteronomously by 'nature'. Because respect is defined here by consciousness of the will's moral determination, it *reflects* the will's moral determination, rather than producing it or constituting a kind of prior attitude to it; respect accompanies this moral action and is entailed by it, in so far as it is a by-product of action taken solely for the sake of the moral law. In the same note, however, Kant expands respect to include both the will's immediate determination by law and the consciousness of this determination. 'The immediate determination of the will by the law, and the consciousness thereof, is called respect, [which] is regarded as the effect of the law upon the subject and not as the cause of the law' (ibid.). Respect is here the law's subjective effect, rather than a prior cause of the law. Yet, in identifying respect with the act of determination and the reflective act of consciousness on this act, Kant seems to envision diverse accounts of the relation of respect to law, for the former use would seem to constitute moral action itself, rather than an attitude preceding moral action or an effect of moral action, like the latter. If respect is merely an effect of moral action, as in the latter interpretation, then it cannot be involved in the determinability of the moral subject. However, what Kant says is that respect is not an effect of moral action but, rather, an effect of the law upon the subject. Both the law's determination of the subject and the consciousness thereof are respect; hence, moral action is inseparable from respect.

By demonstrating that sublimity involves moral respect, I will connect sublimity to moral determinability. I argue that Kant's 'moral' account of respect is identifiable with the allegedly non-moral, sublime feeling of respect in their common negative relation to the inclinations (for example, the link of respect and sublimity to sacrifice in GMM and CJ), their connection with intrinsic worth and their relation to the determination of the will.

The case for this identification of respect in CJ and GMM is very strong, as is the connection between respect and sublimity. In §27, Kant explicitly defines 'the feeling of the sublime in nature [a]s respect for our proper determination' (CJ: 257). Whether sublimity ultimately is identifiable with, or merely generates, respect, the latter is defined in terms remarkably similar to GMM, and it is clear that respect in both texts involves the same consciousness of power, domination and powerlessness involved in sublimity. In GMM, respect is defined by the consciousness of the subordination of my will to law, while in CJ, '[t]he feeling of the incommensurability [inadequacy, *Unangemessenheit*] of our power to the attainment of an idea, which is law for us, is **respect**' (ibid.). The subject's powerlessness, revealed in the sublime, leads to respect, for the 'subject's proper lack of power [*Unvermögen*] uncovers the consciousness of an unlimited power [*Vermögen*] of the same subject, and the mind can judge the latter aesthetically only through the former' (CJ: 259). Our imagination's failure to comprehend 'a given object in a whole of intuition . . . proves its limits and inadequacy, and yet at the same time proves its determination to effect adequacy with the idea of reason as a law' (CJ: 257). A law of reason imposes the idea of comprehending every given appearance as a whole, in so far as reason recognizes the absolute whole as the only determinate, fixed, universally valid measure. The imagination's striving for this comprehension, to exhibit the idea of reason, demonstrates both its boundaries and incommensurability to reason's idea, and its determination (*Bestimmung*) to adequacy (*Angemessenheit*) to the idea as law.

One might object that this idea of reason is cognitive rather than moral and that, as Rachel Zuckert argues, Kantian sublimity is a self-regarding (and hence, non-moral) feeling (Zuckert: 229n10). Critics can correctly claim that the rational determination here involves the power of cognition, rather than practical reason, but, as I will show in my discussion of the mathematical sublime later in this chapter, this relationship to the cognitive power also carries out moral functions. However, critics wrongly claim that this form of respect is not moral. Kant seems to undermine the connection between sublimity and moral respect in saying that

> we show [this respect for our determination] to an object of nature through a certain subreption ([wrongly] exchanging respect for the object for respect for the idea of humanity in our subject), which as it were makes intuitable for us the superiority of the rational determination of our power of cognition over the greatest power of sensibility. (CJ: 257)

But what he is arguing is that while the experience of the sublime arises often from the experience of things in nature, this is itself a misplaced form of respect for the idea of humanity in us, a directly moral respect for the humanity in our own person (the formula of humanity in GMM). Our attribution of sublimity to things in nature merely externalizes respect for our own internal determination by subreption ('the intellect's trick of slipping in a concept of sense as if it were the concept of an intellectual characteristic' (Kant, *Inaugural Dissertation* (1770); cf. Pluhar, introduction to CJ: 114n22)). The experience of the sublime, in producing the feeling of that which is infinitely greater, moves us to respect for practical reason's supersensible power, but this is respect for the transcendent moral law, for the moral law is practical reason in its supersensible determination. The exhibition of imaginative weakness and rational power constitutes respect for our proper, moral determination, in that it makes intuitable our supersensible determination and produces a type of respect defined in terms of the moral formula of humanity. The sublime reveals 'our superiority to nature', defined by our 'power to judge independently of nature', and through this power of self-preservation, this power of mental resistance to natural power, the humanity in our person remains undegraded, although the human being must be subject [*unterliegen*] to that violence [or domination (*Gewalt*), in physical terms] . . . [nature is judged as sublime] because it calls up our force [*Kraft*] (which is not nature) in us to regard that for which we are concerned (goods, health and life) as small and therefore its might [*Macht*] (to which we are indeed subjected in regard to these matters) as still nevertheless for no such dominance for us and our personhood [*Persönlichkeit*] under which we would have to bow if it came to our highest principles and their maintenance or abandonment. (CJ: 261–2)

Consciousness of the subordination of my will under law in GMM becomes in CJ the consciousness of an unlimited power or capacity (*Vermögen*) over nature that elevates us above any natural command. These definitions are clearly convertible, for they both declare that the subject shall be commanded only by reason through the adherence of the will (the unlimited power) to the moral law, not by nature. Sublimity preserves the humanity in our persons not merely as a means subject to nature's might, but also as an end in itself, a possible rational will, according to the moral formula of humanity. Hence, contra Zuckert, sublimity is no merely self-regarding feeling, and, even if it were, that would not in itself make it immoral for Kant, since he enjoins duties both to self and others. Sublimity moves us to subject ourselves voluntarily to moral law (CJ: 264) by generating consciousness of this determinative independence from natural laws and inclinations and giving the rule to the inclinations of pleasure–displeasure. In uncovering an inability and displeasure in our power of judging, the sublime allows the subject to discover its supersensible power to determine nature autonomously. This awareness of an independent reason (CJ: 258), combined with the pleasure and displeasure occasioned by the sublime, lead 'much more to admiration and respect than to positive pleasure [*positive Lust*], that is, to negative pleasure [*negative Lust*]' (CJ: 245). Since sublimity is the sole condition of respect, which is the necessary condition of morality, sublimity constitutes the necessary condition for the proper attunement to the moral law and, thus, for the possibility of properly determining the moral law in action. It is not that sublimity generates freedom or the moral law, but that the subjective attunement of sublimity generates awareness of our supersensible moral power and constitutes the internal relations of powers necessary for moral action.

Sublimity's problematic relation to moral feeling

The real problem with linking sublimity to respect is not that respect in the third *Critique* is non-moral, but that Kant identifies respect in CJ with *moral feeling*. As Clewis argues, 'Kant considers respect for the moral law to be synonymous with the moral feeling' (citing Guyer 1993; Clewis: 358); for Kant, 'the capacity to take such an interest in the law (or respect for the moral law itself) *is the moral feeling* properly speaking' (Clewis: 127, citing CprR: 80, 86 and CJ: 257). But, in correctly identifying respect and moral feeling in CJ, Clewis misses the fact that they are clearly differentiated in GMM (see Clewis: 126–45). Although Crowther, Pillow, Kirwan, Pluhar and Banham all derive sublimity from the universal capacity for moral feeling (Crowther: 126–7; Pillow 2000: 106; Kirwan 2004: 91; Pluhar, introduction to CJ: lxx–ii; Banham: 94) and Kirwan, Recki and Clewis identify respect and moral feeling (Kirwan 2004: 82; Recki: 277; Clewis: 127), none of them recognizes that this identification is highly problematic. If sublimity is derivative of moral feeling, and moral feeling in CJ refers to the feeling identified in GMM as heteronomous and, hence, inadequate to morality, then sublimity can have no role in moral determinability. It would seem at first glance that, by moral feeling, Kant means respect, since respect is a feeling necessary for an action to count as moral, that is, the only moral feeling. However, in GMM, Kant distinguishes moral feeling from respect and argues that the former is inadequate to morality. Respect is autonomous, for it is self-produced by a rational concept, as '[t]he immediate determination of the will by the law, and the consciousness thereof' (GMM: 401n14); by contrast, moral feeling in GMM, as an empirical interest that we take in moral laws, which promises to aid our well-being or happiness, is superficial, heteronomous, non-uniform, an insufficiently universal measure of good and evil (GMM: 442/442n30) and inadequately determined, as 'some obscure distinction of judgement which it calls feeling' (GMM: 450–1). Moral feeling is associated with pleasure or even defined by it. Far from providing a standard for our moral judgement, then, moral feeling 'must be regarded much more as the subjective effect that the law exercises upon the will, for which reason alone furnishes the objective grounds of such moral feeling' (GMM: 460). Interestingly, this account of moral feeling as the law's subjective effect on the will is identical to the account of respect in

GMM: 401n14 above and, indeed, Kant says that moral feeling, 'this alleged special sense', is closer to morality and dignity than happiness, because it does not tell virtue 'to her face that it is not her beauty but rather only our advantage that binds us to her' (GMM: 442–3). Yet, as we have seen, Kant elsewhere in GMM distinguishes respect quite clearly from moral feeling; indeed, he rejects any foundation of morality on moral feeling on grounds that it would destroy the sublimity of morality. As an empirical principle of happiness borrowed from 'the particular constitution of human nature' or chance conditions, moral feeling effaces the universality of laws in founding 'morality upon incentives that undermine it and annihilate its whole sublimity' (ibid.).

However, if moral feeling is, in most passages, clearly distinct from respect and sublimity in GMM, this is not the case in CJ. As Pluhar argues, in CJ, '[r]espect for the moral law, together with our awareness that we have the freedom to obey or disobey it, is what Kant calls "moral feeling" (cf. Ak.267)' (Pluhar, introduction to CJ: xliv). We saw in CJ: 257 above that in respect we recognize the mind's transcendence over nature and, in CJ: 268, Kant defines moral feeling as the mind's feeling of its determination to transcend nature. Hence, moral feeling and respect are the same in CJ, even though they are different in the moral works. It seems, then, that Kant equivocates in referring to moral feeling in the third *Critique* and GMM. Kant's attitude toward other feelings is similar in GMM and CJ. For instance, his rejection of fear or dread in morality (GMM: 410/419) supports his distinction of fear and sublimity in the third *Critique*. But, in CJ, Kant always associates moral feeling with respect and sublimity whereas, in GMM, he explicitly dissociates respect and sublimity from moral feeling, attributing respect to the rational power and moral feeling to some unspecified empirical process subversive of morality. If sublimity and morality cannot coexist with heteronomous moral feeling in GMM, then Kant cannot be referring to the same feeling in CJ when he grounds aesthetic judgement in the sublime on the moral feeling of a transcendent mental determination (CJ: 268). Assuming that Kant has neither changed his mind on any relevant, substantive issue, nor simply erred in relating sublimity to a moral feeling that transcends nature, he must construe moral feeling in the sublime only as a form of respect identifiable with or akin to the moral works, not as the heteronomous empirical principle of happiness ('moral feeling' as an alleged special sense) disparaged in GMM and CPrR. Indeed, it would be quite odd if the moral form of respect that Kant so often identifies with the feeling of the sublime were some other feeling entirely than the morally obligatory form of respect.

Against this background, it becomes possible to assess the psychologistic critiques levelled by Paul Guyer and Paul Crowther in regard to the connection of sublimity, morality, moral feeling and respect. Crowther questions the role of moral feeling and respect in sublimity on universalistic and, hence, anti-psychologistic grounds. According to Crowther, Kant offers no strong argument to believe that moral feeling should have a priori status; if simple moral feeling is not a priori, then sublimity can apply only to complex moral feeling, which is not necessarily identical to the specific, complex structure of 'respect', and negative and positive aspects of complex moral feeling would not necessarily be exactly the same in all persons (Crowther: 127). For sublimity,

> even if *we* experience the feeling of respect in response to some overwhelming natural item, we have no a priori entitlement to demand a similar response in others. They can be expected to have moral feeling but not necessarily our particular kind of moral susceptibility and insight. (Ibid.)

For Crowther and Guyer, another deduction is needed to justify the claim that moral feeling alone is needed. According to Guyer, '[t]he universal imputation of the judgement of sublimity presupposes that all persons have the same limits on their imagination, and that this Faculty will interact with reason in the same way in the case of any given object' (in ibid.). Kant's 'criteria of [judgements of sublimity] are *psychological* inasmuch as they hinge on "indeterminate" lessons of moral significance which we learn from our cognitive engagement with nature' (Crowther: 132). Along these lines, Guyer questions the legitimacy of demanding moral feeling from others. He identifies moral feeling as necessary to moral action in parts of CJ, but not in the ethical theory, where the demand is on an intention's conformity to duty, rather than on feeling. The only feeling that might be demanded is respect, which is a mixed feeling *motivating* moral action; moral feeling, in contrast with respect, is a pure pleasure *produced* by moral action. Hence, it seems that there can be no direct demand to experience moral feeling or a feeling conducive to moral feeling (Guyer 1979: 360–1; cf. 368).

However, his remarks, along with those of Crowther, are clearly mistaken on a variety of key issues, including the relevance of moral feeling and the question of psychologism. Guyer fails to see that the moral feeling necessary to moral action in parts of CJ is precisely the respect necessary to moral action in the ethical theory, rather than a pleasure produced by moral action, as in GMM. If moral feeling in CJ is the same as respect in GMM, contra Guyer, then there obviously *is* a direct demand to experience moral feeling, since Kant argues in GMM: 439–40 that moral action requires as its sole drive (*Triebfeder*) respect for the moral law. Respect is a morally necessary feeling because it derives from reason alone and involves consciousness of the will's determination by the moral law. If reason is the source of respect and moral feeling alike, and both respect and moral feeling are defined by the will's subordination to a higher power generative of law, then respect and moral feeling are identical in the third *Critique*. Hence, sublimity can be linked simultaneously to respect and moral feeling. And, because respect is identifiable with moral feeling in CJ, there can be a universal demand to experience moral feeling as construed in CJ without thereby adding 'yet another form of feeling'.

While Kant earlier regarded an aesthetics as necessarily psychologistic, sublimity in CJ should not be regarded primarily in psychological terms like empiricist accounts, because of its universality, its connection to an a priori morality and its definition by certain powers and functions. Sublimity's universal validity is non-objective and, therefore, requires no object with universally agreed upon qualities. Hence, the attention to variances in objects arousing the sublime, as in Crowther (e.g. Crowther: 127, 132), rather than to the internal relations of powers definitive of the sublime, obscures Kant's basic concern in the sublime. Because the sublime concerns a certain subjective liking for our power of mind (*Geistesvermögens*, CJ: 262), it is not even meaningful to say that the subject is in the presence of a genuine sublime object; there is no external test for sublimity. The universal validity of sublime judgements depends purely on an internal relation within a being with the a priori power of purposes (the will). Contra Guyer, sublimity depends neither on the specific psychological limits of imagination (only that the imagination involves finite material representation), nor on its interacting with reason in the same way with any given object (it is subjective, only certain objects arouse the sublime and they do so in different ways), nor again on moral 'lessons' gleaned from cognition of nature (the exhibition of freedom and production of respect are not moral lessons and no cognition is involved; its universality and necessity depend on its basis in our a priori moral capacities, the will and moral feeling). Kant rejects his earlier view of taste as psychologistic, while retaining from GMM both his rejection of a moral role for beauty and his acceptance of a moral role for sublimity. He undermines the psychologistic reading by defining moral feeling in CJ as a universalizable feeling that the mind has a supersensible determination. Sublime liking concerns only the self-uncovering of 'the *determination* of our power', a disposition inherent in our nature; our obligation is to develop and use this disposition (ibid.). The sublime carries with it a certain moral obligation to the development and use of our disposition or determination to a power over nature, even though we can 'uncover' or experience this power only in so far as we are safe and nature is not overwhelming. Conversely, 'the human being may be conscious of his present actual powerlessness [impotence, *Ohnmacht*]', in reflecting on it (ibid.), but this actual state of external powerlessness against the forces of nature does not obviate the internal power of acts of will, nor the moral obligations whose conditions are made clear by the experience of the sublime. Moral feeling in CJ is linked to sublimity's displeasure and situated at the basis of moral action; it is not 'an unmixed pleasure resulting from moral action', as Guyer argues. Sublimity's transcendence of feelings of fear and danger means that it is independent of the validity or external adequacy of any personal feelings. The universal validity and necessity (CJ: 266) of sublimity rest on the judging subject's autonomy in regard to pleasure (CJ: 281). Hence, sublimity answers the non-psychological, justificatory question '*quid juris*' by referring to moral grounds (CJ: 282–3), namely, the will's a priori purposiveness in relation to cognition (CJ: 280). The sublime has a moral right to claim universality in its uncovering of the freedom of the will. By contrast, empiricist art critique exemplifies a merely physiological or psychological aesthetics in focusing on empirical rules of the process of taste, rather than the transcendental critique of the power of judging involved in taste and the sublime (CJ: 286). It is by reference to sublimity's connection to morality, then, that Guyer himself undercuts the psychologistic reading of sublimity's relation to moral feeling and supplies a justification for the identification of respect and moral feeling in CJ. He assumes that 'we are justified in presupposing the existence of the faculty of reason in everyone else – and in equating reason as the source of the moral feeling with reason as the source of limitless ideas in general' (Guyer 1979: 266).[4] Sublimity eludes psychologism, then, by its link to moral powers.

Thus, sublimity's relationship to moral feeling as construed in CJ is unproblematic for Kantian morality. The sublime, as a form of aesthetic, universally valid judgement, refers to subjective grounds, resists sensibility for the ends of practical reason and is purposive in relation to moral feeling by leading us to esteem practical reason's ends, even against any sense interests (CJ: 267). Sublimity refers to subjective bases purposive for moral feeling, in the sense that their resistance to sensibility supports the will's autonomy from nature and thereby serves the purposes of practical reason. Sublimity's reference to moral feeling also grounds its moral universality, for it shows that a judgement about the sublime is not produced or introduced by culture or the conventions of human society but, rather, 'has its foundation in human nature and indeed in that which one can require and demand of everyone at the same time as sound understanding, namely the disposition [*Anlage*] to the feeling for (practical) ideas, i.e., to moral feeling' (CJ: 265). Therefore, the singular judgement of sublimity ('this representation is sublime' (cf. CJ: 244)) demonstrates the universal disposition to moral feeling and justifies the universal moral claim that we possess this disposition. The connection of sublimity to moral feeling also confirms sublimity's relation to moral determinability, for moral feeling is the subject's determinability and sublimity alone exhibits or produces moral feeling. If moral feeling in CJ were identical to moral feeling in GMM, this relationship would cast doubt on both sublimity's transcendental character and its relationship to morality. But, as we have seen, moral feeling in CJ is different from moral feeling in GMM and identical to respect in both texts. Hence, sublimity's relation to moral feeling in CJ only confirms the former's role in the moral subject's determinability.

This account of the relationship of sublimity to moral feeling and respect provides more reason to exclude beauty from exercising crucial moral functions in the Kantian system.

> [T]he feeling for the beautiful is not only differentiated specifically [in kind] from moral feeling (as it actually is as well), but even the interest

that one can connect to it can be [bound] only with difficulty with the moral interest, and in no way through inner affinity. (CJ: 298)

Thus, Richard Kuhns is wrong to argue that Kant resolves the incompatibility between beauty and sublimity in moral terms, since morality is a major ground of the *division* between beauty and sublimity. Kant argues that in order to conceive the universal communicability of what is specific to sensation and referred to cognition, it is necessary to assume 'that everyone has [the] same sense as our own' (CJ: 291). But we cannot make this assumption with sensation, because there are those who lack, for example, the sense of smell, and there is no way of knowing that others receive identical sensations even of objects. Hence, the passive reception of pleasure (agreeableness or disagreeableness) deriving from sensation of objects cannot demand universal validity, because of its origin in sense (CJ: 291–2). When the liking of an act derives from its moral character, it is no mere pleasure of enjoyment, because it arises rather 'from our spontaneous activity [or self-agency, *Selbstthätigkeit*] and its conformity with the idea of its determination. But this feeling, which is called moral [*sittliche*] feeling, demands concepts and exhibits no free, but rather lawful purposiveness'; therefore, this feeling must be mediated through reason, for pleasure can be communicated 'universally only through very determinate practical concepts of reason' (CJ: 292). There would have to be a conceptual link and a rational mediation or basis for feeling to be tied properly and universally to the moral.

> The pleasure in the sublime in nature, as pleasure of reasoning contemplation, also makes claim to universal participation, but still already presupposes another feeling, namely, that of its supersensible determination, which has a moral foundation, however obscure [dark, *dunkel*] it may be. (Ibid.)

Sublimity's claim to universality depends on the feeling of our supersensible determination, our determination of self-agency, which is founded in morality, although Kant ought really to say that our supersensible determination *is* moral and that it *enables* morality, rather than that our free power is itself *founded* in morality; otherwise, he would be basing the enabling condition of morality (freedom) on what it conditions (morality). But there must be some internal basis for the universality of the sublime. Its liking cannot be presupposed universally in the rough magnitude of nature, since nature itself is terrifying. Consideration for the moral disposition entails that we require this liking of everyone on the basis of the moral law, which is grounded on rational concepts (ibid.).

The clear parallel between taste and moral feeling does not extend to interest. Taste concerns pleasure or displeasure in aesthetic judgement's power to judge forms non-conceptually with a liking that stands as a universal rule, but this liking is not based on, and does not arouse, an interest. Moral feeling similarly concerns the pleasure or displeasure in

> a power of an intellectual judgement to determine *a priori* for mere forms of practical maxims (insofar as such maxims qualify of themselves for universal legislation) a liking that we at the same time make into law for everyone without our judgement being grounded on some interest, although it still produces such an interest. (CJ: 300)

But here the forms of liking associated with beauty and moral feeling differ in that the latter produces an interest, while still serving as the basis for a universal law. Reason's interest in natural harmony (beauty) is moral,

> and he who takes an interest in the beautiful in nature can do so only in so far as he has beforehand already well grounded his interest in the moral good. Hence one has cause to suspect that whomever the beauty of nature interests immediately [has] at least a disposition [*Anlage*] to a good moral sense [attitude, *Gesinnung*] . . . an object of nature interests us by its beauty only insofar as an accompanying moral idea is affiliated with it. (CJ: 300–2)

Thus, beauty's relation to moral feeling is contingent on a prior moral idea, rather than producing such an interest. Disinterested judgements of taste (such as beauty) present their liking a priori as proper for humankind in general, yet their interest is free, for they are subjective, whereas the interest of moral judgement from concepts 'is grounded on objective laws' (CJ: 301).

Although beauty and sublimity are both 'purposive in relation to moral feeling', then, beauty 'prepares us to love something, even nature itself, without interest', whereas sublimity prepares us 'to esteem it against our (sensuous) interest' (CJ: 267). Because it opposes our interests and constitutes respect, rather than love, sublimity's esteem (*hochschätzen*) or respect harmonizes with moral action. Hence, sublimity alone is grounded on moral feeling (CJ: 268). Sublimity's necessity and universality are grounded on the subject's moral determinability, which is or is announced by what Kant here calls moral feeling.

> so we say of he who remains unmoved by that which we judge to be sublime that he has no *feeling* . . . judgement therein relates the imagination to reason as the power of ideas, and so we demand feeling only under a subjective presupposition (but which we believe ourselves justified to require of everyone): namely, that of the moral feeling in human beings, and so we even attach necessity to this aesthetic judgement. (CJ: 265–6)

Hence, sublimity both generates and presupposes moral feeling and an attunement to moral ideas, for the universal subjective presupposition of moral feeling warrants the existence of feeling and the attunement of sublimity.

Sublimity's negativity and contrapurposiveness

Common readings of sublimity have erred in identifying its negativity and contrapurposiveness as destructive of any, or at least any non-analogous, moral functions. This interpretation fails to recognize that sublimity's negativity is just what entails its positive moral functions. The fact that the sublime 'is entirely negative in regard to the sensible' (CJ: 274; cf. CJ: 245, 269, 271), that it is negative to inclinations (Kirwan 2005: 56–7), is a necessary condition for any moral role, for it preserves the purity of will and autonomy requisite for morality. Kant argues that 'autonomy is the sole principle of all moral laws' (CPrR: 33) and the admission of positive inclinations into the will implies heteronomy. Hence, for Kant, the only case that can be proclaimed moral with reasonable certainty is that in which an act accords with duty and is contrary to all inclination or pleasure (GMM: 398). Sublimity can generate respect for that which is absolutely great only because it produces a negative pleasure or displeasure, which, like the good, moves us to a seriousness that repels charms, incentives and limits in its alternation between attraction and repulsion for the object (CJ: 271). This combination of pleasure and displeasure generates a mental movement crucial to sublimity's moral function. Whereas the aesthetic judgement of the beautiful in nature 'presupposes and preserves the mind in *calm* contemplation' (CJ: 247, cf. CJ: 258), the representation of the sublime in nature produces a feeling of movement or agitation in the mind (cf. CJ: 245, 226). Beauty's generation of restful contemplation recalls the Aristotelian virtuous activity of the soul, a heteronomous form of 'morality' that Kant rejects in his critical period, while sublimity's mental movement enacts the Kantian critical moral requirement of negating sensibility and affirming reason. Rather than calm contemplation, the sublime brings with it a mental movement comparable, especially at first, to a violent shaking or vibration, a 'swiftly changing repulsion and attraction even for the same object' (CJ: 258). The sublime produces displeasure and pleasure, repulsion and attraction or contrapurposiveness and purposiveness, due to the contrast between the felt limits of the imagination and the conscious unboundedness of the power of reason. Intuitive apprehension drives the imagination to an abyssal excess and thus, to fear of its own dissolution; for reason's supersensible ideas, no such excess is possible, since they refer already to maxima in the lawful demand to think the totality. Sublimity's negativity to sense interests undermines the reading that sublimity is somehow selfish or non-moral both by its resistance to natural inclinations and its subjection of the sensible realm to the rational. 'The liking in the sublime in nature is therefore also only negative ([whereas] the liking for the beautiful is positive), namely, a feeling of the robbing of the freedom of the imagination by itself', sacrificing itself in being determined by a higher law or cause than its empirical use (CJ: 269). This shows the imagination's inadequacy to the task, its finitude with respect to the totality, despite its apparent boundlessness. The effect of this violence to sensuous inclinations obstructing the rational power is to free the subject from both natural forces and fanatical epistemological claims.

> [T]his pure, soul-elevating [soul-sublimating, *seelenerhebende*], merely negative exhibition of morality brings on the contrary no danger of *fanaticism* [*Schwärmerei*], which is a *delusion* [*Wahn*] *to want to see something beyond all bounds of sensibility* . . . the exhibition [of morality avoids fanaticism because it] is merely negative. For *the inscrutability of the idea of freedom* cuts off the path of all positive exhibition entirely; but the moral law is in itself adequate and originally determining in us, so that it does not once allow us to look around for a determining ground outside it. (CJ: 275)

Sublimity's negative exhibition of morality removes the threat of fanaticism's claim to know freedom and God. This function is essential to morality, because theoretical knowledge of an omnipotent being's existence would destroy morality, and theoretical knowledge of freedom would lend it no further basis in referring only to a prior practical power of freedom standing as the true ground of morality.

Thus, negativity, the recognition of limits, essentially distinguishes the sublime experience of enthusiasm (*Enthusiasm*) from the non-sublime experience of fanaticism (*Schwärmerei*). Whereas fanaticism, as a mode of principled dreaming or 'raving with reason' (CJ: 275), claims to go beyond all the limits of sensibility, enthusiasm, like respect, is merely negative in relation to sensibility and is produced by reason. Unlike fanaticism, enthusiasm involves an affect, a kind of passing madness (*Wahnsinn*) occasionally occurring even in the healthiest understanding, in which the imagination's power is unrestrained, rather than ruleless, as in passions, which constitute a deranging sickness, a mania (*Wahnwitz*). Enthusiasm associates the idea of good with an affect, the mind's movement in establishing free reflection on principles for its self-determination (CJ: 271–2). It carries with it no danger of fanaticism (*Schwärmerei*), because it rules out any positive, sensible exhibition of freedom or the infinite beyond sensibility (CJ275). The sublime, aesthetic affect of enthusiasm serves reason as 'a tension of forces through ideas, which give to the mind an impetus [*Schwung*] that works far more powerfully and lastingly than the drive [*Antrieb*] through sense representations' (CJ: 272).[5] By contrast, passions, inclinations belonging to the power of desire, 'make it difficult or impossible for all determinability of the power of choice through principles' (ibid.). The sublime works its effects through exhibitions that are entirely negative toward sensibility. Reason feels that all barriers are removed and its powers unlimited in the necessity of transcending the sensuous; this feeling of unlimited power exhibits the infinite, albeit entirely negatively, and thus extends the soul. The sublimity of the Jewish law, like that of the 'Mohammedans', against making images or even likenesses of anything on earth, below the ground or in heaven derives from this negative stance toward imagination and sensation. This law is sublime in recognizing the impossibility of constructing images of the infinite.

However, it is not merely its negativity that enables sublimity's moral functions. The inherent link between its negative and positive functions is also necessary. The sacrifice and violent suffering inherent in sublimity positively subject all inclinations to the dominance of the moral power. Thus, sublimity 'is a violence that reason exerts on sensibility only in order to expand it commensurately with reason's own domain (the practical one)' (CJ: 265). This explains why the sublime is attractive to reason and repellent to sensibility. Sublimity's displeasure engenders a form of morally necessary violence against sensibility. In constituting reason's violent domination of sensibility, sublimity enables reason's own practical or moral function, for 'human nature does not of itself harmonize with that good, but only through the violence that reason does to sensibility' (CJ: 271). Hence, 'this same violence that happens [*widerfährt*] to the subject through imagination is still judged as purposive for the whole determination [*Bestimmung*] of the mind' (CJ: 259). Sublimity's negativity simultaneously clears the way for and makes possible the recognition of a practical power higher than mere nature.

> This might actually makes itself aesthetically knowable [or recognizable, *ästhetisch-kenntlich*] only through sacrifices (which are a theft [*Beraubung*], although on behalf of inner freedom, that, by contrast, uncovers in us an unfathomable depth of this supersensuous power with its consequences stretching themselves into the infinite [the unforeseeable, *ins Unabsehliche*]): thus is the liking negative from the aesthetic side (in relation to sensibility), i.e. against this interest, but observed from the intellectual side, positive and bound with an interest. (CJ: 271)

This contrast between sublimity's natural and moral functions is deliberate, for sublimity's moral functions depend on its negative relationship to nature. The quality of the sublime is a feeling of displeasure (*Unlust*) with regard to the aesthetic power of judging an object represented as purposive. Yet, the subject's ownmost incapacity (*Unvermögen*) uncovers consciousness of an unlimited power, which can be judged aesthetically only through this incapacity. In this two-step process, failure is essential to the aesthetic recognition of the subject's unlimited power. The mind feels aesthetically confined when a magnitude approaches the limits of intuitive comprehension, and imagination is called upon to comprehend a greater unity aesthetically, yet by means of numerical magnitudes, 'for which we are conscious of our power as unlimited' (CJ: 259). The displeasure at this limitation is crucial to sublimity's purposiveness, for in regard to the necessary expansion of the imagination to adequacy with that which is unlimited in our power of reason, namely, the idea of the absolute whole, the displeasure [occasioned by the sublime], and hence the unpurposiveness of the power of the imagination, is still represented as purposive for the ideas of reason and their awakening. But it is just through this that the aesthetic judgement itself becomes subjectively purposive for reason as [a] source of ideas. (CJ: 259–60)

Hence, the unpurposiveness of the imagination's power (*Vermögens der Einbildungskraft*) is equally represented as purposive. This representation of imagination's unpurposiveness as purposive for reason enables aesthetic judgement's subjective purposiveness, because reason is source of ideas and an absolutely great intellectual comprehension, against which 'all aesthetic comprehension is small' (CJ: 260). The condition of the possibility of this purposiveness and pleasure in the object's apprehension as sublime, then, is displeasure at the imagination's incapacity. Displeasure and the unpurposiveness of imagination are thereby represented as purposive, which seems to dissolve the links between pleasure and purposiveness, displeasure and unpurposiveness. This explains the alternation of pleasure and displeasure in the sublime, in that what is unpurposive (the imagination's inability to grasp totality as a real idea) prompts the awareness of our power of grasping totality as a real idea through reason and, hence, is purposive or associated with a pleasure.[6] The aesthetic judgement is the basis once again for an intellectual comprehension. This relation indicates that sublimity serves extra-aesthetic (moral, intellectual) functions, contra Allison, who regards the sublime as serving only as an aesthetic analogue to morality (Allison 2001: 343). The aesthetic link to the intellectual provides the transition from the realm of sensibility to that of reason.

Sublimity's contrapurposiveness consists in its combination of a negative relationship to external nature and a positive relationship to internal nature. Sublimity 'indicates nothing purposive whatever in nature itself, but only in the possible use of its intuitions' (CJ: 246). Nature functions then to excite the mind to a purposive attunement without itself being purposive.

> [J]ust as imagination and *understanding* in the judging of the beautiful [produce a subjective purposiveness of the forces of the mind] through their unanimity [*Einhelligkeit*], so do imagination and *reason* here [in the

sublime] produce a subjective purposiveness of the forces of the mind through their conflict [*Widerstreit*]: namely, a feeling that we have a pure, independent reason, or a power for estimating magnitude, whose excellence can be made intuitable by nothing other than the inadequacy of that power that is itself unbounded in the exhibiting of magnitudes (of sensible objects). (CJ: 258)

Sublimity is negative aesthetically in its opposition to the interest of sensibility, but positive intellectually in its production of rational interest in the moral good (CJ: 271); it executes moral functions by simultaneously destroying natural incentives and uncovering our supersensible moral power. The power of setting purposes or ends (the will) constitutes the a priori basis of the purposive power of cognition found in judgements of the sublime in nature (CJ: 280). These functions, which are moral and not merely intellectual, in their reference to the will, are neither contradictory, nor mutually destructive, for the same reason that the moral subject can be simultaneously subject and sovereign without contradiction. Observed subjectively, the striving to grasp 'a measure of the great [magnitude, *Größen*] in a single intuition' in the sublime is contrapurposive ('*subjektiv betrachtet, zweckwidrig*') as a painful experience that fails to grasp the totality; however, observed objectively, '*for the entire determination of the mind*', this estimation of magnitude is purposive (CJ: 259). Sublimity is contrapurposive or disharmonious with respect to nature, for it nullifies our animal importance, but purposive or harmonious with respect to our supernatural moral powers, for it makes it possible for us to feel 'a purposiveness within ourselves entirely independent of nature' (CJ: 246), that is, 'to be superior to nature within ourselves, and hence even to nature outside us' (CJ: 269), in leading us to consciousness of our internal, supersensible, moral purposiveness for practical reason.[7] Thus, sublimity's contrapurposiveness explains both its moral function and its critical marginalization.[8]

Universality and anthropology

The two standard universalistic arguments against a moral role for sublimity depend on the view that sublimity requires cultivation or anthropology and, thus, is restricted to a narrower class of cases than Kantian morality. Despite the necessity and universality of sublimity's basis in moral feeling, then, Allison faults the sublimity–morality connection on grounds that the cultivation necessary for sublimity is incompatible with the general accessibility of morality. All rational beings can be moral, by this account, but only the cultivated elite can experience sublimity. Hence, sublimity cannot be a necessary condition of morality, 'since there is no reason to believe, for example, that the "good and otherwise sensible" Savoyard peasant would be incapable of fulfilling his duty in trying circumstances' (Allison 2001: 343).

This argument enjoys some textual support, for Kant concedes that 'we might even have suspected in advance that knowledge of what every human is obligated to do, and hence also to know, would be the affair of every human, even the most ordinary' (GMM: 404). He extends practical judgement to the most ordinary understanding, even in preference to the philosopher, whereas he conditions sublimity on non-universal, cultivated feelings. If ordinary understanding 'excludes all sensuous incentives from practical laws', practical judgement may correctly determine 'the worth of various actions' by reference to its single principle. Because philosophers would add only extraneous considerations to this principle,

> [w]ould it not, therefore, be more advisable in moral matters to let the ordinary rational judgement take its course [*bewenden zu lassen*] and at most to bring in philosophy only for the purpose of rendering the system of morals all the more complete and intelligible and of exhibiting its rules in a way that is more convenient for use . . . but not with the practical intention of bringing common human understanding away from its happy simplicity [in moral affairs] . . . [?] (Ibid.)

Hence, Kant seems to accept Allison's argument that morality must be accessible to all in ways foreclosed to sublimity, for '[t]he attunement of the mind to the feeling of the sublime requires the receptivity of the mind to ideas . . . In fact without any development of ethical ideas that which we, prepared by culture, call sublime, is found merely repellent by rough [*rohen*] human beings' (CJ: 265). Unlike the beautiful in nature, with the sublime in nature, we cannot expect the unanimity (*Einstimmigkeit*) of our judgements with everyone else's (CJ: 264), because sublimity requires much greater cultivation of aesthetic judgement and the cognitive power grounding aesthetic judgement (ibid.). By cultivation, Kant means the mind's receptivity for ideas (CJ: 265).

> What is repellent for sensibility, which is yet at the same time attractive, consists in the inadequacy of nature to the ideas, and this only under the presupposition of the same and of the striving of the imagination to treat nature as a schema for them. (Ibid.)

This inadequacy produces the contrary effects of repulsion and attraction in sensibility, as reason's violence to sensibility enables its extension to adequacy with reason's proper, practical region, turning us toward the infinite, 'which is an abyss for sensibility' (ibid.). But, in order to experience this violence as purposive, the mind must already be cultivated by ethical ideas. Hence, Kant expressly sets sublimity beyond the ready capacity of uncultivated human beings. On Allison's account, this elevation of sublimity beyond the level of the 'good' Savoyard peasant rules out any essential moral role for sublimity, because it raises morality beyond the level of the masses, a move that Kant could not accept.[9]

However, Allison goes too far in attaching programmatic moral significance to Kant's description of the Savoyard peasant as 'good'; no doubt, 'good' here connotes little more than common and uncorrupted, as in Nietzschean etymology, since what keeps the peasant from experiencing the sublime is precisely the *lack* of ethical ideas. Hence, the problem for Allison is that this remark from CJ: 265 demonstrates the exact opposite of what he is arguing. For this reason, there is no basis here for a distinction between a form of sublimity accessible only to the elite and a universally accessible mode of morality. Sublimity requires the very ethical ideas necessary for morality. As Clewis argues, 'Kant grounds sublimity on moral or rational ideas' (Clewis: 126). Since we cannot differentiate sublimity from morality by their accessibility, setting ethics upon sublimity hardly contradicts Kant's extension of ethics to all. If the uncultivated merely experience repulsion from nature and horror at the sublime, it is their lack of developed ethical ideas that prevents them from recognizing reason's moral violence to sensibility. The properly cultivated attunement to sublimity combines this horror with the attraction attendant on reason's extension to its practical powers. Thus, Kant links sublimity's requirement of cultivation closely to moral action.

A second problem is that, by setting the development of ethical ideas as a condition of sublimity, Kant seems to refute the notion that sublimity is the condition of the possibility of ethical ideas. However, his grounding of sublimity on ethical ideas enables sublimity's transcendental moral functions, for he argues not that sublimity depends on morality, but that it enables the determinability of morality, and the cultivation of ethical ideas is necessary for the implementation of both morality and sublimity. Kant reinforces this view in asserting that although 'the judgement about the sublime in nature required culture (more than the judgement of the beautiful), it is still not produced first by culture and introduced into society merely conventionally', given its origins in human nature (CJ: 265). Sublimity's requisite cultivation of ethical ideas is independent of cultural conventions, because it is rooted in the natural human disposition to moral ideas. Clewis even argues that 'the sublime is grounded in positive practical freedom in the sense of a capacity to obey the moral law' (Clewis: 216, cf. 224, 226); 'this positive practical freedom' is required to feel the sublime, for it 'is a necessary condition of the experience of the sublime' (ibid.: 219). This condition for the sublime would be identical to the first condition for morality. Sublimity presupposes the disposition to ethical ideas, yet it is on a level with morality, in so far as both are rooted in human nature and require the cultivation of ethical ideas. Lacking developed ethical ideas, the 'good', intelligent Savoyard peasant fails to recognize the sublime, because, '[i]n the demonstrations of the violence of nature in its destruction and the great measure of its power, against which his own power disappears into nothingness, he will see just the toil, danger and hardship [necessity, *Noth*], which would surround humans who were confined therein' (CJ: 265). The peasant neglects the moral dimension in failing to recognize that Saussure, unlike other travellers, endangers himself with the intention of teaching humanity and adding the soul-elevating (sublimating, *seelenerhebende*) sensation, which he then communicates to his readers (ibid.). The disposition to moral ideas grounds the necessity of the universal agreement on the judgement of the sublime (ibid.).

This claim does not mean that there is any actual universal agreement on the sublime. Just as we ascribe lack of taste to those indifferent to beauty in nature, we judge those unmoved by the sublime to have no feeling (ibid.). But, although actual universal agreement on judgements of the sublime does not exist, we still require of every human being taste and feeling for the sublime, and, indeed, we presuppose taste and feeling for the sublime in 'cultured' individuals (CJ: 265–6). If this cultural requirement grounds

Allison's claim that the allegedly elitist standards for sublimity remove it from the absolutely universal sphere of morality, even here Kant *expects* of every human being taste and feeling for the sublime, limits sublimity's universality for specifically moral reasons and grounds the necessity of sublimity on our universal disposition to moral ideas.

The universal expectations for beauty and sublimity differ because they involve different relations of powers and a different relation to morality. We require taste universally, because judgement relates the imagination to understanding as a power of concepts, whereas we require feeling only under the subjective presupposition of moral feeling in human beings, because the sublime consists in the relation of imagination to reason as power of ideas (CJ: 266). Hence, the presupposition of moral feeling in humans remains subjective and, therefore, lacks universality or, rather, lacks *objective* universality. Yet, we believe ourselves justified in requiring sublimity of everyone and therefore assign necessity to sublime aesthetic judgement as well (ibid.). The necessary modality of sublime aesthetic judgement is crucial, because it warrants sublimity's place in a critique of judgement. The necessity of sublime aesthetic judgements elevates or sublimates them beyond the realm of empirical psychology, 'in which they would otherwise remain buried under the feelings of pleasure [*Vergnügen*] and pain', because it reveals a priori principles at their ground and, thus, places them within transcendental philosophy (ibid.). Hence, Kant's response to the psychologistic critique relies on sublimity's connection to morality, in so far as it depends on the modality of sublime aesthetic judgements, and this necessity is itself grounded on the universal disposition to moral ideas.

In turning back to Kant's moral philosophy, we see again that the cultivation required for the sublime is the development of ethical ideas and that both sublimity and morality require cultivation. Indeed, Kant grants a significant role to philosophical corrections and clarifications of morality. He stresses that '[i]nnocence is indeed a magnificent thing; only it is also very bad in that it cannot be preserved well and is easily led astray. On that account, even wisdom ... needs science' (GMM: 404–5). For this reason, it is necessary, even on practical grounds, to establish the moral laws and to eliminate ambiguities in common use by articulating the conditions of a metaphysics of morals. Just as formal logical languages claimed to eliminate the ambiguities of so-called 'natural' or ordinary languages, Kant claims to eliminate the uncertain meanings of ordinary morality through a systematic determination of the form of all morality. The natural dialectic, the struggle between reason and inclination, generates a quibbling with strict laws of duty and their purity on behalf of inclinations. As a result,

> common human reason itself is driven to go out of its sphere and to take a step into the field of a practical philosophy, not through some need for speculation ... but rather on practical grounds themselves in order to receive information and clear instruction on the source and correct determination of its principle in opposition to maxims that are based on need and inclination, so that reason may get out from the dilemma [*Verlegenheit*] of opposing claims and run no risk of losing all genuine moral principles through the ambiguity into which it easily falls. (GMM: 405)

Because ordinary reason is incapable of resolving this dialectic, Kant argues that 'peace will be found only in a complete critique of our reason' (ibid.). Hence, Kant is far from asserting morality's universal extension, unaided by cultivation, contra Allison.

Indeed, Kant sets the bar for morality and its verification extremely high. While human nature is already noble enough for the disposition of morality, we cannot by any means declare victory in advance, for 'when we pay attention to the experience of the actions of human beings, we meet frequent and – as we ourselves admit – correct complaints that there cannot be cited a single sure example of the disposition [*Gesinnung*] to act from pure duty' (GMM: 406; cf. GMM: 459), let alone that of the common person, for example, the Savoyard peasant. 'In fact it is absolutely impossible to make out a single case with complete certainty where the maxim of an action otherwise conforming to duty has rested solely on moral grounds and on the representation of one's duty' (GMM: 407). The impossibility of verifying the secret incentives of our actions leads Kant even to the point of questioning the very possibility of morality. There is always the possibility that the will is determined by some 'secret impulse [*Antrieb*] of self-love', because 'we can never, even by the strictest examination, completely get behind the secret incentives [of our actions] ... the concern is not with the actions, which one sees, but rather with their inner principles, which one does not see' (ibid.). Because there can be no experience of the noumenal will, the possibility that nature lies behind all of our actions cannot be excluded. But, if the will is situated within the sphere of natural causality, then all 'actions' are necessarily heteronomous and morality is an illusion.

By referring the existence and duties of the will to natural purposes, Kant's essentially pre-critical retention of teleology in morality lends further credence to this subjection of the will to nature. His account of the imperfect duties of self-improvement and helping others relies on natural purposes, for he grounds these obligations on the 'fact' that nature has given us powers for all sorts of purposes. He generalizes this re-importation of nature into morality in saying that 'the human being is subjected only to his own, and nevertheless universal, legislation, and ... is bound only to act in accordance with his own will, which, however, according to natural purposes, is universally legislative' (GMM: 432). The whiff of natural teleology, which eludes any possible sensible foundation, is unfortunate here. If we are subject to the will's legislation because this constitutes natural purposes (which we cannot know), then all Kantian morality is reducible to natural 'obligation'. But this would commit the fallacy of hypostatization and the naturalistic fallacy, in that it attributes intentionality to nature as if it were a being and takes an alleged fact of nature as the basis for a claim to what ought to be the case. However, all that Kant needs here is the view that the will, by its very nature, its essence or identity, as the power to set purposes, is legislative. There is no need to refer at all to natural purposes, since the will is the power to act purposively.

While these doubts as to the existence of any such moral actions should not cast doubt on the *conditions* of moral action in reason's commands (GMM: 408), they suggest strongly that the standards for morality exceed those of sublimity. Indeed, on my account, sublimity establishes only the determinability of the moral subject, which determinability is a necessary but *not* a sufficient condition for moral *action*. Allison's notion that morality is more generally accessible than sublimity, then, is clearly false. While the experience of sublimity is quite common, Kant's standards for acting morally and for verifying that an action is moral are virtually unattainable. To act morally is more difficult and rare than to experience the sublime. Hence, there is no clear reason to exclude a moral role for sublimity on grounds of universality or accessibility. The fact that not everyone is affected equally by sublimity and moral sense does not destroy the universality and necessity of sublime and moral judgements. As we have seen, we are entitled to demand sublimity of everyone with a healthy understanding, because of its connection to moral feeling (GMM: 408); the requirement of culture proves merely that sublimity and morality must be cultivated in order to actually exist. Finally, as a question of Kant-interpretation, if we were to grant that the accessibility of sublimity was a problem for any account of the relation of sublimity to morality, that would show only that no such relation should be asserted; it would not mean that Kant himself rejected such a relation, for it would not outweigh the many texts in which Kant attaches such moral roles to sublimity. Indeed, as we have seen, he locates sublimity in the very structure of morality in arguing that sublimity mimics or constitutes the position of the moral subject.

An alternative, universalistic ground for rejecting the relevance of sublimity to morality derives from its allegedly anthropological character. Allison argues that sublimity includes considerations specific to human beings and, therefore, incompatible with the general applicability of Kantian morality to all rational, not merely human, beings. According to this argument, if sublimity were a necessary condition for morality, then Kant would be subjecting morality to anthropological considerations, contrary to his clear intentions. Indeed, Kant argues that a major problem with popular morality is that it commonly includes 'the particular determination [*Bestimmung*] of human nature', as well as the idea of a rational nature, but only the latter belongs properly to morality (GMM: 410). '[W]e must not let it come into our mind to want to derive the reality of this principle [of morality] from the particular characteristic of human nature' (GMM: 425). The universality and a priori necessity of morality require the exclusion of anthropology.

> [W]ith what right can we bring into unlimited respect as a universal precept for every rational nature what is perhaps valid only under the contingent conditions of humanity? And how should laws for the determination of our will be held as laws for the determination of the will of a rational being in general and only as such also for our own will, if these laws were merely empirical ... (GMM: 408)

> the proper worth, elevated [sublimated, *erhabene*] beyond any price, of an absolutely good will consists precisely in the fact that the principle of action is free of all influences from contingent grounds. (GMM: 426)

Hence, Kant insists on the non-anthropological character of his morality. Yet, he seems to admit many anthropological elements into it. For instance, his formula of humanity, which he claims is convertible with his other formulations of the categorical imperative, commands that we treat humanity in our own person or in that of another '*always at the same time as an end and never merely as a means*' (GMM: 429) and he says that 'the moral law interests us because it is valid for us as human beings, since it has sprung from our will as intelligence and hence from our proper self' (GMM: 461). Thus, Kant is himself responsible for the anthropological critique of Kantian morality. Nevertheless, it is not at all clear that these remarks demonstrate Kant's use of anthropology, for what he means by the proper self identifiable with the will as intelligence, in the latter case, and the humanity in our own person, in the former, turns out to be *reason*, not any contingent, anthropological qualities.[10] Hence, the proper self of men and the formula of humanity are really formulae applicable to all rational beings, stripped of any anthropological considerations. Immediately prior to stating the formula of humanity, then, Kant expresses rationality as the general condition of morality, humanity being solely one type of rational being. Only a thing whose existence has absolute worth, as an end in itself, can ground determinate laws and, thus, can ground a categorical imperative or practical law; such a being is the human being and every rational being (GMM: 428). The principle of humanity and rational nature in general as end in itself 'is the supreme limiting condition of every man's freedom of action ... not borrowed from experience ... because of its universality, inasmuch as it applies to all rational beings generally, and no experience is capable of determining anything about them' (GMM: 430–1).

Hence, Kantian morality's apparent reliance on anthropology turns out to reduce to necessary powers of reason, rather than contingent, human elements. It would seem, then, that Kant's morality is actually non-anthropological and, thus, is incompatible with his anthropological account of sublimity.

Yet, closer inspection reveals that the laundry list of specific anthropological elements in sublimity not only includes several powers necessary to Kantian morality, at least as presented in most of GMM, but also involves a far broader category of being than human being. Kant claims to exclude any anthropological considerations even in *applying* morality to humans, on grounds that this task involves giving a priori laws to humans as rational beings. But, while Kant elsewhere attempts to reduce morality to purely rational considerations, he acknowledges that morality becomes a question, a 'should' rather than a 'would', only for rational beings also subject to natural inclinations. Hence, consideration of the non-rational forces operative in beings subject to both rational and natural forces is essential to Kantian morality. As we have seen, the application of morality relies on judgement, sharpened by experience: 1) to determine the applicable cases and 2) to access and influence the human will so as to put the moral law into practice against heteronomous inclinations (GMM: 389). In granting such an important role to judgement, Kant seems to involve his moral philosophy in anthropological considerations, in that judgement, as a power of moving back and forth from universals to singulars, concerns the transition between understanding or reason and sensibility or imagination, a range of powers extending beyond reason and possibly specific to humans. Although Kantian morality excludes imagination, sensibility and inclination ('[t]he dependence of the power of desire on sensations' (GMM: 413n3)) from the determination of action, moral obligation presupposes the existence of natural inclinations, and moral action involves these powers in various ways. Indeed, specific dimensions of our humanity are relevant both to the contingent implementation of morality through a judgement sharpened by experience, as Kant says in GMM, and to the very question of how a categorical imperative is possible, for Kantian morality depends on the twofold reflection in which we regard ourselves on the one hand as a mere appearance governed by natural laws and on the other as an intelligence, with a will, governed by laws of freedom. This is not the case for a purely rational being, because such a being exists utterly independently from natural desires and inclinations; this being is conscious of morality only as 'a necessary *would* insofar as he is a member of an intelligible world', and does not experience the moral *ought*, since the latter depends on the being's 'regard[ing] himself at the same time as a member of the sense world' (GMM: 455). Morality does not exist as a problem for a purely rational being, in so far as such a being acts necessarily according to the moral law. This explains why Kant continually refers to the human being as placing himself at one time under one set of laws and at another under another set of laws (GMM: 457). The problem of morality consists in the struggle for self-determination, a struggle that can exist solely for rational beings subject to natural inclinations. Kant's specific demand that we act out of respect for the moral law demonstrates his recognition of the necessity of incorporating anthropological considerations into his morality. Indeed, he says explicitly that

> all morals, which require anthropology for their application to humans, must be completely expounded at first independently of anthropology as pure philosophy, i.e., as metaphysics ... [without metaphysics] the attempt is impossible, I shall not say to determine exactly for speculative judgement the moral element of duty in all that accords with duty, but rather even in the mere common and practical use, especially of moral instruction. (GMM: 412)

The suggestion, then, is that while morality must be articulated independently of anthropology, the application of morality depends on such considerations (GMM: 411–12). Perhaps the best way of resolving these ambiguities is to recognize that the general problem is not anthropology, but the power struggle between rational and natural determination. Kant clearly seeks to eliminate anthropological considerations from morality, while asserting the necessity of attending to rational–natural tensions relevant equally to morality and sublimity.

If Kantian morality excludes all such anthropological considerations (GMM: 410), then it seems at odds with sublimity, whose subjective universality is dependent specifically on the particular powers of human beings, namely, imagination, reason and feeling (pleasure, pain, moral feeling/respect), and possibly even specific structures or functions of the senses and feeling as well. Thus, Kant argues that the language of *intellectual* beauty or sublimity is incorrect, in so far as pure intelligences lack the power of sensibility and, thus, are denied aesthetic modes of representation such as beauty or sublimity (CJ: 271). Sublimity would have to be rational, rather than anthropological, to stand as a necessary condition for the determinability of the moral subject in general, since morality applies to all rational beings, not merely all human beings. These anthropological connections imply that the (hypothetical) class of non-human, rational beings subject to natural inclinations (the other beings for whom a moral ought would apply) might not necessarily be able to experience the sublime. Hence, it seems that sublimity can at best be a sufficient, not a necessary, condition for the determinability of the moral subject. However, the general category of sublimity, like those of humanity and morality, is remarkably abstract, and abstract in a way particularly suitable to morality. Sublimity pertains to all simultaneously rational and natural beings, in so far as they would experience the tension between natural and rational powers of determination, regardless of whether they shared our particular forms of sensibility and imagination; pure intelligences (that is, purely rational, non-natural beings) would not present things aesthetically in beauty or sublimity (ibid.). This implies that Kant's morality and sublimity cover the same rational–natural beings, for only such rational–natural beings are subject to the 'ought' of morality. Purely rational beings not subject to natural determination experience morality only as a 'would', since their sole mode of determination is rational and, thus, moral. Non-natural, rational beings experience moral commands as a 'would', rather than a 'should', in the sense that they necessarily act according to the moral (rational) law, since they lack any non-rational form of determination. Therefore, it is arguable both that sublimity and morality extend equally to all rational–natural beings and that Kantian morality is directed primarily at such beings, in that purely rational beings are incapable of acting non-morally.

Mathematical and dynamical sublimity

However, if sublimity is a non-anthropological condition of the determinability of the moral subject, one might still restrict the scope of sublimity's moral functions by granting the connection between *dynamical* sublimity and morality (Makkreel: 313–14),[11] while disputing the connection between *mathematical* sublimity and morality (e.g. Budd: 69; Zuckert: 218; Pillow 2000: 72–3, 107), on grounds that mathematical sublimity applies merely to theoretical cognition, rather than practical desire. The contrast between Kant's examples of the dynamical and mathematical sublime, all of which are familiar to eighteenth-century aesthetics, seems to support this view. In the dynamical sublime, our power of resistance is insignificantly small in comparison with the might of overhanging, threatening boulders, thunderclouds, thunder and lightning, volcanoes with their destructive violence or dominance (*Gewalt*), hurricanes leaving devastation, the boundless ocean in storms and the high waterfall of a mighty river (CJ: 261). The more fearful the phenomenon, the more attractive the view, if we are safe. 'The *astonishment*, which borders on terror [*Schreck*], the horror and the holy shiver [*Schauer*], which seizes the observer in the sight of massive mountains climbing skyward, deep ravines and raging waters within, deeply shadowed wastelands inviting melancholy reflection and so forth', is not 'actual fear', because he knows that he is safe; the imagination's consideration of these terrorizing scenes is always tempered in the sublime by consciousness of our safety (CJ: 269). While physical resistance against these forces is futile, these objects are called sublime because of their effect on the strength of the soul, when they raise it 'beyond its customary measure and let us discover in us a power to resist of an entirely different type', enabling our mind to measure up to the seeming omnipotence (*Allgewalt*) of nature (CJ: 261). This effect, which depends on the absence of any actual danger or genuine threat of destruction (the genuine sublime is aroused here only by the appearance of danger), is the positive, moral complement of Kant's negative definition of a mighty nature defined as dynamically sublime through its inadequacy with respect to our moral power. Thus, the ideas of might and power in the dynamical sublime seem to link organically to moral discourses. Because reason's power is desire, rather than cognition, and only the dynamical sublime refers to desire, it would seem that only the dynamical sublime could relate to morality.

An apparent exception to the moral role of the dynamical sublime comes from Kant's view that no one could call moral conceptions of God's will derived 'from such characteristics as desire for glory and dominion bound with the frightful representations of might and vengeance. Any system of morals based on such notions would be directly opposed to morality' (GMM: 443). Here we see the possibility in Kant of a violent form of dynamical sublimity (nature as might) unrestrained by any moral scruples, which is the major concern in recent Continental accounts of the Kantian sublime. But even though this case seems to oppose dynamical sublimity to morality, there is no real exception here, because Kant argues in the third *Critique* that such frightful representations of God's might and vengeance cannot be called sublime. Rather than sublime elevation, the mental attunement toward God's violence, in contrast to the attunement toward natural violence, usually marks subjection (*Unterwerfung*), depression and a feeling of powerlessness; this comportment of contrition, fearful gestures and voices is manifested typically, though not necessarily, in religion (CJ: 263). Sublimity and morality would be destroyed by knowledge of the actual presence of God. Yet, the right moral attitudes can still transform the experience of divine greatness, like the experience of war, into something dynamically sublime. It would be 'foolishness and sacrilege' to imagine ourselves superior in our minds to the effects and intentions (*Absichten*) of God's fury, in storms, earthquakes and so forth (ibid.), for sublimity involves the awareness of a human mental power that transcends *natural*, not divine, violence. To attribute sublimity to the experience of divine greatness, then, requires replacing the attitude of fear attributed to one's internal offense to the irresistible will of divine might with quiet contemplation and free judgement, awareness of an upright, God-pleasing attitude or even a certain self-critical, self-improving humility (CJ: 263–4). The religious subject conquers the terror of the superstitious subjection to the will of superior might, which the superstitious experience as alien to their own will, by conforming its will to that of God (CJ: 264). Superstition produces only a flattery with no moral content, and thus cannot serve as a basis for 'a religion of good life-conduct' (ibid.). The stance of heteronomous obedience is a lowering, not an elevating, attitude. However, a sublime mental attunement can be constituted by 'humility [*Demuth*] as the merciless [*unnachsichtliche*, stronger than uncharitable or unindulgent] judgement of one's flaws, which could easily be cloaked otherwise in the consciousness of good attitudes toward the fragility of human nature', in so far as one 'subject[s] oneself willingly [*willkürlich*] to the pain of self-reproach in order to eradicate the causes for that little by little' (ibid.). This form of humility, in contrast to a humiliating lowering of the subject, involves the sublime, because it tacitly elevates the subject through the recognition of its self-critical powers. Hence, dynamical sublimity harmonizes with the experience of religious might, given the following three conditions: the subject feels power only over nature, not God; it exercises free judgement over non-rational feelings, such as fear and terror; and it conforms its will freely to God, without superstitious fear, since the latter cannot be a basis for a moral religion.

Moral functions seem quite removed, by contrast, from the mathematical sublime, in so far as the latter concerns the ability to think the totality in the face of imagination's inability to grasp the magnitude of pyramids, mountains, stars and the universe as a whole. The division of the sublime, unlike the beautiful, into the mathematical and the dynamical depends on whether the imagination refers the sublime mental agitation attached to the judging of an object to the *cognitive power* (the mathematical sublime) or the *power of desire* (the dynamical sublime), the one relating to magnitude, the other to might. Since mathematical sublimity refers to the cognitive power, which is allied to understanding, rather than the rational power of desire, and concerns the seemingly supramoral category of quantity (magnitude), the exclusion of mathematical sublimity from any moral role is plausible. Indeed, in the discussion prior to CJ: 255, the aesthetic estimation of magnitude in the mathematical sublime, even in its revelation of a supersensible mental power, seems purely theoretical and only tenuously related to a *practical, moral* power through its production of emotion.

Yet, there are many moral links within the sections on the mathematical sublime. Furthermore, Kant suggests negatively the possibility of extending moral powers to both mathematical and dynamical sublimity by referring frequently to sublimity's moral powers without specifying whether these powers relate to the mathematical or dynamical sublime. Still, this could be an oversight on Kant's part, and perhaps he is always tacitly referring to dynamical sublimity when he invokes the moral functions of the sublime. Hence, a positive account of the role of morality in the mathematical sublime is essential to disproving this restriction of moral sublimity. But this account is certainly present, for Kant himself begins his explanation of the moral functions of dynamical sublimity by likening dynamical to mathematical sublimity. 'In the immeasurability of nature and the inadequacy of our power [*an der Unermeßlichkeit der Natur und der Unzulänglichkeit unseres Vermögens*][12] to an aesthetic estimation of magnitude', in the mathematical sublime, we recognize in our rational power a non-sensible measure, a 'superiority in our mind over nature itself in its immeasurability' (CJ: 261). Everything in nature is small, as compared to this non-sensible measure, which subsumes the infinite as unity under itself (ibid.).

> In the same way, the irresistibility of nature's might also gives us, observed as natural beings, to know [*erkennen*] admittedly our physical powerlessness [*Ohnmacht*], but uncovers in us at the same time a power to judge independent of nature and a superiority [*Überlegenheit*] over

nature that grounds a self-preservation of an entirely different type than is that one which can be contested and brought into danger by nature outside us, whereby the humanity in our person remains undegraded, although the human must be subject [*unterliegen*] to that violence [or dominance, *Gewalt*, of nature]. (CJ: 261-2)

Nature's irresistible might (the dynamical sublime) both engenders *knowledge* (cognition) of our physical impotence to resist, in so far as we are regarded as natural beings, and reveals our free power of judgement over nature. This presumably non-cognitive, non-conceptual awareness of judgement's freedom manifests an entirely other power of self-preservation, which sustains the humanity in our person even against nature's physical dominance over us as humans. Kant is clearly referring to the formula of humanity from GMM. It is possible to treat the humanity in our person as an end in itself, not merely as a means, only by recognizing the sublime freedom definitive of our humanity. Thus, nature is judged as sublime not in arousing fear but, rather, in calling up in us our force (*Kraft*), which is not nature, to regard various objects of natural concern, property, health and life as small, as not dominant over us, as persons, in so far as we need not bow to them with our highest principles at stake (CJ: 262). 'Here nature is called sublime [*erhaben*], merely because it elevates [sublimates, raises, *erhebt*] the imagination to the exhibition of those cases in which the mind can make it possible to feel the proper sublimity [*Erhabenheit*] of its determination itself over nature itself' (ibid.). So, in first examining whether mathematical sublimity can be linked to morality as much as dynamical sublimity, we see that the moral power of dynamical sublimity is, in fact, already established by analogy to the moral power of mathematical sublimity. Hence, the connection of morality to the mathematical sublime is actually prior to that of the dynamical sublime.

Thus, Kant associates morality with *mathematical* sublimity both implicitly at the end of the second *Critique* (CPrR: 161–2) and explicitly in CJ:§§25–7 on the mathematical sublime. In §26, the second section on the mathematical sublime, Kant argues that the aesthetic estimation of magnitude plays a role in the practical, moral power.

> A power to be able to think the infinite of supersensible intuition (in its intelligible substrate) as given, surpasses all measure of sensibility and is

great beyond all comparison with the power of mathematical estimation; admittedly not in a theoretical intention on behalf of the power of cognition, but still as expansion of the mind, which feels itself able [*vermögend*] to transcend the limits of sensibility with another (a practical) intention. (CJ: 255)

The power of thinking here emerges as practical, not merely theoretical. Judgements that seem connected only to cognition may actually found moral or practical judgements, because Kant's notion of quantity has a general significance applicable to all possible appearances, both intellectual and sensible. The judgement of great and small applies 'to anything, even to any characteristics of things', including beauty, in so far as they are exhibited or represented aesthetically as appearances in intuition according to judgement's prescription, and thus are a quantum (CJ: 249–50; cf. CPrR: A162–6/B202–7, Pluhar's note). This relation to the cognitive power serves a practical or moral aim in the mathematical sublime. In its quantitative dimensions, sublimity unveils our moral power, for the agitation and strife occasioned by the sublime give rise, as we have seen, to the feeling that we possess an independent power of reason for estimating magnitude (CJ: 258). Hence, the apparently theoretical significance of Kant's references to quantity and the cognitive power in the 'Analytic of the Sublime' is misleading, for he is referring to the subject's practical power of *reason*. This moral reading of the mathematical sublime is evident in §25 where Kant connects the representations of the absolutely great (or large) with respect and the absolutely small with contempt (CJ: 249). The concern here is with our moral ideas. Because no adequation to a standard is possible when the quantum concerns the absolutely large, the sublime is to be sought 'not in things of nature but rather solely in our ideas' (CJ: 250). The imagination's inadequacy to estimating absolute magnitude in the mathematical sublime engenders in us 'the feeling of a supersensible power in us', a power that '*surpasses any standard of the senses*' (CJ: 250; cf. CJ: 254–5).

The judgement of the sublime harmonizes imagination with indeterminate ideas of reason (through their conflict) in order to produce, as we have seen, a 'mental attunement that [conforms to and is compatible with] that which the influence of determinate (practical) ideas would effect on feeling' (CJ: 256). In §27, the final section on the mathematical sublime, Kant then explains that this mental attunement is respect for our own determination. In the mathematical sublime, respect is referred to an object of nature, rather than the idea of humanity in us, through a certain subreption or aesthetic substitution (CJ: 257). But this aesthetic experience, as we have seen, 'makes intuitable for us as it were [*gleichsam anschaulich macht*] the superiority of the rational determination [*Vernunftbestimmung*] of our cognitive power [*Erkenntnißvermögen*] over the greatest power of sensibility [*das größte Vermögen der Sinnlichkeit*]' (ibid.).[13] At the same time, the representation of the sublime in nature produces a mental agitation defined by repulsion and attraction for the same object, which is purposive for the determination of the mental power through its violence to inner sense, its exhibition of reason's dominance over our physical nature (CJ: 258–9). Therefore, the mathematical sublime, like the dynamical sublime, leads inexorably to the moral ideas, to consciousness of our supersensible power and to respect for the moral law. Hence, I would argue against Clewis's view that

> [t]he traditional division of the sublime into the dynamical and the mathematical, while undoubtedly rooted in Kant's text, is too narrow to account for other forms of the sublime that are also found in the third *Critique* – the moral sublime and its subset, the sublime of mental states. (Clewis: 216)

There is no need to separate out a moral sublime from its other forms, as Clewis does, for the mathematical and dynamical sublime already incorporate within them the moral possibilities of the sublime.

This relation of the sublime to morality elucidates Kant's puzzling stricture on the mathematical sublime, viz. that it must concern the absolutely great (or large), in the sense of the infinite as a whole; it cannot concern the absolutely small, for the absolutely small produces *Verachtung*, contempt, rather than *Achtung*, respect (CJ: 249). For Kant, '[w]e call *sublime* that which is *absolutely* [*schlechthin*] great [*groß*, large]' (CJ: 248); '*sublime is that in comparison with which everything else is small*' (CJ: 250). The sublime is linked necessarily, then, to the idea of the absolutely great, to what is great beyond all comparison. The connection to respect lies in the fact that the identification of an object as great is a merely reflective judgement on the object's representation, not a mathematically determining judgement; it is subjectively purposive for the use of our cognitive forces in estimating magnitude. Hence, 'we thereupon connect with the representation at every time a type of respect [*Achtung*], just as we connect with that which we simply [*schlechtweg*] call small, a contempt [*Verachtung*]' (CJ: 249). This universal application of the judgement of magnitude undermines any restriction of a moral role to the dynamical sublime, for it extends the judgement of great and small in the mathematical sublime to anything, including virtue, public freedom and justice. For what is *absolutely* great, great beyond all comparison in every respect, that is, sublime, we can seek only an internal measure, not a commensurate, external measure. The absolutely great is a magnitude equal only to itself. To say that something is absolutely great or great (*Größe*) beyond any comparison (*absolute, non comparative magnum*) differs from saying that something is simply (*schlechtweg, simpliciter*) great, as *magnitudo* and *quantitas*. To be great, small or medium brings with it no cognitive principle, and thus signifies neither a pure concept of the understanding, nor a concept of reason. Absolute greatness must signify or derive from a concept of the power of judgement and 'lay at the ground a subjective purposiveness of representation in relation to judgement' (CJ: 248). Hence, it is possible to find the sublime only in our ideas, not in things of nature. This difference in feeling rules out the sublimity of the absolutely small and grounds the sublimity of the absolutely great, for without respect, 'these principles condemn human beings to self-contempt and inward abhorrence' (GMM: 426). The imagination in sublimity 'is a might [that allows us] to assert our independence against natural influences, to degrade as small what is great according to the imagination in its first [role] and so to posit the absolutely great only in his (the subject's) own determination' (CJ: 269). Everything in nature, howsoever large or small, may be degraded to the infinitely small or magnified to the scale of worlds, by comparison with greater or smaller measures, as evidenced by telescopes and microscopes.[14] Therefore, no possible object of the senses can be called sublime on this ground. In striving for the infinite, conceived not as a magnitude, but as the totality, the imagination runs against its own limits, despite its supposedly boundless nature. And this occasions in us a feeling that we are small, yet have a supersensible power within us that is absolutely great, the power to regard nature as 'small in comparison with ideas of reason' (CJ: 257). Sublimity engenders wonder for this absolutely great substratum, which lies outside of the category of existence and, therefore, may cause a purely disinterested respect for the moral law of the supersensible. The experience of sublimity generates an unconditioned intellectual liking for 'the moral law in its might, the might that it exerts in us over each and all of those drives of the mind that precede it' (CJ: 271). Thus, sublimity's *might* exerts power over all natural drives, and thereby effaces the obstacles to morality. In exclusively exhibiting the moral law's absolute might over us, the sublime uncovers the immeasurability of our supersensible power (ibid.), indicating our absolute moral autonomy. But, in order to reveal our moral power, sublimity must first determine our own inadequacy with respect to the boundless, absolute totality, and second, exhibit our power to think this totality.

Conclusion

I have argued that the relation of sublimity to morality is crucial to Kant throughout his career. But it is only in his critical period that he solves the problem of providing a non-psychologistic account of sublimity and morality and, in so doing, articulates a fundamental role for the sublime in the critical project, that of conditioning the determinability of the moral subject. The reflective judgement of sublimity generates the necessary conditions for determining the moral law, for it proves the existence of a moral sense, produces in the subject the necessary attunement of respect for the moral law and demonstrates to the subject that it possesses a determination (*Bestimmung*) surpassing nature – a moral power. Sublimity constitutes a necessary condition of moral choice; it does not show what morality or duty requires, either in general or in specific cases, for these are functions of reason and determinative judgement. While the experience of moral obligation is supposed to prove the existence of freedom for practical purposes, since 'ought' implies 'can', this experience cannot elevate the subject from the phenomenal to the supersensible sphere or generate the morally necessary attunement of respect for the moral law, for the experience of obligation does not entail the exhibition of our supersensible moral power or the determination of respect for the moral law. Whereas the experience of moral obligation provides an indirect, practical link to our freedom, the experience of sublimity provides a direct, practical proof of freedom, in that it makes us aware of our supersensible power to act independently of nature, rather than merely presenting the abstract feeling of ought or the specific feeling that we ought to do A, rather than B. This role of sublimity in morality does not mean that moral action presupposes the experience of sublime, threatening clouds, towering mountains or pyramids. No externally originating judgement of sublimity is necessary to morality, for the internal experience of the moral law itself occasions the experience of sublimity, and thus carries with it all of the necessary conditions for acting morally. It should be recalled that the difficulties that Kant raises for *acting* morally and *proving* that we acted morally are insuperable, since by Kantian standards we cannot *prove* practically or theoretically that there has been a single instance of moral action in human history. The experience of sublimity does not resolve the epistemic question of knowing that we have acted morally. Nevertheless, it establishes the conditions for the determinability of the moral subject in revealing the subject's powers and situating the subject in the paradigm case for morality, as sovereign and subject, acting in accordance with duty, against all inclinations, solely for the sake of the moral law. Hence, sublimity's relation to morality resolves a troubling problem in Kant scholarship by completing the critical project of determinability.

This interpretation of Kantian sublimity is also significant in re-enforcing the recent turn in Kant scholarship by Allison and others away from the reading of Kantian morality as independent of its disciplinary and experiential conditions, as if it were an innate, pre-formed power, which both supporters and critics of Kantian morality have argued. However, this strong moral reading of the sublime goes beyond recent Kant scholarship in uncovering the essential conditions for the determinability of the moral subject, from our attunement to morality and the production of respect to the awareness of freedom, resisting the argument that sublimity's analogy to morality obviates any significant moral functions, restoring sublimity's systematic dimensions and criticizing the view that beauty is closer or more comparable to morality. Indeed, Kant's claim that the sublime is an aesthetic analogue to morality should be read to support, rather than undermine, the importance of its moral functions, for there can be no epistemic ground of moral freedom, and practical reason can neither provide for the motivation to act morally, nor generate the transition between nature and freedom.

Only the aesthetic judgement of sublimity can generate the feeling of respect, the motivation to sacrifice nature to the higher laws of freedom and reason, the awareness of our freedom and the transition between nature and freedom that are necessary for the determinability of the moral law. Hence, we should abandon the attempt to dismiss a significant moral role for sublimity by referring to it as a mere aesthetic analogue to morality. My strong moral reading of the sublime also undermines the erroneous assumption in contemporary philosophy and art history that beauty is moral and sublimity useless or anti-moral. However, in substituting sublimity's moral functions for those of beauty, it problematizes recent attempts to efface moral ideology from aesthetics by turning from a moralized beauty to a non-moral sublimity. If Allison is right, then sublimity and all aesthetic judgements are impotent aesthetic analogues to morality, lacking any role in morality. But if my reading is correct that morality and all its instantiations are necessarily sublime and that only a sublime aesthetic analogue to morality can constitute the conditions for the determinability of morality, then there is a need for a paradigm shift in the way in which aesthetics' scholarship treats sublimity's relationship to morality and morality's relationship to experience.

Part III:
Sublimity and Morality in German Idealism and Recent Continental Philosophy

6 • Post-Kantian Continental Work on Sublimity and Morality

The post-Kantian Continental tradition of aesthetics shares many of the problems of recent analytic Kant scholarship on the relationship between sublimity and morality, except that the former also includes within it substantially accurate interpretations of Kantian sublimity, as well as interestingly different directions for the expression of sublimity in morality and politics. To write a chapter on post-Kantian Continental work on sublimity and morality is to restore a neglected, even repressed, element of the history of sublimity and to show the significance of Kantian sublimity and morality to later Continental aesthetics. For no clear reason, scholars ranging from Jared Moore, Paul Guyer (1979) and James Kirwan to D. A. Russell have peddled the myth that Kant's work marked the end of the history of sublimity. As we shall see, this could not be farther from the truth. What did change after Kant was that the *predominant* concern in aesthetics from 1800 to 1960 shifted from sublimity to beauty and, among Anglo-American philosophers, treatments of sublimity almost disappeared. While virtually every significant eighteenth-century critic or philosopher wrote extensively on the sublime or associated ideas, many prominent nineteenth- and twentieth-century Anglo-American philosophers wrote nothing directly or indirectly on the subject.

However, if discourse on the beautiful clearly became more common than that on sublimity, the reasons for sublimity's loss of prominence are disputed. In a representative 1948 *Journal of Philosophy* article, 'The sublime and other subordinate esthetic concepts', Jared S. Moore attributes the marginalization of sublimity to the inherent marginality of its own concept, describing beauty as the 'central concept of esthetics' and relegating sublimity to one of a group of subordinate formal concepts concerned with outward or sensible beauty, as opposed to the inner, expressive concepts, such as tragedy and comedy, concerned with inner beauty (Moore: 42).

Moore's position, taken from Kant, represents the mainstream position in Anglo-American aesthetics. Yet, as we shall see, the inherent marginality of the concept of the sublime is precisely why Continental philosophers, especially Jacques Derrida, have found the Kantian sublime so interesting. James Kirwan, who accepts the notion that Kant marked the death of the sublime, the end of the golden age of sublimity and the elimination of the topic's vibrancy (Kirwan 2004: 1–2), blames Kant himself, rather than problems inherent in the concept. But it is hardly credible to say that the most rigorous and influential statement on the sublime, Kant's 'Analytic of the Sublime', could have done all that. Russell's explanation, that in the nineteenth century sublimity's aesthetic primacy faded from its ubiquity, sounds too much like Yogi Berra ('no one goes there anymore; it's too crowded'). It makes no sense to say that sublimity was both ever-present and absent at the same time, but it is clear that the very qualities of boldness, lawlessness and originality deemed shocking and innovative to eighteenth-century critics had become old hat, discussed to death (Russell, introduction to Longinus 1964: xlviii). Indeed, it is arguable that eighteenth-century discourses on the sublime, with the exception of Kant's 'Analytic of the Sublime', proliferated to an extraordinary level without engendering adequate critical disagreement or justificatory apparatus to sustain the discussion.

However, the Russell-Guyer-Kirwan narrative overstates the case for the neglect of sublimity in general and Kantian sublimity in particular by ignoring post-Kantian continental philosophers and 'non-philosophers'. Guyer argues that 'even if there is a historical interest in Kant's discussion of the sublime, I think it is safe to assume that his analysis of this particular aesthetic merit will not be of much interest to modern sensibilities' (Guyer 1979: 400n). But while there was a shift from sublimity to beauty and analytic philosophers almost entirely neglected the sublime until the 1980s, academic databases indicate that the sublime has been a popular topic since the late seventeenth century. WorldCat registers a continuous stream of books on the sublime since the 1700s, the great majority, both in the eighteenth century and after, written by non-philosophers. Academic and artistic interest in the sublime seems only to have increased since the eighteenth century, and especially in the past fifty years. WorldCat lists 293 books referring to the sublime or sublimity in the 1950s, 565 in the 1960s, 617 in the 1970s, 1,002 in the 1980s, 2,145 in the 1990s, and 3,391 in the 2000s. Strikingly, fewer than twenty books refer to the sublime and philosophy in each of the decades prior to 1980, as against 180 in the 1990s and 460 in the 2000s. Indeed, within the academic discipline of philosophy from 1940 to 2011, the number of works on beauty is vastly greater and most works on the sublime have appeared only in the past thirty years. The *Philosopher's Index* records over 21,000 entries on aesthetics, over 13,000 on art and around three thousand on beauty or the beautiful, versus just 637 on the sublime, 82 per cent of which date from 1980 to 2011 (296 since 2000, 179 in the 1990s, 49 in the 1980s, 46 in the 1970s and 22 in the 1960s). Beauty was a far more popular topic in the twentieth century, and sublimity became fashionable again only within the past thirty years, as a wider JSTOR search confirms.[1]

Although Anglo-American philosophers wrote few explicit works on the sublime from 1800 to 1978, prominent post-Kantian continental philosophers such as Friedrich Schiller, Johann Gottfried von Herder, Georg Wilhelm Friedrich Hegel, Søren Kierkegaard, Friedrich Nietzsche and Theodor Wiesengrund Adorno continued to write on the sublime. If much of the attention given to the Kantian sublime is 'historical', it is certainly not narrowly historical, to the exclusion of articulating matters of present significance or attempting to identify the nature, limits and uses of sublimity, and commentators are wrong to think that the history of sublimity concludes around 1800, for this historical interest frequently extends from the post-Kantian period to the present.[2] Nor is it reasonable to dismiss the diverse nineteenth- and twentieth-century interpretations of the sublime as derivative of earlier periods (as if most eighteenth-century interpretations of the sublime were not also derivative of earlier accounts!), given the concept's application to so many unanticipated literary, artistic and philosophical developments since Kant's time. Indeed, many works link the sublime not only to Kant and pre-Kantian figures such as Shakespeare, Christopher Marlowe and Burke, but also to post-Kantian figures and movements such as Romanticism, most famously in Caspar David Friedrich's paintings, European and American nineteenth-century landscape painting (for example, works on the Hudson River School, or the periods 1820–80 and 1850–75), the Victorian era, nineteenth-century American literature (for example, Moby Dick), James Joyce, postmodernist philosophy and literature (for example, Lyotard, Derrida, John Barth, Toni Morrison, Christa Wolf), twentieth-century American women's poetry, twentieth-century American painting (Robert Motherwell, Barnett Newman), sculpture (Louise Bourgeois) and urban life. To take even a fraction of this multifarious work seriously as indicative of interest in sublimity is to recognize that the sublime has remained exceptionally important in culture and criticism since Kant. As Jean-Luc Nancy argues, sublimity is 'a fashion that has persisted uninterruptedly into our own time from the beginnings of modernity', as a break within aesthetics (Nancy 1993: 25; cf. Shaw: 148).

As I have already examined many claims from recent analytic readings of Kantian sublimity and I cannot hope to treat the tremendous range of non-philosophical, post-Kantian writings on the sublime, I restrict this chapter to the legacy of Kantian sublimity and its relation to morality in post-Kantian continental philosophy. In the first part of the chapter, I examine Kant's successors in the German idealist tradition. I describe Schiller's early moral readings of Kantian sublimity, defend Kant against Herder's critique and look at Hegel's influential interpretation of sublimity as symbol. In the second part of the chapter, which covers influential Continental philosophers since the 1960s, I articulate the rise of sublimity as a limit concept in deconstruction and postmodernism; describe how Adorno's generally accurate reading of Kant tends to conflate beauty and sublimity, while neglecting the uses of the latter in his own philosophy; demonstrate that Jacques Derrida's and Lyotard's accounts of Kantian sublimity inaugurated the resurgence in philosophical attention to sublimity, with mixed results for its moral dimensions; and, finally, examine Slavoj Žižek's interesting political reading of sublimity and his incorrect conflation of sublimity and evil. I argue that Continental interest in the sublime derives from its preservation of tensions between opposing elements such as nature, consciousness, art, reason, sensibility and imagination, its status as a limit function testing the boundaries of these same intellectual elements and its problematization of representation. Although Continental philosophers have largely neglected the radical potential for moral-political readings of sublimity, sublimity's tension, its limit functions, its problematization of representation and its questioning of the subjective powers and their relation to emotion, nature and technology provide fertile ground for developing Continental moral-political theory. While moral readings of Kantian sublimity figure prominently in post-Kantian Continental philosophy, none of these readings captures its systematic moral functions, and some of the most influential Continental interpretations of Kantian sublimity ignore or misconstrue its moral dimensions.

I: Sublimity and Morality in German Idealism

The publication of Kant's *Critique of Judgment* in 1790 inspired a series of prominent German idealist works on the sublime. Among the first were works by Friedrich Schiller (1759–1805). In 'Of the sublime: toward the further development of some Kantian ideas' (1793) and 'On the sublime', first published in 1801 and composed between 1794 and 1796 (see Hinnant), Schiller, unlike Herder and Hegel, offers an explicitly Kantian reading of the sublime, stressing its moral dimensions by explicit distinction with the beautiful. While Eric Baker argues that Schiller departs from Kant in reading sublimity objectively, allowing for degrees of sublimity and shifting the discussion from the transcendental to the empirical (Baker: 530–1), I would argue that their differences lie elsewhere, for Kant and Schiller both refer at times to an objective sublime, to degrees of sublimity and to the human experience of sublimity.[3] But Schiller certainly diverges from Kant in his solution to natural violence.

Schiller argues in 'On the sublime' that what marks us off as human is the power of our will to resist all natural violence (Schiller 1801: 215). In acting violently against us, a person brings into question our humanity, for our humanity depends on our freedom of will to resist all external forces. Since our aspiration conflicts with our physical capacity to enforce our will against all external powers, many of which are greater than our own physical and scientific powers, we experience terror at the prospect that natural power will destroy our power to will. The elements of this account are virtually identical to those in Kant. However, Schiller's resolution of the problem is largely heteronomous, by Kantian standards. Schiller argues that culture provides for our liberation from natural violence. Yet, the fact that nature can always overcome our physical force leaves us the sole option of destroying the concept of physical force by submitting voluntarily to its power. This is called moral science. Hence, solely 'the morally cultivated man' is free (ibid.: 216).

Despite this heteronomous subsumption of the will to natural power, Schiller's association of moral cultivation and sublimity is akin to Kant's. Sublimity, like beauty and morality, requires cultivation, for the rational capacity of apprehending greatness and sublimity hinges on the acquisition of an adequate supply of concepts and principles, in the maturation of taste. If sublimity requires more cultivation than beauty, cultivation of the former is nonetheless possible for all and, therefore, the potential to experience sublimity is universal. Moreover, Schiller makes no distinction between morality's and sublimity's requirements of cultivation. Both require the slow maturation of innate capacities through the development of concepts and principles. For this reason, Schiller would reject the attempt to drive a wedge between sublimity and morality, since in Schiller the requirement of cultivation does not distinguish sublimity from morality at all. Where Schiller differs from Kant is in arguing that freedom includes not only superiority to nature, but also *identity* with nature, as in Henry David Thoreau's 'Walking'. Kant would reject this notion of freedom as voluntary submission to natural forces, since that is his definition of heteronomy. For Kant, it is the fact that we know that we need never give in to any force, howsoever great, that constitutes our sublime independence from nature. Schiller, who praises the stoic Cato as one of a few men of sublime reason in history, provides an account closer to stoic acceptance of fate's power over us:

> This frame of mind which morality teaches as the concept of resignation at necessity, and which religion teaches under the concept of submission to the divine judgement requires, however, if it is to be a work of free choice and deliberation, already a greater clarity of thought and a higher energy of volition than the human is accustomed to exercise in practical life (Schiller 1801: 216–17);

> Good for him if he has learned to bear what he cannot alter, and to surrender with dignity [*Würde*] what he cannot save! (Ibid.: 227)

But if Schiller's notion of freedom as surrender to external forces diametrically opposes Kant's notion of freedom as self-law and, thus, opposes the foundation of Kantian morality, Schiller argues to something closer to a Kantian notion of freedom in rejecting beauty's power to bring us freedom from nature. This account distinguishes beauty from sublimity largely on moral grounds amenable to the Kantian account. Despite its disinterested character, which Kant defines as indifference to the existence of objects, beauty lacks freedom from nature, because it remains connected to the object from which its semblance is derived. Satisfaction in the beautiful remains dependent on natural power in the existence of beauty and goodness.

> That mental attunement [*Stimmung*] which is indifferent whether the beautiful and the good and the perfect exist, but demands with rigoristic strength that the existing be good and beautiful and perfect, is above all called great and sublime because it contains all the realities of the beautiful character without sharing any of its limitations. (Ibid.: 217–18)

Whereas the beautiful requires the existence of the morally good, the sublime is indifferent to its actual existence, a view consonant with Kant's account of moral standards that may never be attained. Moreover, the beautiful involves play within the constraints of the physical or sensible world, rather than solemn elevation beyond 'the power of nature' in which reason acts solely from its own laws, as in the sublime. For Schiller, sublimity's combination of contradictory perceptions of rapture and melancholy 'demonstrates our moral independence in an irrefutable manner' (ibid.: 219). Since contradictions cannot arise from the same object, they depend on two different ways in which we ourselves are affected by the object. The contradiction between reason and sensuousness demonstrates our intelligible power, a function that exceeds the capacity of beauty's harmony between 'reason' and sensuousness.[4] Although a person driven by beauty might very well act in accordance with the moral law by some fortunate harmony between sensuousness and reason, there is no outward difference between this person and another driven merely by self-interest; a negative turn of fortune's wheel might easily plunge the beauty-driven moral actor into action contrary to morality. Here in words nearly identical to Kant's in GMM and elsewhere, Schiller agrees entirely with Kant in criticizing a morality motivated by pleasure in the beautiful.

> This discovery of the absolute moral capacity which is bound to no natural condition endows the melancholy feeling by which we are seized at the spectacle of such a man with the quite unique, inexpressible charm which no pleasure [*Lust*] of sense, however ennobled it might be, can offer in competition with the sublime. Thus the sublime affords us an egress from the sensuous world in which the beautiful would gladly hold us forever captive. (Ibid.: 221–2)

Sublimity reveals for us this absolute moral capacity in liberating us from sensuous nature. By enacting this function foreclosed to beauty, on account of the latter's connection to sensuous nature, the sublime enables the soul to recognize 'its true determination [*Bestimmung*, as in Kant]' (ibid.: 222).

> The capability of perceiving the sublime is thus one of the most masterful [*herrlichsten*] dispositions [*Anlagen*] in human nature, which because of its origin in the independent powers of thought and volition is worthy both of our respect and of the most perfect development because of its influence on the moral human being. The beautiful is valuable only with reference to the human being, but the sublime with reference to the pure daemon in him; and since it is certainly our determination, despite all sensuous limitations, to be guided by the law-book of pure spirits, the sublime must complement the beautiful in order to make aesthetic education into a complete whole and to enlarge the perceptive capacity of the human heart to the full extent of our determination; even beyond the world of sense. (Ibid.: 228–9)

For Schiller, then, sublimity exercises essential moral functions. Morality is not merely sublime or linked to sublimity; rather, moral action is made possible by the experience of sublimity, in that the latter reveals for us our moral determination as rational beings free in thought and action to determine our will independent of nature.[5] If Schiller at times expresses this freedom in terms of identification with nature, he primarily adopts an explicitly Kantian morality, in contrast to the virtue ethics and utilitarianism of all of Kant's predecessors that I have identified. However, Schiller differs from Kant in ignoring the systematic functions of sublimity in reflective judgement.

In sharp contrast to Schiller's highly Kantian work on sublimity and morality, Johann Gottfried von Herder's late work *Kalligone* is a polemic against Kant's 'Critique of Aesthetic Judgment'. In attacking Kant, Herder is clearly reacting negatively to the Kantian critical turn, not to Kant's pre-critical philosophy, for, in a 1768 letter in which he refers Kant to a French version of Burke's occasionally 'deeper' *Philosophical Inquiry into the Sublime and Beautiful*, Herder praises Kant's aesthetics very highly, describing Kant's pre-critical 1764 *Observations on the Feeling of the Beautiful and Sublime* as a contribution to 'the culture of our century', superior to Burke's text in its ability to generalize and contrast the beautiful and sublime (Kant 1997: Herder to Kant, November

1768: no. 41, X.77).[6] After the appearance of the third *Critique*, Herder took quite a different line. According to Rachel Zuckert, Herder's two lines of criticism of the 'Analytic of the Sublime' were that: 1) Kant fails to explain the feelings of the sublime, and 2) his problem is methodological (Zuckert: 218); a transcendental a priori method cannot 'articulate the necessary conditions for the possibility of such an experience' (Zuckert: 219). Herder's general critique of Kantian sublimity is precisely the same as his critique of Kantian morality. He rejects Kantian sublimity on grounds that it posits contradictory and, hence, unattainable ends in identifying itself by an impossible, formless, natural form (Herder: 877–8; cf. Zuckert: 218) and seeking to *comprehend* an absolute, non-relative size (Herder: 877–8, 880, 885, 891, 902, 905, 907). Because size involves measure and, therefore, is necessarily comparative (Herder: 880, 905), and natural objects, governed by natural law, are necessarily subject to form, the Kantian sublime could produce only displeasure, contempt and pity at our failure to attain the absolute magnitude of sublimity (Herder: 877–8, 885, 891, 902, 907). For the same reasons, Kant's rational morality, invoked by the dynamical sublime, is unattainable and unrealizable, and thus as self-contradictory as his account of sublimity (Herder: 911–12). Kantian sublimity and morality fail, because they set unattainable goals. They claim to transcend nature, yet Herder argues, similarly to Schiller, that 'we belong to nature; we can know no sublime fully beyond her' (Herder: 898). The sublime depends upon contingent facts about our bodies. Hence, Herder rejects Kant's subjectivism by saying that '[t]hough the subject's standpoint, attitudes and responses are intrinsic components of the experience of the sublime, such attitudes and responses are responses to characteristics of objects' (Zuckert: 221).

Yet, in conceiving sublimity in terms of responses to objective conditions, Herder fails to recognize that Kantian sublimity and morality depend on internal relations of powers independent of objectivity, and hence, require no impossible objective correlates. Kant's morality depends on no actual attainment, for he states explicitly that he seeks only to provide a standard against which actions may be judged, regardless of whether there has yet been an action adequate to this standard. While Herder is correct that failing to achieve this goal might bring displeasure, he misses both that Kant explicitly conceives of sublimity as involving displeasure in the imagination's incapacity to attain to reason's ideas and that, for Kant, pleasure cannot be the basis or motivation for moral action. Pleasure may be a legitimate result of moral action, but actions for the sake of pleasure, even if in accordance with the moral law, fall into the immoral third case of action from some immediate inclination. Indeed, the fourth and only licit case of action in Kant's GMM involves displeasure, as action *against* inclination. For this reason, Kantian morality, contra Herder, depends neither on achieving unattainable goals, nor on pleasure, since that would be heteronomous, involving dependence on nature.

Similarly, Kantian sublimity, as an object of aesthetic judgement, requires no relationship to impossible formless or absolutely large natural objects. Although certain types of nature may arouse in us the feeling of the sublime if our mind is suitably prepared by various ideas, sublimity does not presuppose the intuition of nature as infinite. Phenomenal nature necessarily lacks the unconditioned, which reason thinks only as a noumenon. Hence, the absence of the unconditioned in phenomenal nature 'recalls to us that we have to do only with nature as appearance', even though this appearance 'must be regarded still as mere exhibition of a nature in itself', which yet exists for us only as an idea of reason (CJ: 268).

> But this idea of the supersensible, which we admittedly do not determine further, [and] consequently do not cognize nature as exhibition of the supersensible, but rather can only think, is awakened in us through an object, the aesthetic judgement of which strained the imagination to its limits, [whether] extension (mathematically), or its power over the mind (dynamically), in that the aesthetic judgement grounds itself on the feeling of a determination of the mind, which entirely transcends the domain of nature (moral feeling), in regard to which the representation of the object is judged as subjectively purposive. (CJ: 268)

It is not that nature presents us with absolute magnitude but, rather, that certain experiences of what is great or powerful lead us towards our own incomparable supersensible powers. Hence, the inherent tension between imagination's striving for totality and the impossibility of intuiting this totality is what is subjectively purposive for Kant. The imagination strives to comprehend the infinite totality, even as we perceive its incommensurability to this unlimited power. The absolute totality of nature, which for nature as appearance is infinity comprehended, is at the same time the unchanged basic measure of nature.

> But because this basic measure is a self-contradictory concept (on account of the impossibility of the absolute totality of a progression without end) . . . that magnitude of a natural object, to which the imagination finds its whole power of comprehension applied fruitlessly, must lead the concept of nature to a supersensible substrate (which lies at the same time at the ground of nature and our power to think), which is great beyond all measure of senses. (CJ: 255)

Notice here not only that Kant recognizes what he takes to be the impossibility of the absolute totality of an infinite progression, which is Herder's objection, but that it is the imagination's failure to attain to this totality (the element of failure and displeasure) that leads us to our incomparably great powers. Kant's notion of purposiveness without purpose means that sublimity entails no attainment of some purpose, contra Herder, but only the recognition in us of supersensible powers (the source of our *telos* or *Zweck*). This is not to say that failure and, therefore, displeasure are absent from sublimity. On the contrary, pleasure and displeasure are both intrinsic to Kantian sublimity. The sublime generates displeasure from the imagination's constitutive inability to comprehend the entirety of reason's ideas or natural objects or powers arousing the experience or feeling of sublimity within us. Simultaneously, alternately, or successively, however, sublimity generates pleasure from our ability to think absolute size or power. Hence, Kant never claims any impossible achievement or argues that sublimity directly generates pleasure from our incapacity. Kant argues that

> [t]his striving [for totality in ideas] and the feeling of the unattainability of the idea through the imagination is itself an exhibition of the subjective purposiveness of our mind in the use of the imagination for its supersensible determination and necessitates us to think of something supersensible without being able to bring about this exhibition objectively. (CJ: 268)

As Zuckert notes, sublimity (in a sense) 'makes sensible the supersensible aspects of our nature', namely, our rational ideas and ends (Zuckert: 218). Imagination's failure to exhibit the idea objectively, then, is what exhibits the mind's subjective purposiveness in using the imagination, for it reveals the mind's power to transcend the sensuous sphere and thereby achieve its supersensible determination. This process cannot be objective, because the unconditioned, absolute magnitude, which reason demands, is absent from nature in space and time (CJ: 268); we cannot meet with the unconditioned, the absolute or the infinite objectively in outer experience. Thus, contra Herder, Kant is quite explicit both that we cannot attain any impossible objective correlates of reason's ideas in the sublime and that the displeasure generated by this failure is itself essential to the supersensible uses of sublimity. To be sure, historical accounts of the sublime, and not merely the Kantian sublime, have always been defined largely by tensions and contradictions, and Kant defines sublimity as the discordant harmony of imagination and reason. But, in judging Kantian sublimity by reference to a bivalent standard, Herder fails to recognize that: 1) it is possible to experience contradictory feelings, as in the sublime, 2) the dominant tension in sublimity involves the conflict of independent powers, rather than direct contradictions, and 3) Kantian critique adopts a mediating position between sceptical, non-teleological accounts of nature and dogmatic physico-teleological reductions of nature to supersensible purpose.

Nevertheless, Herder provides an early indication of the moral significance of Kantian sublimity by reading sublimity and morality in similar formal terms. Herder and Kant also agree that the sublime is related to moral determination (Zuckert translates *Bestimmung* as vocation) and perfectibility (Zuckert: 225), as well as to superior moral characters (Herder: 867–8; cf. Zuckert: 219). Hence, Herder says that, for Kant, one could find oneself the most sublime of all (Zuckert: 225). However, for Herder, Kant's moral person is tyrannical, in so far as he exerts power over others and lacks any recognition of a debt to the world, culture and others (Herder: 911–12; cf. Zuckert: 226). The latter is an interesting objection, which takes us into Hegelian and communitarian critiques of Kantian morality. Indeed, the sublimity of Kantian morality *requires* the latter's utter independence from nature, its strict derivation from the sovereign will and the absolute mastery of moral law and reason over will and nature. Yet, to be fair, Kant condemns the use of arbitrary or tyrannical power over other persons (as rational beings) in the formula of treating humanity as an end in itself and in the derivation of society from contract ('On a supposed right to lie because of philanthropic concerns', Ak.427). The subject's moral power consists in reason's command of the will over the forces of internal and external nature, where other autonomous beings are accorded equal status to oneself. Moreover, Kant himself recognizes cultural and social debts and obligations in many passages, ranging from our perfect duty to tell the truth to others and our imperfect duty to help others, to the *sensus communis* and our mature reason's dependence on a long education generating horizons harmonizing our aims, ends and inclinations in logic, aesthetics and ethics (Kant 1800: *Logik*, IX40–3). Therefore, we cannot accept Herder's objection to Kantian morality as tyrannical in its relationship to others.

Herder's 1800 response to Kant is said to mark the end of explicit philosophical discussions of sublimity (Kirwan 2004: 1–2). Yet, the sublime remained a live topic in German idealism. G. W. F. Hegel's relative inattentiveness to sublimity is clear from the fact that Paul de Man ('Hegel on the sublime', 1983) can demonstrate the allegedly fundamental significance of sublimity to the Hegelian system only by placing great weight on Hegel's *marginalization* of the sublime (see Donougho). De Man argues that 'the enslaved place and condition of the section on the sublime in the *Aesthetics*, and the enslaved place of the *Aesthetics* within the corpus of Hegel's complete works, are the symptoms of their strength' (de Man: 118). However, Hegel discusses sublimity at length in his *Aesthetics* and his *Lectures on the Philosophy of Religion*. Whereas Herder's account of the sublime opposes Kant from within the parameters of Kantian and Burkean aesthetics, Hegel's account criticizes Kant from a non-Kantian paradigm.[7] Hegel's account focuses exclusively on symbolic art, rather than the disharmonious effects of natural and mental representations on the subject's mental powers.[8] Yet, he argues that the symbolic structure of sublimity precludes the emergence of free, moral subjectivity, and the moral-political consequences of this claim are significant, for he links sublimity in art and religion to particular, allegedly deficient cultures. Hegel's *Aesthetics* and *Philosophy of Religion* identify Judaism as the religion of sublimity (Hegel 1985: v.1, 363/II.495).[9] He places it prejudicially before, rather than after, Greek beauty, as Yirmiahu Yovel and Slavoj Žižek note (Žižek 1989: 202), while Hegel's *Aesthetics* associates the sublime symbol also with 'the East'; *Morgenlande* (ibid.: 298/H.406), formerly translated as 'the Orient', cf. *morgenländischen*, glossed as ancient Persian, Indian, Egyptian (ibid.: 304/H.413). These identifications of sublime art carry negative connotations, for Hegel argues that the sublime stage of art, like Eastern and Jewish culture, is inadequate to the concept. Despite the symbol's natural, if one-sided, relationship to the idea – e.g. the lion is the symbol of courage, rather than the totality of possible leonine characteristics (ibid.: 300/H.408) – no determinate form can correspond to the determinate, measureless, transcendent idea's abstract universality. This transcendence of determinate, outer existence through its non-correspondence to the symbol defines the sublime (ibid.: 298–9/H.407). Hence, 'Eastern' symbolic artworks cannot be read superficially according to their 'bizarre, playful, grotesque', immediate appearance (ibid.: 305/H.416), given their enigmatic one-sidedness and isolation of meaning from concrete appearance (ibid.: 367/H.501). Sublime cultures, in their 'infancy [*Kindheit*]', remain incapable of expressing religious ideas more purely through beautiful forms, yet their symbolic images indeterminately veil more complex meanings with the aid of these 'fantastic and grotesque' forms (ibid.: 304/H.413–14). The image itself holds neither pleasure, nor satisfaction, because the artwork's esoteric meaning requires transcending the sensuous image (ibid.: 304/H.413). These 'essentially symbolic' myths, 'produced by the spirit', find their justification in revealing 'general thoughts upon the divine nature . . . philosophemes'; myths 'justify human being in their spiritual images and representations', despite the accidental elements remaining from imagination and history (ibid.: 305/H.416). A rational basis and genuine religious ideas underlie the veil of mythology, even if these have not yet been thought abstractly. A universal thought provides the real meaning and basis of true works of art. However, as soon as a critical spirit attains this meaning, the art work is destroyed, for the meaning is what is truly significant about the work.

The overcoming of the pure symbol and, hence, the overcoming of sublimity, with its vagueness and indeterminacy, occurs in the representation of the gods in classical Greek art. Representation in art develops through the emergence of the free, individual Greek Gods, and the symbol disappears. Hence, despite exhibiting the transcendence of finite necessity, as in Kant, sublimity for Hegel cannot represent 'free, enclosed individuals, independent in themselves' (ibid.: 308/H.419), for it remains on the symbolic stage, caught in vague and indeterminate ideas unable to express this difference from the universal. This incapacity to express the moral person reflects the difference between the Hegelian and the Kantian moral agent. Whereas the Kantian moral agent remains on the abstract, universal level, with the exception of the developmental suggestions of Kant's notion of horizons, the Hegelian moral person is a kind of concretized universal, constituting a transition between universal law and free individual. This concretized agency is lacking in the sublime, for the stage of the symbol begins from the contingent outer appearance and moves to the abstraction of the idea without exhibiting the activity and movement of spirit. For this reason, the symbolic sublime leaves off 'where instead of indeterminate, universal, abstract representations, free individuality makes up [*ausmacht*] the content and form of exhibition [*Darstellung*]' (ibid.: 308/H.419). The symbol's enigmatic character prevents its exhibition of the intrinsic clarity of the active subject (ibid.: 308/H.419). The universal, absolute character of the gods is revealed through the determinate and, hence, non-sublime representation of independence; nobility and elevation exhibit their transcendence of finite necessity, despite their natural, sensuous form. Sublimity in the classical ideal is grounded in beauty. Yet, if beauty marks the harmony of the spiritual and the corporeal, the outer, formal manifestation of inner moral goodness, beauty also contains within itself the seed of its destruction, in exhibiting tacitly the discord between spiritual grandeur and corporeal beauty.

Symbolic art fails to exhibit real individuality, except as empty semblance because, even if it involves sensation and thought, it treats the immediate sensuousness of physical objects as images of a detached, immaterial, invisible, general power. Symbolic art cannot homogenize the heterogeneous elements of sensation and pure conception, for Hegelian matter and form, like the Kantian sublime, are locked in ceaseless strife even as they seek harmony. In recognizing this conflict, the pure or unconscious, irreflective symbol of 'Eastern' art passes into the conscious, reflective symbol of comparison or allegory, where the idea and image are conceived clearly as distinct. Thus, whereas Derrida stresses Kantian sublimity's simultaneous claims to transcend and to exhibit comparisons in identifying sublimity as what is absolutely large or great, beyond all comparison, for Hegel, sublimity's indeterminacy and its failure to reconcile the difference of its formal and material, universal and particular, elements situates it immediately *before* the stage in which comparison is possible. The stage of strife definitive of Hegelian and Kantian sublimity in each case leads to transcendence of the merely natural. The difference is that for Hegel this movement destroys sublimity, because of its inadequacy to moral personhood, whereas for Kant sublimity's transcendence unveils our moral freedom.

II: Sublimity and Morality in Contemporary Continental Philosophy

Contemporary Continental philosophy of the sublime always refers back to Kant and/or Hegel, while going beyond either in its use of psychoanalytical, structuralist and post-structuralist methods. Theodor Adorno's work on the sublime sets the paradigm for recent work influenced by both Kant and Hegel. In *Aesthetic Theory*, certainly the richest statement of Frankfurt School aesthetics and nearly complete at his death in 1969 (Adorno, AT (the remaining citations refer to the German edition): translator's introduction, xx), as well as other texts, Adorno provides an exceptionally accurate, detailed moral reading of Kantian sublimity.[10] In its emphasis on Kant, its accuracy and its moral focus, Adorno's account stands apart from those of other Continental philosophers, with the exception of Schiller and Derrida. But what is original about Adorno's reading is that it is a *Hegelian* reading of Kantian sublimity. While Jacques Lacan and Slavoj Žižek have given Hegelian readings of sublimity, Adorno uses Hegelian structures and terminology to criticize and transform Kantian sublimity. The consequence of combining Kantian concepts with Hegelian accounts is that Adorno ultimately undermines the possibility of the Kantian moral reading of the sublime.

Despite his Hegelian methods and concepts, it is clear that Adorno works from a Kantian account of the sublime. Adorno refers directly to Kantian sublimity in many works throughout his career, ranging from his first book, *Kierkegaard: Construction of the Aesthetic*, to *Dialectic of Enlightenment* and *Aesthetic Theory*. Throughout these texts, Adorno is consistent in identifying moral functions as the essence of the Kantian account. In contrast to recent attempts to separate Kantian morality and aesthetics, Adorno argues that in the sublime external to the artwork, Kant sought 'the infiltration of the aesthetic with the moral' (*Ästhetische Theorie* (AT): GS7.79). Hence, Adorno characterizes Kantian sublimity in terms of its moral functions. 'For Kant, what is sublime in nature is nothing but the autonomy of the spirit in the face of the superior power of sensuous existence' (AT: GS7.143). The subject recognizes its autonomy in the encounter with overpowering nature or sensuous existence, and the recognition of autonomy is a necessary condition for moral action. This reading of moral functions as essential to Kantian sublimity depends on the view that even the hard cases for moral readings of sublimity – objective nature, quantitative magnitude (read: mathematical sublimity) and intellectual functions – mark subjective, moral autonomy over nature. Thus, Adorno argues that Kant compares abstract magnitude to the moral law (AT: GS7.110) and that Kantian sublimity is 'not quantitative magnitude as such' but, rather, 'the spirit's resistance to superior force' (AT: GS7.296). Mathematical and dynamical sublimity equally exhibit the spirit's resistance to natural and even political violence. In the dynamical sublime, as in the mathematical sublime, resistance against nature restores 'power and hope' to the powerless (Adorno, *Musikalische Schriften I–III: Kriterien der neuen Musik*: GS16.226), for the sublime is conditioned on the subject's power (AT: GS7.364). Sublimity's exhibition of the unboundedness of wild nature is simultaneous with 'the emancipation of the subject and thereby the self-consciousness of the spirit' (AT: GS7.292). The triumph of the intelligible over the sensuous in the sublime enables the emergence of the subject's eternal, 'universal determination', that of the spirit (AT: GS7.295). The sublime marks the 'triumph of the free and autonomous spirit' (Adorno, *Kriterien der neuen Musik*, GS16.227).

Yet, Adorno's highly Kantian moral reading of sublimity ultimately conflicts with his Hegelian structure and terminology. Indeed, in explicitly criticizing the Kantian account of sublime moral autonomy on Hegelian grounds, Adorno suggests the impossibility of any Kantian moral use of sublimity. He criticizes the 'formal subjectivism' of Kant's account of the sublime (AT: *Frühe Einleitung*, GS7.496n5), speaks of Kant's 'questionable proposition [that] "nothing sensuous is sublime"' (AT: GS7.140), dismisses Kant's association of great magnitude with sublimity and small magnitude with contempt, citing Karl Rosenkranz's 1853 text *Ästhetik der Häßlichen* (Adorno, *Kierkegaard: Konstruktion des Ästhetischen*: GS2.33–4), and suggests, with Karl Kraus, that there is something ideologically bourgeois about the fascination with great quantitative magnitude (AT: GS7.110). Although he also criticizes Hegel's aesthetics, for dissolving the objective artwork entirely in the unity of spirit (AT: GS7.140), Adorno's reading of sublimity is Hegelian in its dialectics, its focus on art, rather than Kantian nature, and its language of spirit, abstraction, concreteness and autonomy. Adorno's view that sublime nature's 'autonomy is achieved only in the spiritualized artwork' (AT: GS7.143) agrees with Hegel in locating spirit and the autonomy of natural sublimity dialectically in their opposites, art objects (that is, subjective spirit is found in the object, nature in art). For Adorno, certain spiritualized artworks manifest the spirit concretely, rather than abstractly, without collapsing into 'subaltern thematic material' (AT: GS7.143). Thus, he describes the autonomous artwork as the realization of sublimity, whereas Hegel describes it as the *destruction* or overcoming of sublimity. However, the structure of their arguments is identical, for both apply the terms 'realization', 'destruction' and 'overcoming' to this act of the reconciliation of opposites. Although Adorno historicizes the association of sublimity with art by associating it with a post-Kantian spiritualization of nature (AT: GS7.292; in contrast to Hegel's location of the sublime in ancient Eastern and Jewish architecture), Adorno suggests that this passing over into its other is inherent in the *Kantian* account, for Kant's moral philosophy depends on the contradiction that the free and sublime subject is simultaneously an entity in unfree nature (Adorno, *Negative Dialektik*, GS6.181). In thus denying the possibility of separating the free sublime subject from unfree, objective nature, Adorno asserts the impossibility of the Kantian account. Sublimity's exhibition of an autonomous moral subject is necessarily illusory, if there can be no radically free moral self. If sublimity is possible, it is only through a non-reductive interconnection of subjectivity and objectivity in which difference and relation exist simultaneously. Sublimity requires the subject's relation to the object. Autonomy cannot be understood in Kantian terms as absolute disconnection.

In then sustaining sublimity's *moral* possibilities on the same grounds as he argues to sublimity's very possibility, Adorno adverts to quite a different conception of moral autonomy. According to his negative dialectical account, what makes sublimity possible and grounds its moral functions is its exhibition of tension, rather than the strict separation between subjectivity and objectivity that is posited by Kantian autonomy. Adorno agrees with Kant that sublimity exists and that it is dissociated from evil, because it is not supposed to harmonize or unify the tension of opposites, as in beauty. Yet, for Adorno, moral autonomy consists in this recognition of tension, not in liberation from nature. This position derives from his identification of critique as the highest moral function. For Adorno, a critical philosophy, in contrast to an ideology, functions by exposing conflicts, revealing the distorting powers of ideological operations and exhibiting possibilities for their resistance. Sublimity enacts these critical functions by exhibiting the inherent tension between subjectivity and objectivity, reason and imagination, leading the subject to recognize its autonomous power of moral resistance against external powers and motivating it to moral action from the seriousness, rather than mere play, of its emotion (citing Kant, Adorno, *Dissonanzen. Einleitung in die Musiksoziologie: Kritik des Musikanten*, GS14.72). These critical functions dissociate sublimity from evil and constitute its 'autonomy'. Spiritualized artworks serve critical functions because they 'reveal [in what has been stigmatized by bourgeois society] that nature whose suppression is what is truly evil' (AT: GS7.144). Sublimity resists evil by revealing the natural strife that bourgeois ideology seeks to conceal. This explains why Adorno particularly admires sublimity's exemplary liminal status in Kant's definition of sublimity as a 'trembling [*erzitternd*] between nature and freedom', for '[t]his ambivalence is registered by every genuine aesthetic experience' (AT: GS7.172). What distinguishes modern works is their exhibition (*qua* ugliness) of the tension between spiritualization and its opposite, 'what is most distant from spirit' (AT: GS7.144). Spiritualization purifies art of 'the topical preferences of philistine culture: the true, the beautiful, and the good'; for Adorno, though, spiritualization serves moral purposes in transcending truth, beauty and goodness, because this distance enables its critical function; in 'art's social critique or *engagement*, all that is critical or negative in art, has been fused with spirit, with art's law of form' (AT: GS7.144).

However, Adorno recognizes that sublimity can itself be transformed into an ideological function, as in bourgeois tourism, for 'even the abstract magnitude of nature, which Kant still marvelled at [*bewunderte*] and compared to the moral law, becomes' an element of bourgeois striving for quantitative records (AT: GS7.110). The great magnitude of the Alps is denatured by its transformation into a ranked system of mountains of a definite size. Thus, it is necessary to unmask the fact that sublimity can become 'only the fruit of ideology, of respect before power and magnitude' (AT: GS7.224). But this assimilation of sublimity to unthreatening, domesticated, quantitative comparisons or even servile acceptance of external, hierarchical power relations remains observer dependent. To a different observer such as Nietzsche at Sils Maria, the magnitude of nature in exhibiting the weakness of our drives might become a reminder of the limits of human mastery of nature

(AT: GS7.111). It is contingent, then, whether sublimity will exercise moral-critical or evil-ideological functions; both possibilities inhere in sublimity.

Conflicts within this account may be due in part to the fact that it is reconstructed from isolated, paratactic remarks. Adorno never gives a single, sustained treatment of the sublime. Nor does he refer specifically to sublimity's systematic function in establishing moral determinability through reflective judgement's transition from nature to freedom. Yet, in emphasizing that a moral enterprise is at the root of the Kantian account of the sublime and in articulating how sublimity functions to exhibit and inspire our moral powers, Adorno provides arguably the best moral reading of Kantian sublimity among recent continental philosophers, despite the fact that his construction of sublimity owes as much to Hegelian dialectical accounts as to Kant.

In the generation following Adorno's death, virtually every major postmodernist or post-structuralist philosopher has worked on sublimity. As Philip Shaw argues, sublimity is involved in Jacques Derrida's discussion of *parerga*, Paul de Man's rhetoric, which with Peter de Bolla treats sublimity as an 'effect of the transformational or combinatory power of language' (Shaw: 89), Lyotard's unpresentable, Jean-Luc Nancy's offering, Jacques Lacan's *thing* (ibid.: 11), Rodolphe Gasché's Kantian account of sublimity 'as the minimal synthesis in order for there to be a mediation between concepts of nature and concepts of freedom' (Gasché 1990: 112–13) and Žižek's discussions of ideology and 9/11. This interest is due primarily neither to the psychological or linguistic concerns of Continental philosophers, as Shaw argues (Shaw: 131), nor to the influence of Barnett Newman or Lyotard, as Zuckert argues (Zuckert: 228n2). While psychological and linguistic concerns are *contingently* relevant to continental discourses on the sublime, sometimes at issue, other times not, I would argue that continental interest in sublimity is intrinsic to the subject, in so far as both Continental philosophy and sublimity are defined by aporetic questions concerning the limit and the unlimited, the presentable and the unpresentable (Lyotard 1984: 81).[11] Continental philosophers are drawn to the sublime, because in their reading, it constitutes a site for the working out of the limit questions characteristic of continental philosophy. Hence, it is unnecessary to refer to psychological and linguistic questions to explain Continental attention to the sublime and, indeed, such questions are not always at issue in, for example, Derrida or Žižek.

As for Zuckert's claim that Newman or Lyotard is responsible for postmodernist attention to the sublime, the actual history is more complex. As we have seen, interest in the sublime, whether in the arts or academia, never truly waned outside the field of Anglo-American philosophy. Hence, there were always many possible influences on recent Continental philosophers. But Kant and Hegel are clearly the strongest influences both on Continental philosophy in general and Continental philosophy of sublimity in particular, as is evident both in citation measures and in the specific themes and ideas of Continental philosophers.[12] Few Continental philosophers, aside from Lyotard, have discussed Newman's work on sublimity. Now, Lyotard has wielded considerable influence on recent Continental philosophy of sublimity, for his work on sublimity is by far the most cited in the past thirty years. Yet, Lyotard conceives himself to be merely 'explicating' Kant's own text, not constructing his own new account. Moreover, in time, method, subject matter and Kantian focus, Lyotard, like subsequent Continental writers on the sublime, follows closely Jacques Derrida's prior work on sublimity in the 1970s.[13] Lyotard's only major departure from Derrida and, hence, the only position in later Continental philosophy that can be derived strictly from Lyotard, is his flawed, anti-moral reading of the sublime.

Derrida's essay, 'The Parergon', first published in French in 1978 in *La Vérité en Peinture*, and in English as a stand-alone essay in 1979 in *October* (no. 9: 3–40) and in *The Truth in Painting* in 1987, provides a long deconstruction of Kantian sublimity. This essay is to my knowledge the first extended treatise explicitly on the sublime by an influential philosopher since Hegel. However, a good deal of the essay is not on the sublime, but on beauty, art, the aesthetic and the relationship between art and nature. As I have learned from Alan Schrift, these were the very topics of the 2e written composition for the 1967 French *Agrégation* programme (the introduction and 'Analytic of the Beautiful' from Kant's *Kritik der Urteilskraft* (in German) were required reading for the 1977–8 exams and all of Kant's written works, including the *Critique of Judgment*, had to be studied for the 1974–5, 1982–3, 1990–1, 1996–7 exams).[14] At the time, according to Schrift, Derrida was the *caiman* at the École Normale Supérieur, responsible for preparing *normaliens* for the

Agrégation, and one of Derrida's students at the time, Jean-Louis Fabini found that *The Truth in Painting* followed his own 1967 notes very closely. Indeed, Derrida refers directly to the *Agrégation de philosophie* on the second page of the 'Parergon' essay. In the interim between 1967 and 1978, Derrida seems to have discussed portions of 'The Parergon' in a 1973–4 seminar (Derrida 1987a: 19–20: all Derrida references are to this edition, except as noted) and he published a shorter version, excluding the fourth section, 'The Colossal', in *Digraph*e 3 and 4 (1974) (ibid.: 16n). Derrida's essay may not have initiated discussion on the Kantian sublime, but it did mark the beginning of a turn to Kantian sublimity, on the part of both Anglo-American and Continental philosophers. Prior to the mid- to late 1980s, there was no single focal point for work on the sublime. There were about as many original works on sublimity as works on the sublime in Kant, Burke, Hegel, Longinus or Romanticism. But, by the late 1980s, most philosophical work on the sublime was about Kant. Counting historical-analytic writings, beginning in 1980 with Kant scholar Allan Lazaroff and continuing in 1982 with Paul Guyer and William Hund, at least three hundred works on the Kantian sublime have appeared since Derrida's 1970s texts. Whether or not Derrida's influence prompted this outpouring, Continental works on the Kantian sublime soon appeared from Lyotard from 1982–91, Paul de Man in 1983, Rudolf Makkreel in 1984, Jean-Luc Nancy in 1985 and 1993, Slavoj Žižek in 1989, Rodolphe Gasché in 1990 and Philippe Lacoue-Labarthe in 1991. According to Shaw, postmodernists such as Derrida, de Man, Lacoue-Labarthe and Lyotard criticized Kantian sublimity by shifting sublimity's locus from transcendence to immanence, exhibiting the unrepresentable as internal to representation and conditioning sublime consciousness on language. Nevertheless, their work focused on Kant and retained Kantian parameters (Shaw: 3–4, 7).

Derrida's influence over subsequent interpretations of sublimity depends primarily on his arguments that Kant's account of sublimity: 1) determines the limits and essence of his account of beauty (at the same time as it unseats the logic of limits and essences, so as not to merely invert a transcendental logic), rather than constituting a mere appendix to the critique of taste, 2) is self-deconstructing, and thus is best read deconstructively (Derrida 1987a: 71, 73), 3) exhibits the dependence of critical reason on aesthetic judgement, and 4) articulates the limits of representation. Here I examine how these arguments shed light on a less influential aspect of Derrida's deconstructive reading of Kant's 'Analytic of the Sublime', namely, how it addresses moral-political elements in Kant's work. In 'The Parergon', as in all of Derrida's work prior to the late 1980s and his so-called 'ethical turn', there is little direct attention to moral-political issues, except for a brief account of certain moral functions of the Kantian sublime. Yet, Derrida's discussions of logical and metaphysical-epistemological questions, here as elsewhere, implicitly deal with moral-political issues in a way that builds on but also goes beyond Kant's own moral uses of sublimity.[15] In particular, Derrida's examination of the problem of representation and his attention to the marginalization of difference and otherness imply a distinctive, radical moral-political stance against homogenization and domination within the formal and structural assumptions of Kantian aesthetics.

Derrida's indirect moral reading of Kantian sublimity posits an ethics of difference that is largely alien to Kantian morality, yet is *implied* by Kant's construction of sublimity as the representation of the unrepresentable. Derrida argues that sublimity involves the ethical quandary of how to attend to otherness and difference without reducing them to unity or sameness. The implicit ethical-political problem involved in failing to recognize difference as such, without reduction, cannot be treated explicitly as a problem within Kant's *universalistic* morality, except to the extent that it amounts to disrespecting the autonomy of the other. Derrida also departs from Kant in criticizing both the self-sufficiency of reason in morality and the individualistic focus of ethics, which are at odds with the anti-rationalism of post-Nietzschean Continental philosophers and the anti-individualistic, social-political focus of post-Hegelians. Hence, Derrida's ethics of difference is quite distinct from Kantian morality, even if Derrida is drawn to Kantian sublimity precisely by its recognition that the conditions of morality exceed rational boundaries. In the past thirty years, Derrida's attention to marginalization has come to seem quite conventional. But what continues to set the Derridean position apart is its extension of questions of political domination to metaphysical identities underlying political domination and its performative moral-political operation of restoring the suppressed powers of the marginal *parerga* to their constitutive role in defining the 'nature' of the beautiful work.

In Derrida's reading, Kant's definition of sublimity as the presentation of the unpresentable brings to the fore the problem concealed in all presentation of what is other than the sign, image or presentation, namely, that presentation or representation claims to identify or re-present what is *ex hypothesi* different. Kant's colossal sublime makes this problem explicit. In the colossal, the claim is to present what is too large for comprehension and almost too large for presentation and apprehension (Derrida 1987a: 125–6). The presentation of a non-thing, an almost unpresentable concept, by reason of its size, is colossal (ibid.: 125). Unlike the monstrous or prodigious, the colossal (*kolossalisch*) does not through its size nullify or annihilate the end constitutive of its concept but, rather, presents a concept 'almost too large for any presentation' (ibid., citing Kant, CJ: 253). Thus, for Kant, sublimity is in the most correct sense to be found in our own presentation of the inadequacy of our power of presentation to reason's ideas (Derrida 1987a: 131–2). This self-cancelling, or almost self-cancelling, move exhibits the limits of the representation of difference as the tacit form and content of any sublime representation. The failure to replicate, replay or signify what by its size exceeds our capacities of representation establishes that representation is limited, that it cannot grasp all possible objects or experiences or reduce differences to a single identity in present-tense experience. But, in this failure, sublime representation indicates the very existence of the indeterminate differences that it cannot exhibit or reduce to unity with its sign. Hence, for Derrida, the colossal sublime makes explicit the irreducibility of differences within the representational process of unifying sign and significatum. The colossal sublime thereby enacts the incessant deconstructive project of restoring the irreducible character of difference(s), otherness and marginality, and prompting the ethical-political-epistemological recognition of their existence and significance.

Derrida's account of the mathematical sublime revisits the problem of the representation of difference through the problem of comparing the incomparable. The Kantian mathematical sublime concerns what is absolutely, non-comparatively large, but to define it as large, to exclude what is infinitely small and to prefer this magnitude to others is to posit sublimity as simultaneously exclusive and inclusive of comparison (ibid.: 136). Sublimity's magnitude lacks any dimension and hence, is neither equal, nor comparable to anything else; it is 'inadequate to anything measurable' (ibid.: 135).

In Kant's exhibition of the irreconcilability of difference with unity, through the refusal of comparison and equality, Derrida recognizes a properly ethical understanding of the problem of representation. The impossibility of reducing differences to the unitary basis of comparison, at least in the absolute magnitude of the mathematical sublime, coupled with the claim to a self-defined, independent quantity, establishes an absolute or intrinsic value. But what is valued absolutely is really the condition of sublimity and morality, the autonomous self. Hence, Derrida reads the mathematical sublime as undergirding both Kantian morality and a general ethics of difference. However, he criticizes Kant's subsequent reduction of this sublime incompossibility. In describing sublimity both as the quantum of the absolutely large and as that *'in comparison with which all the rest is small'* (Kant, CJ: 250; cf. Derrida 1987a: 138), Kant brings sublimity under the aegis of comparison, 'comparing the comparable with the incomparable' much as St Anselm does in his proof of the existence of God (*'aliquid quo nihil majus cogitari potest'*) (Derrida 1987a: 137). Comparison, analogy and representation reduce otherness to unity by identifying heterogeneous entities as the same or by measuring them according to the same standard. Thus, the Kantian sublime articulates a mode of difference irreducible to unity, in the figures of the unpresentable and incomparable, and then annuls this philosophy of difference, reducing difference to unity by claiming to present the unpresentable and to compare the incomparable. In the first step, there is a clear ethical-political concern to preserve the ineradicable singularity of what is different, while in the second step, the metaphysics of identity reasserts itself, violating the Derridean ethical-political attention to singularity.

Again, in Derrida's argument that a dominant, centralized essence, whether in epistemology, metaphysics or aesthetics, depends ultimately on its excluded, marginalized others, there is a clear concern for the non-reductive, non-hierarchical, political and ethical recognition of oppressed or colonized others. Derrida criticizes Kant's alleged privileging of essentialist elements (the *ergon* or work) over their inessential or marginal conditions (the *parergon* or frame of the work). He argues that the metaphysics and epistemology of the sublime depend on a certain self-undermining 'logic' of the limit in which the frame defining the limits or boundaries of the work (say, a gilded or decorated frame of a painting or the columns of a frieze) is regarded as inessential to the identity of the work it defines. The response is not to argue that the marginalia constitute the 'true' essence of the work, but to argue to the reciprocal constitution and problematization of 'interior' and 'exterior'. This approach treats metaphysical-epistemological questions in criticizing Kantian claims to the being, essence and knowledge of the sublime. But it examines moral-political claims in attending to the recognition, preservation or destruction of the singular being, essence and knowledge of the sublime.

In Derrida's reading, the moral-political functions of the beautiful and the sublime follow from their relationship to the Kantian *parerga*. The beautiful artwork is defined as a work by the marginalization of its *parerga*, the incidental charms, flourishes, columns or frames surrounding the *ergon* or work. Hence, this identification of the crucial defining functions of the marginalized others first demonstrates their suppressed importance. The beautiful requires the domination of the other in order to be what it is. This means that Kant assigns the *parerga* the crucial role of providing the beautiful work its determination by framing, outlining and limiting it (ibid.: 127). Understood as a dialectical reversal, this Derridean move could be criticized for merely inverting the relationship of essence and marginalia, while sustaining an hierarchical, essentialist account; the marginalia would lose their inessential status, supplanting the essence of the work without altering this hierarchical, essentialist, indeed transcendental, logic. However, Derrida resists this claim, arguing that the relationship between the *parerga* and the *ergon* constitutes a non-hierarchical, non-essentialist, non-transcendental logic, a *reciprocal* logic implicating the new conditions of the possibility of the work in the work itself, each functioning as condition and conditioned. Although Kant seems never to allow for such a logic, since his transcendental argument is classically linear in conditioning the work on the conditions of its possibility, his third form of relation in the table of judgements, community, itself constitutes such a reciprocal logic. In Derrida's deconstruction of beauty, the attempt to set a final boundary between essential work and marginalized borders fails, because the borders define the nature of the work and thus, are implicated within the work.

Hence, the sublime functions according to an entirely different 'logic', in Derrida's reading of Kant. The Derridean sublime is much closer to *parergon* than *ergon*, as an appendix to the critique of judgement. However, the sublime resists the roles both of margin and essence, and hence seems to fall neither within the dominating, nor the dominated. Whereas the limits of the beautiful are determined by its marginalized others, 'there cannot, it seems, be a *parergon* for the sublime' (ibid.), because a *parergon* of the sublime would necessarily stand outside of it and frame or define it, and the sublime exceeds any boundaries. In the sublime, the form is finite and determinate, yet what is presented is necessarily infinite and indeterminate, and this indeterminacy, this formlessness, is what is to be presented in its presentation (ibid.: 129). Hence, the sublime neither requires the marginalization of charms or other *parerga*, nor constitutes its own limiting function. As a threshold function, exceeding or overspilling any limits, sublimity eludes the classical master–slave dichotomy implied by the beautiful. Although it is not clear that Kant allows for such a logic in other contexts, the logic of Kantian sublimity preserves radical difference by undoing the polarities essential to bivalent constructions of sameness and otherness. Recognition of this logic, then, would be the basis for an indirect, deconstructive ethics or socio-politics of Kantian sublimity.

However, Derrida also provides a *direct* moral reading of the sublime that is largely consonant with Kant and inclusive of many of his key points, if incomplete and absent sublimity's systematic function of establishing the determinability of the moral subject. The basis for this reading consists in Derrida's recognition that Kantian sublimity entails the morally requisite negative relations to the inclinations of pleasure, attraction and fear, and the morally useful positive relation to the disinclination of displeasure. He argues that for Kant the reason that in sublimity nature cannot be overwhelming or great enough to nullify the end constitutive of its concept, as in the monstrous or prodigious (*ungeheuer*), is that this nullification would admit fear or 'attraction' into sublimity (ibid.: 124–5). This incompatibility with fear and attraction is crucial to sublimity's moral functions for Kant, since he rejects any foundation of morality on inclinations. To act in accordance with the moral law from fear is to act heteronomously from inclination. Hence, the devout believer acting in fear and trembling from knowledge of God's infinite existence cannot act morally for Kant. Her action is unfree, determined by her corporeal nature. Similarly, action in accordance with the moral law from pleasure or attraction is based on inclination and, thus, is heteronomous and contains no moral content. But, because beauty, unlike sublimity, is accompanied by a positive pleasure, action motivated by beauty would for the same reason be heteronomous. Therefore, Derrida's examination of the introduction to the third *Critique* and the 'Analytic of the Beautiful' stresses the liminal role of disinterested pleasure, a characteristic of all aesthetic judgements. The essence of aesthetic judgement consists in 'the relation of the representation . . . to the *subject* and to its affect (pleasure or unpleasure)' (ibid.: 44). Aesthetic pleasure is disinterested in the sense that it is detached from the existence of the object. But the question remains whether this strict detachment of pleasure from its object is possible or whether aesthetic pleasure entails some dependence on the object's existence (ibid.: 45). If, as Derrida argues, it is impossible to detach the pure or essential sense of beauty from 'the circumstance of the object being talked about', if it is impossible to detach the parergonal frame from the work itself (ibid.), then we may conclude that beauty cannot give rise to a Kantian moral judgement that is defined by its violence to sensibility. However, if we have seen both direct and indirect arguments against assigning beauty a moral role, there are times at which Derrida does allow for such a role. He holds that for Kant

> absolute interiority and absolute morality intervene as conditions of the ideal of beauty . . . [for] [i]f the human form and it alone has the right to ideal beauty, it is because it expresses the inside and this inside is a relation of reason to a pure moral end. (Ibid.: 114)

The ideal of beauty (the inner character of a human being) expresses the moral, and without this basis 'the object would not please at once universally and positively' (CJ: 235; cf. Derrida 1987a: 114). Yet, as Derrida recognizes, the purity of ideal beauty is impossible; pleasure is necessarily attached to beauty, and this pleasure is basic to Kant's exclusion of beauty from a moral role. Kant's attempt to detach the work itself violently from its inessential charms or frames would enable a moral role for beauty, in so far as this detachment of the marginalia from the work would purify and determine the identity of the work independently of the pleasure of charms. Hence, Kant's failure to justify an independent analysis of work and frame, essence and marginalia, defeats his attempt to liberate beauty from pleasure, and thereby provide it a moral role.

However, this argument is almost certainly superfluous, given Kant's own explicit association of beauty with positive pleasure and sublimity with negative pleasure. As much as beauty's moral role is radically restricted by its association with positive pleasure, sublimity's moral role depends on its negative relation to pleasure, for this negative relation brings to light sublimity's association with the autonomous, rational will and announces our moral powers. Derrida rightly argues that the negativity, and thus, seriousness of the *Wohlgefallen* or, as he freely translates it, '*pleasing-oneself-in*' the sublime (Derrida is referring tacitly to CJ: 269, which does not contain an expression translatable as 'pleasing-oneself-in'), in contrast to that of the beautiful, 'suspends play and . . . [thereby] constitutes an occupation related to the moral law. It has an essential relation to morality (*Sittlichkeit*), which presupposes also violence done to the senses' (Derrida 1987a: 130). Although this violence is committed by imagination, rather than reason, imagination's self-sacrifice 'lets itself be commanded by a law other than that of the empirical use which determines it with a view to an end' (ibid.: 131). Hence, the sublime is related to the non-empirical, moral law and the autonomous, rational will. As Derrida argues, for Kant, the power to recognize that 'the whole of nature . . . is and appears as small in the eyes of magnitude' awakens us to 'the feeling of a supersensible faculty' (CJ: 257; cf. Derrida 1987a: 138). Judgement enacts a transitional function in moving between the realms of nature and freedom, making it possible for the realm of freedom to 'have an influence on the former', even as the realm of nature 'can have no influence on' freedom (CJ: 176; cf. Derrida 1987a: 36).

Sublimity's middle position between reason and sensibility enables its moral role by sustaining simultaneously its relationship to concepts, its emotional, motivating force and its free power to dominate inclination. Although Hegel, in Derrida's reading, criticizes Kantian 'subjectivism' for attempting to explain substance's sublation of interpretation (that is, sublimity) according to finite subjectivity, Kantian sublimity itself overcomes the limits of the subject in revealing the autonomous will as transcending all natural phenomena and, thus, transcending all subjective and objective appearances. For Hegel, if Kantian sublimity is non-phenomenal, then it cannot be presented and it is nonsensical to refer to it. Therefore, Hegel thinks of the sublime without presentation as unpresentable, whereas Kant claims to present what is without measure inadequately as unpresentable (Derrida 1987a: 133–4). For this reason, despite his frequent exemplification of the sublime through architecture, Kant argues in §26 of the 'Analytic of the Sublime' (CJ: 252–3) that there is no '"suitable" example of the sublime in the products of human art'; art depends on purposive human determinations of form, dimensions, limits and ends in view, whereas the sublime exists by overflowing any limits, surpassing any measures, by its disproportion 'to man and his determinations' (Derrida 1987a: 122). The Derridean reading of Kantian sublimity deconstructs the limits of the subject–object dichotomy, then, displacing the attempt to situate morality within the locus of the subject, in opposition to the object. This move enables a radical or radically destructive account of morality and politics, for, if there is no subject, then there is no publicly or phenomenally accessible locus of free, moral decision and there is also no place open to determination by objective nature. The notion of individual responsibility and the division between individual and society, concepts basic to most moral and political systems, become meaningless or, at least, highly problematic. It is unclear, then, what moral or political functions Derrida may concede, other than the somehow non-subjective, non-objective responsibility to deconstruct dominant claims to centrality, and thereby to reveal the unacknowledged existence and significance of otherness, differences and marginalia in the constitution of centrality.

However, if Derrida provides a more rigorously Kantian and, thus, moral reading of Kantian sublimity than subsequent Continental philosophers, Jean-François Lyotard has proven the most directly influential recent philosopher on discourses of the sublime.[16] But, this influence is problematic, for his reading of Kantian sublimity as anti-moral or evil is deeply mistaken (Lyotard 1991: 229/189). Listed in sixty-five entries of the *Philosopher's Index*, as against eighteen for Adorno, eleven for Derrida and just six for Guyer, Lyotard's work on the sublime has been cited far more over the past twenty-five years than that of any other philosopher on the sublime, other than Kant and Burke.[17] The primary reason that Lyotard's direct influence far outweighs Derrida's is that Lyotard concentrated on the topic for a decade, publishing at least a dozen articles, chapters or books on the sublime from 1982 to 1991, many of which were translated with his help into German and

English, including prominent early pieces in *Artforum* and *Artforum International*, whereas Derrida to my knowledge devoted only part of a single, long essay to the sublime.[18] Lyotard, like most recent Continental writers on the sublime, omits any mention of Derrida's work in his own *Lessons on the Analytic of the Sublime* (a volume in a series directed in part by Derrida), describing his work as '*explication de texte*', as if Kant were its only influence. However, as Shaw argues, Lyotard's approach to the sublime owes a lot to Derridean deconstruction (Shaw: 116), and Lyotard follows Derrida temporally, methodologically and materially in deconstructing Kant's 'Analytic of the Sublime'. Aside from its far greater detail and greater similarity to conventional textual exegesis, Lyotard's text differs from Derrida's primarily in its denial of sublimity's moral functions. But this is a crucial difference, for the moral functions of Kantian sublimity are essential to it and Lyotard's far greater direct influence on the subject has made the anti-moral view standard among Continental philosophers.

Kirwan regards Lyotard's (allegedly) purely aesthetic reading of Kantian sublimity, like those of Crowther and Pillow, as an asset, in contrast to the moral readings of Derrida, de Man, Žižek and others (Kirwan 2005: 158), because the aesthetic readings attempt first to establish what sublimity is, avoiding issues tangential to sublimity such as morality. But this view is doubly mistaken. The notion that morality is tangential to sublimity ignores the fact that sublimity has virtually always been constructed in moral terms, from Longinus to Addison, Kant and Schiller. Moreover, the question in reading Kant is not whether sublimity can be rigorously distinguished from morality, but whether Kant makes such a distinction. Since he relentlessly links sublimity to morality, as I have shown, we cannot rate highly any 'close reading' of Kant that denies sublimity's moral functions, as in Lyotard. The latter argues that Kant must show 'the sublime ... to have no moral value' (Lyotard 1991/1994: 75/55). Because sublime feeling, as an aesthetic feeling, is necessarily distinct from moral feeling (respect), sublimity can play no moral role (ibid.: 148/118–19); 'the "soul-stirring delight [French: *satisfaction exaltante*]" felt by "rationalizing [*vernünftelnd*]" ... thought in the sublime is not respect for the moral law itself ... [but rather] a sort of echo of respect in the order of the aesthetic', contemplative, not practical (ibid.: 281/234). For Lyotard, sublimity cannot be appropriated for Kantian morality, because sublimity marks the destruction of moral universality by the move to aesthetic 'universalization', and the destruction of aesthetic universalization by the move to moral universality. 'The sublime feeling is neither moral universality nor aesthetic universalization, but is, rather, the destruction of one by the other in the violence of their differend', which cannot itself 'be communicated by [*d'être partagé par*] any thought' (ibid.: 286/239). In other words, the violence of the relationship between reason (the source of moral universalization) and imagination or feeling (the source of aesthetic universalization) forecloses the possibility of either mode of universality, and no crossing between the domains of aesthetics and morality is possible. In sublimity, reason cannot attain its universal ideas, nor imagination or sensibility the universality of a *sensus communis*, because sublimity is constituted by the tension of reason and imagination. But Lyotard fails to see either that Kant provides for no fixed separation between the domains of aesthetics and morality or that the tension and violence of sublimity are crucial to its moral functions. Kant's definition of sublimity concerns the violence done by reason to sensibility, but he is clear that this very tension constitutes a type of harmony or purposiveness in that it reveals our supersensible moral powers as regnant even against the unbounded might of nature.

Lyotard's anti-moral, subjective reading of sublimity tends to recognize these functions, while denying their moral power on grounds that otherwise they would violate the strict separation between aesthetic functions concerning the power of feeling pleasure or displeasure and moral functions concerning the power of desiring (ibid.: 172/140). His position on sublimity's relation to subjectivity is ambivalent. Temenuga Trifonova has argued that Lyotard's postmodern sublime dissolves the subject in a non-subjective, non-objective, ontological realm prior to ethics and rationality, an account similar to Derrida's in its dissociation of sublimity and subjectivity, whereas Matthew Pacholec argues that Lyotard's account of sublimity involves 'agitated subjectivity'. However, both are correct. Lyotard argues both that sublimity, as a form of taste, is subjective, admitting only of subjective universality, in contrast to duty (Lyotard 1991/1994: 284/237), and that the feeling of the sublime cannot allow for the *deduction* of a sublime, unified subject; 'the properties that prevent the deduction of a sublime subject are the same ones that authorize the maintenance of the sublime in the order of the "subjective"' (ibid.: 37–8/22–3). The judgement of sublimity 'responds clearly, that is, negatively, to the question of the possibility of a subject and an aesthetic temporality (both sublime) constituted on the model of the *Ich denke* [the 'I think', Kant's empirical interpretation of the Cartesian 'cogito'] and the temporality required for theoretical thinking' (ibid.: 37/22–3; cf. 177/144). Yet, if Lyotard here recognizes that the sublime points toward the transcendence of subjectivity implied by the notion of free, supersensible, moral powers, he minimizes the significance of this transcendence and relies on the subjective dimensions of sublimity to deny its moral functions. Thus, he argues that 'what is important is not that the moral maxim . . . "manifest" a transcendence of free will in relation to all other motivation . . . it is more important that the object be grasped as the occasion of a pleasure, which is the case with taste' (ibid.: 283–4/236). This one-sided concentration on sublimity's relation to pleasure and its subjectivity is the basis for Lyotard's distinction of sublime feeling from morality, duty, respect and virtue. Dismissing Kant's own identification of duty and virtue as sublime, Lyotard argues that '[i]f virtue were itself sublime, the sign of the law of freedom in it would not be graspable by subjective thought . . . [for] the phenomenality of the virtuous act . . . would be too great [*grand*] or too strong to be presentable' (ibid.: 285/238). Thus, despite his recognition that sublimity indicates a transcendent will, Lyotard argues that the subjective character of sublimity delimits its moral functions. More seriously, Lyotard also offers an *anti*-moral reading of sublimity, arguing that whereas beauty is analogous (but only analogous) to morality (ibid.: 285/237, 286/239), sublimity is evil and that the only sublime politics consists in terror, as in Nazism (Shaw: 125).

The sole moral function that he allows for sublimity is resistance to natural inclinations. 'All that can be conceded to sublime feeling in the consideration of morality is resistance . . . the resistance of virtue to the passions, to "fear", "superstition", "the frailty of human nature", and its "shortcomings"' (citing Kant, Lyotard 1991/1994: 285–6/238). This form of resistance constitutes an important element in the moral actor's independence from nature. Yet, in making this concession, Lyotard retains his wall of separation between morality and aesthetics, arguing that 'even then it is not morality itself that is felt to be sublime, it is its resistance to temptations, its triumph over them, reducing them to naught'

(Lyotard 1994: 286/238). We have seen that Kant rejects any such wall of separation, identifying morality and moral respect as sublime and assigning sublimity a host of moral functions. There is no ground for a non-moral or morally neutral reading of Kantian sublimity.

Nevertheless, Lyotard's recognition that sublimity involves resistance is the key to efforts by Shaw, Hugh Silverman, Ana Anahory and Alison Ross to provide a moral-political reading of Lyotard on sublimity. Anahory's reading is unusual, in that she argues that Lyotard regarded the 'sublime subject' as providing elements of resistance against political neocontractualism. To accept such a reading, it would first be necessary to explain away Kant's own social contract theory and Lyotard's denial of a 'sublime subject', and then to isolate features of sublimity such as disinterestedness and reason's violence to nature (Lyotard 1994: 180) that resist certain features of neocontractualism such as rational self-interest and atomistic subjectivity. In most readings of Lyotard and, accordingly, in most political readings of Lyotard on the sublime, as in Shaw and Ross, the focus is, rather, on sublimity's unpresentability. Shaw argues that for Lyotard sublimity resists a politics of terror because it exhibits the impossibility of any presentation of supersensible ideas; a sublime, political aesthetics would affirm the unpresentability of ideas (Shaw: 125–6). In *The Postmodern Condition* and in *Just Gaming*, Lyotard describes sublimity as a palliative for the totality and reconciliation of beauty, which forges consensus in capitalist society (ibid.: 125). Disaster arises when indeterminate judgements are treated as determinate; hence, a just politics affirms justice as sublimely unpresentable (ibid.). In this respect, Lyotard's political reading of sublimity seems quite close to the Derridean account. Yet, Derrida's claim is not that such ideas are *un-presentable* but, rather, that they must be presented as unpresentable (Derrida 1987a: 133–4) and, thus, that they operate at the limits of representation, refusing the dichotomy of the presentable and the unpresentable. Sublime ideas, for Derrida, affirm difference in exceeding the boundaries necessary to representation and unification.

Hence, four clear problems arise in Lyotard's moral-political readings of the sublime. First, he neglects the systematic functions of Kantian sublimity in morality. Second, he reads Kantian sublimity as neutral or even evil, rather than as a basis for morality. Third, he relies on a one-sided, dogmatic account of the unpresentable, which cannot explain the tension between rational and imaginative presentations in Kant's work. Fourth, he never accounts for the fanatical possibilities of a view of sublimity as mere unpresentability, whereas Kant limits any such *Schwärmerei* by further restricting sublimity to a purposiveness without purpose at the limits of reason.

Slavoj Žižek's work on sublimity, beginning in 1989 with *The Sublime Object of Ideology*, similarly refers to Kant, recognizes positive and negative moral-political forms of sublimity and adopts other elements from Derrida and Lyotard such as their common emphasis on unpresentability (cf. Elam: 4–10) and Lyotard's identification of sublimity with evil. Yet, in its reliance on the language, issues and structures of Hegelian and Lacanian models, Žižek's account of the sublime constitutes a genuine alternative to the Kantian account of sublimity popular in most recent Continental philosophy. The result is that, even as Žižek discusses sublimity according to Kantian parameters, he turns the discussion toward symbolic, moral-political, psychoanalytic and dialectical issues. By his account, the sublime symbol's ability to exhibit the radical negativity or nullity of the political and symbolic order enables a critique of a totalitarian political unity or total self-presence, as well as its totalitarian possibilities.

Žižek's reading of the sublime follows Hegel's critique of the Kantian sublime in *Aesthetics* I: 362–3 and *Phenomenology of Spirit*: §§343–5, especially Hegel's critique of the sensible–supersensible distinction (Shaw: 138–9). What is problematic in Kantian epistemology and aesthetics, according to this critique, is that they claim to present the unpresentable.[19] Just as Kant's epistemology constructs a category, the noumenon, defined as a presentation of an unpresentable, non-phenomenal entity, his aesthetics defines the sublime as the sensuous evocation of the unpresentable as unpresentable. For Kant, as for Derrida, 'the phenomenon's very inability to represent the Thing adequately *is inscribed in the phenomenon itself*' (Žižek 1989: 203). By inscribing this negativity within the presentation of unpresentability, Kant differentiates sublime enthusiasm, which he defines as the idea of the good with affect (CJ: 271–2), from the fanatical claim to present what transcends all presentation (Žižek 1989: 204). But, for Hegel, the category of the unpresentable, in so far as it is structurally isomorphic with the concept of the supersensible or noumenal, is self-cancelling, for it posits an experience of what cannot by definition be experienced. The Kantian account is inadequate, then, because it remains within the field of representation as the negative limit of the sublime (ibid.: 205). Hence, Žižek rejects the claim in Kantian sublimity to represent internally the impossibility of non-phenomenal representations. The overcoming of phenomenality depends not on transcendence but, rather, on 'the experience of how there is nothing beyond it'; this view displaces the sublime from empirical object to 'embodiment of Nothing' or void (ibid.: 206). The void is expressed by the thought of impossibility or contradiction (Hegel 1998: I.363; Žižek 1989: 6). Hence, for Hegel and Žižek, contradictory formulations best indicate sublimity (spirit as bone, etc.) ((Žižek 1989: 209; cf. Shaw: 139).

Žižek's critique of anti-Semitic ideology translates this sublime operation of exhibiting the impossible into the political sphere. In anti-Semitic ideology,

> the 'Jew' is just the embodiment of a certain blockage – of the impossibility which prevents the society from achieving its full identity as a closed, homogeneous totality. Far from being the positive cause of social negativity, *the 'Jew' is a point at which social negativity as such assumes positive existence.* (Žižek 1989: 127)

Hence, this figure passes between collective negativity in the anti-Semitic 'imaginary' and individual positive being in Žižek's interpretation, and thus destroys their false opposition. This, as we shall see, is Žižek's desideratum in his discussion of political and depoliticized, cinematic representations of the Holocaust. He aims to destroy the opposition between the political and the sublime without thereby politicizing the sublime. In *The Sublime Object of Ideology*, the 'Jew' is the sublime object of anti-Semitic ideology in marking the impossibility of the closure and total self-identity of homogeneous society (ibid.). As the living embodiment of social negativity, the 'Jew' transposes the negativity internal to society onto its positive existence. In this dialectical-political interpretation, sublimity is defined by a figure taken as radical evil, as the impossibility of social unity. Yet, in revealing this structure as such, Žižek uses sublimity to exhibit the purely negative reality of the sublime ideology and simultaneously to destroy the myth of internal societal unity. These are classically Hegelian dialectical moves. Žižek identifies sublimity as the figure of negativity and impossibility, only to argue that this negativity passes over into positivity in the real existence of the 'blockage'. Thus, although he identifies the sublime object as evil, in anti-Semitic ideology, he appropriates this figure for positive moral or political purposes in order to expose the inherent failure of anti-Semitic ideology. But this act of appropriating the sublime for certain positive, moral-political purposes transforms the sublime into something else entirely, which implies that sublimity cannot in itself execute such functions.

Like this reading of anti-Semitic ideology, Žižek's political reading of Hegelian subjectivity depends on sublimity's exhibition of negativity and non-totality. However, this second Hegelian account shifts the problem of political power from ideology to the identification of a twofold subjectivity within the state. The individual subject is prima facie alienated from the state, for '[i]n the immediacy of their lives, subjects as citizens are, of course, opposed to the substantial State which determines the concrete network of their social relations' (Žižek 1989: 229). Hegel resolves this alienation by referring to the two opposed meanings of the term 'subject', a free actor and a person subordinated to a monarch (ibid.). For Hegel, 'subjects are subjects only in so far as they presuppose that the social substance, opposed to them in the form of the State, is already in itself a subject (Monarch) to whom they are subjected' (ibid.); the subject attains its subjectivity and overcomes its alienation to the state, then, by identifying with the fictional sovereign will of the state. Sublimity's indication of the void or empty signifier exhibits this ironic fact, namely, that overcoming the 'irreducible otherness of the State' occurs not through the state's withering away, as in Marxism, but through identification with the state (ibid.). As in Jean-Jacques Rousseau, the particular will of each individual ought to identify with the general will. However, in the absence of any constitutive determination of the state by individual subjects (citizens), it is not clear that Žižek's non-resistant 'resistance' amounts to anything greater than an ironic version of Stoic resignation in the face of external domination, as in Schiller.

Žižek's Lacanian influences merely add a psychoanalytic, structuralist spin to this symbolic, Hegelian reading of sublimity as the symbol of negativity and void. In *The Ethics of Psychoanalysis*, Lacan provides no extended account of the sublime. However, he refers to the significance of the Kantian sublime and promises to write a more substantive account (Lacan: 287, 301; cf. Shaw: 132). Lacan also provides indications of how he might develop this account of the sublime even in the direction of morality. This he does in his semiotic view of the signifier as presenting the impossibility of presenting a noumenal real thing external to the network of mental signifiers, in accordingly determining the sublime as 'an object raised to the level of the (impossible-real) Thing' (Žižek 1989: 202–3), in explicitly opposing morality and pleasure (Lacan: 20) and in associating the sublime with desire, love (ibid.: 259, 322) and psychoanalytic sublimation (ibid.: 218, 301).[20] By his own tenets, Žižek's *The Sublime Object of Ideology* cannot claim to overcome this absence of a full Lacanian account by providing the real Lacanian reading of sublimity. What Žižek offers instead is an idiosyncratic Hegelian-Lacanian reading of the sublime, which attempts 'to "save" Hegel ... through Lacan ... [providing a] Lacanian reading of Hegel and the Hegelian heritage' in order to overcome '"postmodernist" traps' (Žižek 1989: 7). By this view, the real is 'not an external thing that resists being caught in the symbolic network, but the crack within the symbolic network itself' and this crack within the symbolic network, in marking the impossibility or unpresentability of the real and thus exploding the traditional oppositions of the symbolic order, is sublime (Žižek 2007: ch.5). Thus, what is sublime in the 1950s communist paranoia film, *Invasion of the Body Snatchers*, is the tiny detail marking the difference of the aliens from humans, such as an extra fold of skin between the fingers, for in 'magically transubstantiat[ing] its bearer into an alien', this 'mysterious *je ne sais quoi* [is] the unfathomable "something" that makes an ordinary object sublime', Lacan's *petit objet a* (ibid.).[21] To this point, the Lacanian reading of sublimity differs only slightly from the Hegelian reading, which itself 'adds nothing to the Kantian notion of the Sublime; it merely takes it more *literally* than Kant himself' (Žižek 1989: 205). But, while Hegel in fact adds to the Kantian sublime a symbolic focus and a systematic context that annuls the noumena-phenomena distinction, what Žižek's version of Lacan obviously adds is a linguistic, psychoanalytic approach. The sublime is viewed in terms of networks of signifiers and a form of sublimation shifting libidinal desire from the unattainable noumenon to some concrete detail or object now taken as sublime (Žižek 1999: 157; cf. Shaw: 135). Although sublimity thus becomes an objective phenomenon, in contrast to Kant's view that sublimity is a subjective phenomenon, occasioned often by objects but consisting in a relationship between imagination and reason, the notion of the spectral presence of the sublime suggests that the language of objects cannot capture what Žižek has in mind. What he is really after is to use the internalized disharmony and spectral presence of the sublime to mark the impossibility of the closure and total presence of ideological politics, defined not by false consciousness but by '*a social reality whose very existence implies the non-knowledge of its participants as to its essence*' (Žižek 1989: 21). Hence, sublimity's distortion of harmony and its exhibition of the lack at the heart of symbolization serve as a crucial condition for a just politics. This dramatic mark of failure within the project of signification is supposed to undermine from within the propaganda of totalitarian regimes.

As Žižek points out, Derrida would reject this reading as sustaining the metaphysics of presence, because of its 'paradoxical gesture of reducing lack through its affirmation of itself' (Žižek 1989: 154, citing Derrida's *The Postcard*). Žižek's response is that the post-structuralist attempt to situate all texts within 'a decentred network of plural [self-subverting] processes' assumes 'a clearly defined theoretical position which can be articulated without difficulty in a pure and simple metalanguage', rather than non-dogmatic, self-deconstructive strategies (Žižek 1989: 155). Certainly, no post-structuralists would describe their positions in this way, either as articulated without difficulty in a 'pure and simple metalanguage', or as purely theoretical, rather than as performative or as crossing the theoretical–practical distinction. But, while these post-structuralist strategies may ultimately fail the self-critical test, or lapse into vacuity, like Žižek's own proclamation of the lack at the heart of the symbolic, this sort of criticism of post-structuralism or postmodernism, found in Žižek as in his opponent Jürgen Habermas, Michael Walzer and many others, is weak, because it fails to address directly such post-structuralist claims or to link these charges specifically to particular philosophers and texts. What is evident is that the moral-political possibilities of Žižek's Hegelian-Lacanian reading of sublimity depend on an inherently metaphysical account of the 'lack' in the symbolic order and Žižek never delimits the inordinately vague consequences of identifying this lack. Moreover, his analysis relies on a structuralist linguistics which, like the Derridean post-structuralist account, cannot account for non-ostensive understandings of language and, hence, cannot deal with a wide range of social-linguistic phenomena.

However, if Žižek's Hegelian and Lacanian influences determine much of his account of the sublime, he also speaks directly to issues relevant to Kantian sublimity and morality, both in ways similar to and in contrast to Kant. On questions of common concern, Kant and Žižek differ in that Kant considers sublimity in terms of its positive moral functions, rigorously excludes any negative moral functions and regards sublimity as the negative limit of representation, whereas Žižek argues that sublimity can be appropriated for both good and evil moral-political uses, and emphasizes sublimity's possible totalitarian functions, following Lyotard. However, Žižek and Kant both trace sublimity back to the autonomous will; they both regard acts of will as closed to consciousness and causal explanation; and they both view good and evil as interconnected through their dependence on the will.

Žižek's own view of his relationship to Kant is inaccurate with respect both to their similarities and differences. Where Žižek believes that he is following Kant, he is often diverging from him, and, conversely, where he believes that he is departing from Kant, he is often quite close to him. For instance, in stressing Hegel's identification of sublimity with the incompatible and incomparable, Žižek is not really distinguishing his position from that of Kant, contra Shaw (Shaw: 139). While Kant identifies sublimity with the awe-inspiring and great, he, like Žižek, also links sublimity to tension and the incomparable, the absolute measure, as we have seen in Derrida's reading of Kantian sublimity. Ironically, Žižek follows Kantian models perhaps most closely in texts and lectures where he, like Lyotard, unconsciously parts with Kant in associating sublimity with evil. In *Welcome to the Desert of the Real*, Žižek refers to the media construction of 9/11 as 'the sublime victim of Absolute Evil' (Žižek 2002: 137) and in a lecture at the University of New Mexico (30 November 2007), he argues that 'Hannah Arendt was right [about the banality of evil]. Such figures, criminal figures, are not personifications of sublime, demoniac evil. When you look at the person who causes an incredible amount of evil . . . you will always discover some human figures.' In this claim that absolute evil, or its victim, is sublime, Žižek believes that he is in agreement with Kant, when, as we have seen, Kant himself rejects this identification. Yet, Žižek here agrees with Kant in tracing sublimity to free will, as a power beyond all natural determination and thus irreducible to any (natural) causal explanation. Žižek asks whether in these events 'we confront the ultimate abyss of free will, the imponderable fact of "I did it because I did it!" which resists any explanation in terms of psychological, social, ideological, etc. causes?' (Žižek 2002: 137). In this view that it is impossible to trace the causal root of evil actions, Kant and Žižek agree, even though Žižek, like Burke and Lyotard, differs from Kant in associating sublimity with evil. For Kant, we can never know that we are free or from what motive, rational or otherwise, we act. Thus, in *Religion within the Limits of Reason Alone*, Kant regards evil 'as if' it originated solely from human innocence,

> [f]or whatever his previous behaviour [*Verhalten*] may have been, whatever natural causes may have been influencing him, and whether these causes were to be encountered within or outside him, his action is still free and determined by none of these causes; hence it can and must always be judged as an *original* [*ursprünglicher*] use of his will [*Willkür*]. He should have refrained from that action, whatever his temporal circumstances and entanglements; for through no cause in the world can he cease to be a freely acting being. (*Religion with the Limits of Reason Alone*, Kant 1960: 36/VI.41)

In a sense, then, Kant regards the conditions of good and evil as identical; freedom is the condition of good and evil alike. Good is defined by rational determination of the will and evil by a natural determination of the will that presupposes the possibility of rational determination of the will and is contrary in content to rational, universalizable determinations of will. Evil might be described as sublime, according to this logic, in so far as it too derives from the autonomy of the will. However, Kant is quite consistent in denying the sublimity of evil, because he argues that, while evil also derives from the autonomous will, it represents a case of the will's allowing itself to be determined heteronomously by natural inclinations. The sublimity of good depends on the autonomous will's self-determination according to the law of reason.

Although he provides no such delineation of the form of will involved in good and evil action, Žižek's reading of the sublime, transposed to the symbolism and ideologies of concrete events, agrees with Kant that the powers of evil and good are internally connected. In *Welcome to the Desert of the Real*, he argues that George W. Bush's notion of an 'Axis of Evil' embodies America's inability to come to terms with its internal antagonisms (Žižek 2002: 43–4).

The formulation of good (America or freedom) and bad (evil or Al Qaeda) sublime objects is internally connected; they are the obverse of one another, for Žižek (ibid.: 51); historically, the presentation in 2001 of America as embodiment of freedom and Al Qaeda as embodiment of evil was simultaneous.[22] However, Žižek's emphasis on sublimity as indicative of the lack or absence in the heart of presence, the presentation of the unpresentable, in his translation, indicates a way beyond a totalitarian sublime politics (Shaw: 141), as Lyotard might describe it. In *The Fragile Absolute*, the sublime constitutes a kind of spectral presence that destroys the false presence of the symbolic order, with its opposition of good and evil, by exhibiting the impossibility of attaining or presenting the real, as in Lacan (Žižek 2001a: 64–5). Hence, for Žižek, a politics of the sublime could work against totalitarian evil by exhibiting this absence or unpresentability as such, through its contradictory presentation in the sublime.

Yet, to this point, Žižek's indications of the criteria for positive and negative political treatments of the sublime remain far too vague. A clearer view of his political desiderata for the sublime is present in a 1999 talk, 'Laugh yourself to death', in which he again links sublimity to absolute evil on grounds of its incompatibility with explanation or representation. The difference here is that he links the sublimity of the Holocaust, defined by this narrative absence, to its *depoliticization*.

> Holocaust in advance disqualifies all (explanatory) answers – it cannot be explained, visualized, represented, transmitted, since it marks the black hole, the implosion of the (narrative) universe. Accordingly, any attempt to locate it in its context, to politicize it, equals the anti-Semitic negation of its uniqueness. (Žižek 1999)

Any attempt to reduce the absolute, incomparable sublimity of the Holocaust by situating it within political or historical contexts is thus a denial of its constitutive character. But this apparently depoliticizing act of elevating the Holocaust above all comparison may itself entail political functions, for 'this very depoliticization of the holocaust, its elevation into the properly sublime Evil, can also be a political act of utter cynical manipulation, a political intervention aiming at legitimizing a certain kind of hierarchical political relations' (ibid.). Depoliticization or sublimation can serve political aims in various ways, as part of a postmodern critique of autonomous political agency (for example, 'we are all victims'), as a means of effacing the significance of human rights violations in developing countries (for example, 'the Armenian genocide was not so bad') or as a warning against all radical political programs (ibid.).

> In short: notwithstanding the unquestionable sincerity of some of its proponents, the 'objective' ideologico-political content of the depoliticization of the holocaust, of its elevation into the abyssal absolute Evil, is the political pact of the aggressive Zionists and the Western Rightist anti-Semites at the expense of TODAY's radical political potentials. (Ibid.)

This ironic reference to elevation into an abyss depends on Žižek's view that sublimity lacks any moral restrictions, and thus that 'elevation' may serve absolute evil. The very attempt to elevate or sublimate an historical event beyond all possibility of representation, beyond all politics, can itself constitute a political act, in so far as it is applied for political purposes; the structure of sublimity, as the removal from any historical-political context, lends it an absolute (incomparable, supra-historical) significance, making it potentially applicable to any political agenda. The political limits on the application of sublimity are thus effaced by its very conception as an absolute, supernatural function. For this reason, Žižek argues in a similar passage in *Welcome to the Desert of the Real* that '[t]he worst thing to do apropos of the events of September 11 is to elevate them to a point of Absolute Evil, a vacuum which cannot be explained and/or dialecticized' (Žižek 2002: 136). To do justice to this single historical event, we must recognize it as unique and incomparable without thereby reducing it to an exemplar for a general political strategy, using its sublimity as a means of denying the significance of other horrific events, invoking it as a means of supporting political violence, as in the case of Israel, or defeating a range of radical political possibilities through a slippery slope argument (for example, x is wrong, because it will lead to y, which will lead to z, which will lead to the Holocaust). The proper response for Žižek is dialectical, to recognize the passing of opposites (the political and de-political, the Holocaust comedy and tragedy) into one another, and thereby to suspend simultaneously the political and the de-political readings.

> The Muslim [a name for camp inmates acting automatically, having lost their will to live] is thus the zero-point at which the very opposition

between tragedy and comedy, between the sublime and the ridiculous, between dignity and derision, is suspended, the point at which one pole directly passes into its opposite. If we try to present his predicament as tragic, the result is comic, a mocking parody of the tragic dignity, and if we treat him as a comic character, tragedy emerges. We enter here the domain that is somehow outside or, rather, beneath the very elementary opposition of the dignified hierarchical structure of authority and its carnivalesque reversal, of the original and its parody, its mocking repetition. (Žižek 1999)

In this passage, Žižek finally adopts the thoroughly Hegelian strategy of limiting the negative political consequences of the sublime by sublating it and thus passing beyond it. But for Kant there are always already moral and political constraints on the sublime because of its inherent connection to moral ideas. The liking for the sublime, like that of the beautiful, can play a positive social role, since it is universally communicable in promoting an interest with respect to society. Separation from society can be considered sublime but only as a non-antagonistic self-sufficiency that sees beyond all sensuous interest by rising above (*Überhebung*) needs; this form of sublimity necessarily rests on ideas and differs from unsociability, shunning society, the hostility of misanthropy, the excessive, partially hateful, partially contemptible (*verächtlich*) fear of persons (*anthropophobia*) or even the mature turn to utopian dreams of absolute, Robinsonian solitude (CJ: 275–6). Although Kant does not say so explicitly, it is clear that, in contrast to a neutral self-sufficiency, these negative relations to society cannot stand as sublime, because they violate moral conditions of respect for persons (*Achtung* versus *Verachtung*), universalizability, humanism (*anthropophobia* versus *anthropophilia*) and autonomy. Similarly, as we have seen, Kant allows that war can become sublime only in so far as it is conducted in an ordered manner with respect for persons. But here we recognize the weaknesses of a Kantian claim rooted in pre-critical judgements (the sublimity of war), for Žižek would find this notion of sublime, civilized warfare the height of ideology.

We have seen that post-Kantian Continental accounts of the sublime tend to favour political over moral readings, even as they vary widely in their understandings of sublimity's role in morality. Aside from Herder, who rejects Kant's account of the sublime in favour of British models, and Adorno, who provides both Hegelian and Kantian readings of sublimity, the post-Kantian Continental philosophers treated here divide more or less neatly into Kantian and Hegelian-Lacanian camps, with the caveat that the latter is heavily influenced by the former. The Hegelian-Lacanian group, represented here by Hegel, Lacan, Adorno and Žižek, sets forth a broadly critical treatment of the Kantian sublime and its individualist moral associations, treating the sublime less as a tool for the attunement of individuals to their supersensible moral functions than as a symbol exercising politically ambivalent functions. However, the plurality of influences on this group results in considerable differences in its accounts of sublimity's moral-political possibilities. Where Hegel regards the sublime as a necessary, but superseded stage in the history of pre-modern aesthetics, Lacan recognizes the use of the sublime in overcoming metaphysical fantasy and Žižek and Adorno distinguish ideological uses of the sublime, consonant with evil and political terror, from politically and metaphysically resistant exhibitions of the nullity and tension inherent in modern society. Within the Kantian camp, there is significant variation as well, from the highly Kantian accounts of sublimity's moral functions in Schiller, Adorno and Derrida to Lyotard's misreadings of Kantian sublimity as merely analogous to morality and, therefore, useless to it. In recognizing the multifarious moral and political readings of sublimity in German idealism and contemporary Continental philosophy, we see the error in Kirwan's claim that contemporary Continental philosophy restored moral readings exorcized by German idealism (Kirwan: 156). In truth, as we have seen, German idealists offered their own moral-political readings of the sublime, and many contemporary philosophers *renounced* moral-political readings of the sublime, while others (Adorno, Derrida, Žižek) retrieved moral-political readings of the sublime from German idealism. As current Continental mathematical and biological approaches to philosophy are applied to aesthetics, as in Alain Badiou, I would wager that Continental accounts of the sublime will continue to emphasize moral-political questions even as they turn from history of philosophy to scientific models formerly characterized by ahistorical, non-contextual, individualistic approaches, because of the historical, contextual focus of Continental philosophy of science.

The postmodernist contribution to Kantian sublimity is, first, to point out the political dangers inherent in accounts of sublimity lacking the sorts of moral limitations articulated by Kant; second, to identify within sublimity the crucial concern for the marginalized other, a position discernible within the structure of Kantian sublimity without being itself explicitly recognized and incorporated in the 'Analytic of the Sublime'; and third, to question the very possibility of articulating limits on sublimity.

Postmodern misinterpretations of Kantian sublimity, which characterize the latter as unable to limit sublimity's use in political terror, highlight the importance of moral limitations on the definition and functions of the sublime, limitations absent from non-Kantian accounts. Hence, Lyotard, Žižek and others only underscore the worth of the Kantian account in wrongly associating it with evil and terror. They show that accounts of sublimity that lack any moral limitations are dangerously compatible with destructive, anti-moral, political programmes, and that such programmes consciously or unconsciously appropriate the aesthetics of sublimity for terroristic purposes. But, by misreading Kant's account as non-moral, they fail to recognize the possibility of distinguishing unlimited, amoral or anti-moral, psychological forms of sublimity from Kant's non-psychologistic, morally constrained account of sublimity. Of course, the maintenance of this distinction between a genuine, morally requisite sublimity and a false, terroristic aesthetics would not make the latter disappear, but it would recall the possibility of exhibiting an aesthetically overpowering, and not merely rationally convincing, counter to a terroristic aesthetics.

The second contribution of postmodern accounts of sublimity, particularly that of Derrida, is to counter the essentialist marginalization of difference and otherness by exhibiting the impossibility of any such final marginalization. Derrida argues that Kantian sublimity tacitly re-envisions the order of essence and non-essence by positing the marginalized other, the frame, column or *parergon*, as the condition of the *ergon*, work or essence. This restoration of the significance of framing devices in artworks (which are themselves of merely analogical significance, yet also of exemplary status for Kantian sublimity, as Derrida argues) simultaneously speaks to the determinative functions of sublimity itself in aesthetics, for it means that this allegedly inessential, marginal concept frames and thus constitutes the aesthetics of the beauty supposedly essential to the meaning of art. At the same time, sublimity's aesthetic demonstration of the arbitrary character of essentialist discourses carries with it a logic and vocabulary directly applicable to ethical-political questions. If sublimity exhibits the marginalization of difference and otherness as presupposing an unsustainable essentialist discourse, the implication, which has in fact been taken up by a host of subsequent intellectual movements from post-colonialism to gender studies, is that the marginalized and oppressed others of the world, women, the colonized, the dispossessed, the disempowered, are themselves irreducibly significant in constituting the essence and meaning of mainstream culture and society. Sublimity does not prove that any particular social groups played any particular, contingent social functions, but it sets forth a logic, according to this postmodernist reading, that casts into doubt any strict separation between mainstream essence and marginalized other, and thereby prompts attention to determining and questioning the relations within society of the one and the other, the essential and the marginalized.

However, this questioning may adopt non-Kantian methods, for the third postmodernist contribution to Kantian sublimity is precisely to radically critique the very possibility of setting Kantian-style moral limitations on any sublime aesthetics. Derrida's understanding of sublimity as an aporetic function exceeding (or almost exceeding) all measures, boundaries and limitations suggests that there can be no moral or other limitations on the sublime, in so far as the sublime destroys the very possibility of the limit or boundary by exposing its necessary dependence on its others. Although Derrida, perhaps alone among the postmodernists and post-structuralists, recognizes the properly moral functions of Kantian sublimity and argues that sublimity explodes the inner–outer dichotomy, his deconstruction of Kantian sublimity reveals 'within the text' the impossibility of Kant's own claims to moral limitations on the sublime. Hence, in reading Kantian sublimity as destroying any rational or moral limitations on the sublime, and thereby transcending the limits that Kant himself attaches to the sublime, Derrida bridges the gap between Kantian sublimity and the popular Continental associations of sublimity with political terror. He shows why these Continental readings, taken as straightforward interpretations of Kant, are wrong, yet in exhibiting the self-deconstructing character of the Kantian account, he shows that the logic of Kantian sublimity entails the abolition of these same moral limitations. In the end, we are faced with the choice to retain the Kantian self-conception, with its moral functions as well as its questionable articulation of the experience of what is great in number, power or magnitude, or to branch off into a hybrid conception that is derived from a strict reading of the Kantian logic of sublimity and more reflective of experiences of great power and magnitude, yet congenitally (and Continentally) incapable of assigning moral limitations on its correct use. Against the Kantian self-conception, then, what are thought to be the experiences of the sublime are inherently appropriable for moral and anti-moral purposes, and they are so appropriated.

Notes

Introduction

1. Pluhar's valuable translation is not always adequately literal or consistent, and he admits to occasionally shortening or rearranging Kant's sentences and paragraphs (CJ 1987: translator's preface, xx).
2. Cohn and Miles question the standard etymology of 'sublime', 'sublimation' and 'subliminal'.

Chapter 1

1. The tremendous volume of eighteenth-century writings on the sublime precludes an exhaustive genealogy. The figures chosen here were all known to Kant and influential on his work.
2. Thus, if Theodore Wood and Alfred Rosenberg are correct that 'any number of passages by authors writing until 1800 that seem to have been inspired by Longinus actually stem from other sources' (Wood: 9), the fact that Longinus anticipated in comprehensive detail the nature of eighteenth-century, pre-Kantian discourses on the sublime suggests that he is the indirect, if not the direct, source for most eighteenth-century accounts of the sublime. Hence, it is necessary to dispense with the standard view that eighteenth-century treatments of the sublime owed little or nothing to Longinus or his translator, Boileau, 'except the initial impetus to discussion' (Russell: xliii), since this view is based on incomplete and inaccurate readings of Longinus (e.g. Samuel Monk's view that the Longinian sublime is ruleless, Wood: 22). Longinus' own originality is impossible to determine, since his identity is unknown and much of the critical literature of his own time is lost, although his work, like that of his eighteenth-century followers, shows clear traces of Aristotle's *Poetics* and *Rhetoric* and Longinus situates his own writing in the context of extant debates on sublimity.
3. Denis Diderot's 1755 *Encyclopédie* includes an article on the word 'sublime', with extensive reference to Longinus (Wood: 189) and many other contributions discuss the sublime, such as those on taste and style.

Chapter 2

1. Even Kirwan's highly detailed history refers primarily to British sources and cites only English translations of Kant.
2. Prior to CJ, Kant regarded aesthetic judgements as admitting no strict necessity, but he did not describe them as singular; rather, he viewed them as generalizations applicable only within a given society, assuming a certain *sensus communis*.
3. Thus, Cassirer and Zammito seem to overstate Bäumler's critique of British influence, for, while Bäumler certainly tries to minimize it, he does not dismiss it entirely, contra Zammito (Zammito: 29), for he views Burke's influence on Kant as significant (*'der Einfluß Burkes war bedeutend'*, Bäumler: 149).
4. Young calls Addison's 'compositions . . . but a noble preface; the grand work is his death: That is a work which is read in heaven . . . stronger than death, risen higher in virtue when breathing his last' (Young 1966: 104–5).
5. Shaw himself should recognize that Burke's alliance of sublimity with pain and pleasure is derivative, for the former argues that Andrew Marvell's 1674 commentary on Milton already identifies the painful pleasure or delightful horror of the sublime (Shaw: 34). Kirwan criticizes 'the widespread misapprehension that Burke is representative of eighteenth-century speculation on the sublime' (Kirwan 2005: 52) as wrongly implying Kant's originality through his difference from Burke (and thus from eighteenth-century critics).

Chapter 3

1. Zammito notes that Kant and Crusius both rejected Wolff's derivation of the principle of sufficient reason from the principle of identity, distinguished formal logic and ontology, rejected the ontological argument (in Crusius' case, for the un-Kantian purpose of restoring the significance of scripture and revelation), emphasized the boundaries of human understanding and distinguished metaphysical and mathematical methods (Zammito: 18–19).
2. To his logic lectures, conducted over decades, Kant brought a heavily corrected, annotated version of G. F. Meier's *Vernunftlehre* (1752/1762), which he sometimes consulted (according to Gottfried Wenzel Graf von Purgstall, in Hügelmann 1879; repr. Malter 1990: 418–21).
3. Kant read almost everything that Herder wrote (Zammito: 36).
4. Frederick Beiser argues, in contrast, that 'Baumgarten's conception of the arts is essentially Wolffian' (Beiser: 48).

⁵ Indeed, despite his fulsome praise of Burke's observation of nature, Mendelssohn had already formulated his theory by the time he read Burke (Pluhar, introduction to CJ: lxix n58) and he criticizes the latter in terms similar to Kant's subsequent critique as failing to 'explain these observations on the basis of the nature of the soul. One sees that [Burke] was unacquainted with the psychology developed by German philosophers', for Burke allows the slightest contradictory experience to refute the well-grounded account that the intuitive knowledge of perfection is gratifying (Mendelssohn: 146–7).

Chapter 4

¹ Many articles on the sublime touch on moral topics without recognizing or detailing the moral link, particularly on a systematic level. Robert Wicks (1995) and Kirk Pillow (1994) allow for sublimity in art beauty, contra Guyer (1995); for Pillow, the same object can be understood as formally beautiful and ideationally sublime.

² On sublimity's late entry into the third *Critique*, see Guyer 1979: 399; Crawford: 176–7, citing Tonelli; Allison: 303, 343. Guyer justifies his initial dismissal of sublimity by this late entry and its alleged irrelevance to Kantian and current aesthetics (Guyer 1979: 399–400n2). But this view is dubious, since the 'Critique of Aesthetic Judgment' includes sublimity, sublimity exercises significant moral functions, many thousands of pre- and post-Kantian texts and artworks concern sublimity and even many analytic aestheticians, including Guyer, have examined sublimity since Guyer 1979. Whereas Meredith argues that the material on the sublime is among the oldest in CJ, Souriau posits the sublime as the 'very latest exposition of Kant's aesthetic thought', dating immediately prior to publication in spring 1790 and Tonelli argues that the sublime followed the cognitive turn of spring 1789, since it required the full conception of reflective judgement (Zammito: 275). For Zammito, there are elements of truth to each of these accounts. Kant had noted the moral relevance of the sublime as far back as 1764 in unpublished reflections, lectures and critical annotations of Burke; hence, Meredith is correct that some of the material was old, but Tonelli is right that §§23–4, 30 and the first part of the General Remark to §29 were new (Zammito: 276). However, the intratextual evidence that Zammito uses to support his claim that the sublime was a late addition to the third *Critique*, intended to relate aesthetic and ethical experience, is tenuous. He cites differences in Kant's comparisons of the beautiful, the sublime, the pleasant and the good in §§1–5, §23 and the General Remark (Zammito: 278). But the fact that §23 omits the pleasant and the good, while the General Remark includes them, says nothing about whether

the *sublime* was a late addition. More relevant is Kant's omission of the sublime from the comparison in §§1–5, where he discusses the themes of the first half of CJ, for this absence does suggest that the sublime was a late addition. As a general methodological point, examining historical records of Kant's process of composition would provide a far more reliable story of the genesis of the third *Critique*, and, as Paul Guyer points out, Zammito does not do this, despite the importance he places on the order of composition of the third *Critique* (Guyer 1994: 370). However, Zammito correctly remarks that Kant did not just invent his account of sublimity in the latter stages of writing the *Critique of Judgment*. Kant had referred to sublimity occasionally since at least 1764's *Observations on the Feeling of the Beautiful and Sublime* and he makes multiple references to the sublime in other sections of the *Critique of Judgment*. But the remainder of the third *Critique* does not take account of or refer to the sublime *as defined* in the 'Analytic of the Sublime'. As Allison argues, '[a] striking feature of Kant's treatment of the sublime, which is indicative of the last-minute nature of its inclusion, is the paucity of references to it outside of the Analytic of the Sublime itself' (Allison 2001: 304). From §§31–8, Kant refers repeatedly to beauty, but never once to sublimity (perhaps simply because these sections concern the deduction, which is unnecessary for sublimity), and sublimity is almost entirely absent from the rest of the text, which suggests how little sublimity entered into the composition of the *Critique of Judgment* as a whole until the very late stages of its writing and how little, consequently, his late, mature accounts of sublimity were incorporated into the remainder of the text. In §39, the sublime reappears for the first time since §30. After §39, it is arguable that the sublime never appears again in its critical form; the few subsequent references employ sublimity as a characteristic of virtue, tragedy, war and so forth without any clear delineation of its own properties. Indeed, Kant's other references to the sublime in CJ (and there are only three references after CJ: 292 (CJ: 316 and 316n15, 335n76, 380), like his earlier uses of the sublime, lack the specificity or schematic order of the 'Analytic of the Sublime'.

3   Allison rejects emotion's relevancy to agency (Allison 2001: 341–3).
4   I translate *Grundlegung zur Metaphysik der Sitten* (GMM) as *Grounding for the Metaphysics of Morals*, following James Ellington's Hackett edition. Ellington argues that the proper translation of *Grundlegung* would be 'Laying the Foundation', but as this is too awkward, he uses *Grounding*. I do not use *Groundwork*, because Kant did not use the word *Grundwerk*.
5   Other Kantian texts would suggest that the intelligible view of human beings depends on the inability to demonstrate that sensible influences are determining, rather than the actual autonomy from sensible influences.

6   This is Pluhar's gloss on the basic meaning of determinability as well (CJ: ci).
7   Cf. Nuyen: 141; Kearney: 38; Banham: 92; Wilson: 221, 223; Recki: 209; and Zammito: 278.
8   This controverts Lyotard's contention that sublimity cannot have a moral role because it leads to this admiration, which he claims is not part of the moral terminology.
9   Pluhar also recognizes sublimity's subjective purposiveness (Pluhar: lxx–ii), while Zammito regards sublimity as a relation, as relative purposiveness in occasioning subjective reflection (Zammito: 279–80).
10 Guyer translates *Urteilskraft* as the power of judgement, but *Einbildungskraft* as imagination, not the power of imagination, at least here in CJ244.
11 The transcendental object=x provides an ultimate, unifying, non-noumenal referent for all experience of objects.
12 That beauty is subjective is not universally accepted by Kant scholars. For instance, Karl Ameriks stresses Kant's references to beautiful objects (Ameriks 2000).
13 Here 'phenomenological' does not refer to the transcendental conditions of possible experience or an epistemological or logical classification or categorization of mental powers.
14 I augment his brief account with remarks from other sections.
15 Pluhar points out sublimity's relation to reason (Pluhar: lxx–ii).
16 In §27, Kant describes the feeling of the sublime as akin to vibration or rapid alternation.
17 Guyer's *Critique of the Power of Judgment* translates *denken* here as 'conceived'.
18 I translate *Darstellung* as exhibition, rather than presentation (as in Guyer), because Kant glosses *Darstellungen* with the Latin word *exhibitiones* (CJ352).
19 Within the genus of representation (*repraesentatio*, *Vorstellung*), the concept refers mediately to the object by features common to a class of objects; a concept formed from notions (*notio*), namely, pure concepts deriving strictly from understanding, 'and transcending the possibility of experience is an idea or concept of reason' (A320/B377). By this definition, Kant may legitimately shift between 'idea' and 'concept of reason' without equivocation.
20 Because sublimity does not concern objects in nature, there is no question of deriving its subjective purposiveness in attuning our mental powers from a teleological reading of nature's objective purposiveness. Since the transcendental aesthetic of judgement concerns only pure aesthetic judgements, 'the examples must not be taken from such beautiful or sublime objects of nature that presuppose the concept of an end; because then the purposiveness would either be teleological or

grounding itself on mere perceptions [*Empfindungen*] of an object (pleasure or pain), and thus, in the first case, not aesthetic purposiveness, and in the second, not merely formal purposiveness' (CJ269–70).

Kant's ambiguous phrasing here suggests that there are sublime objects of nature that presuppose the concept of an end; these sublime-teleological objects of nature would fall under the category of objects of impure aesthetic judgements or teleological judgements. But in his explicit remarks, Kant always rejects any such possibilities as the teleological sublime, since it would involve determinate concepts, conflict in its external reference with his definitions of sublimity as absolutely great and thereby destroy the awesome aesthetic experience definitive of the sublime. 'If one thus calls the sight of the starry sky *sublime*, one should not lay at the ground of this judgement concepts of worlds inhabited by rational beings, and then [think of] the bright points with which we see the space above us filled as their suns moving in orbits posited very much purposively for them, but rather merely [call them sublime based on how] one sees it, as a vast vault which encompasses everything; and only under this representation must we posit the sublimity that a pure aesthetic judgement attributes to this object' (CJ270). This position has been criticized on grounds that we are unable to see external things except under concepts, whether of magnitude, power or identity, as stars and so forth (e.g. Budd: 87). But Kant is opposing the subsumption of nature under purposive concepts in pure aesthetic judgements of sublimity. It is not that we see without any concepts, but that our concepts must remain indeterminate and non-teleological if we are to experience sublimity in nature. Similarly, we must not think of our view of the ocean 'enriched with all types of knowledge [*Kenntnissen*] (but which are not contained in the immediate intuition); roughly as a vast realm of aquatic creatures, as the great reservoir for the vapours that impregnate the air with clouds for the benefit of the land, or even as an element that admittedly separates continents from one another, but equally makes possible the greatest community among them: because that yields pure [*lauter*] teleological judgements' (CJ270).

We can find the turbulent ocean sublime by observing it poetically in merely visual terms as 'an abyss threatening to engulf everything' (CJ270). As long as we do not ground the determination of judgement or the agreement of the sublime and beautiful in the human figure on concepts of ends, which would pollute the purity of aesthetic judgement, we may preserve aesthetic judgements on this figure, assuming that the limbs do not conflict with these ends (CJ270).

[21] As Iris Murdoch asserts, sublimity's association with reason underwrites its closer relation to morality (Wood: 43).

22 As an inducement to life through pleasure, beauty would undermine morality. Regarding the distinction of pleasure, beauty and morality, if the experience of pleasure is prior to and logically independent of 'that reflection on its intersubjective validity which results in an actual judgement of taste' as Guyer suggests and apparently dismisses later (Guyer 1979: 151–3), then beauty is not merely accompanied by pleasure, but is preceded by pleasure; if there is still a causal, but not a logical connection between pleasure and the judgement of taste, then beauty will be directly opposed to moral goodness, which cannot be prompted by pleasure. But if beauty is prior to and independent of the pleasure that it generates, as Kant sometimes argues, then it is still deficient for moral purposes in, e.g., lacking relation to reason or to any negative stance toward the inclinations.

23 Kant reserves for the teleology, rather than the critique of taste (CJ301), his examination of the basis of this purposiveness.

24 For a discussion of symbolic hypotyposis and its closer relation to sublimity, see Martha B. Helfer, *The Retreat of Representation: The Concept of Darstellung in German Critical Discourse* (Albany: SUNY Press, 1996): 36ff.

Chapter 5

1 Even Zammito, who claims to offer a strongly moral reading of sublimity, shifts the discussion from the moral functions of sublimity to those of beauty, concluding weakly that sublimity merely occasions 'self-consciousness in aesthetic reflection' (Zammito: 278).

2 As we have seen, Lyotard agrees with Allison and Crowther that sublime respect is non-identical with moral respect.

3 Crowther argues that Kant introduces respect into sublimity as a means of bringing in morality, and thus, sustaining the deduction of its necessity.

4 Zammito rejects the psychologistic argument (Zammito: 284) on the grounds of moral feeling's *a priori* constitution from moral law (ibid.: 279).

5 *Schwung* and *Antrieb* can both be translated as drive or impetus or impulse. Guyer translates *Schwung* as momentum (and *Antrieb* as impetus), but what I am trying to get at here is less a form of momentum, generated by an anterior force, than a self-sustaining push or drive or setting of the mind into motion in each case (*Schwung* is more forceful than *Antrieb*).

6 Whereas Guyer regards the feeling of the sublime in Humean terms 'as a succession of distinct sensations' and accentuates the '"pre-reflective"

psychological processes' recognizable through pleasure and displeasure (Crowther: 123), Crowther argues that 'the mental movement of sublimity is vibration, i.e. repeated succession, not succession' (Crowther: 124).

7   Sublimity 'presents merely the subjective play of the mental powers themselves (imagination and reason) as harmonious by virtue of their contrast' (CJ258).

8   Kant's claim that sublimity has no function in the critical project and is not nearly as rich in implications as the beautiful derives from its contrapurposiveness.

9   Allison argues that 'the claim is that since we must presuppose moral feeling in everyone (as a condition of treating someone as a responsible moral agent), and since judgements of sublimity have their foundation in a predisposition to this feeling, it is legitimate to attribute necessity to such judgements' (Allison 2001: 334).

10 For an example of this argument, see, for instance, Craig Greenman, *The Weaker Soldier*.

11 I refer to Makkreel here, rather than to any number of Kant commentators, because he specifically grants a strong connection between *dynamical* sublimity and morality, as opposed to a more general connection between sublimity and morality, which is granted in some form by a host of authors.

12 Note that *ermessen* also means 'estimate' and thus *Unermeßlichkeit* might be translated as 'what cannot be estimated'.

13 Pluhar recognizes sublimity's exhibition of our supersensible moral 'vocation' (Pluhar: lxx–ii), the problem being that he translates *Bestimmung* as vocation, rather than determination.

14 But, it seems, not infinity – though what is really lacking is the absolute totality (CJ249).

Chapter 6

1   A JSTOR search for beauty or the beautiful registers 343,567 entries, as against 44,782 on sublimity or the sublime, 3,568 in the 1960s, 4,739 in the 1970s, 6,464 in the 1980s, 9,222 in the 1990s and 8,217 from 2000–2011.

2   In 1980, T.J. Diffey supposes that 'a majority ... regard the sublime as of merely historical interest' (Diffey: 357).

3   Baker neglects to mention that Schiller, as we will see below, differentiates sublimity from beauty in part according to the former's autonomy from the existence of objects and the latter's dependence on their existence.

4 In stressing the moral function of the contradiction in sublimity, Schiller fails to recognize that the Kantian sublime involves an odd sort of harmony *through* tension, not disharmony. Schiller also differs from Kant in associating beauty with the harmony between reason and sensibility, rather than sensibility and *understanding*.

5 Baker adds that Schiller's three-stage discussion of the horse illustrates the progress of individual and society 'from pristine nature, to domestication, coming to rest in the violent overthrow of servitude' (Baker: 531), but that the sublime is merely a stage prior to the unification or harmonization of nature and humanity (Baker: 533).

6 In the same letter to Kant, Herder also speaks of his admiration of Hume, Pope, Aristotle and Rousseau, among others, and writes of combining Baumgarten's 'rich psychology' with Montaigne's 'experience of the soul' (Herder to Kant, November 1768: no. 41, X76).

7 To describe Herder's critique as internal and Hegel's as external would violate the Hegelian critique of the internal-external dichotomy, while obscuring Hegel's similarities to Kant and Herder's rejection of various Kantian assumptions about the sublime.

8 Articles on Hegel and the sublime include Paul de Man's deconstructive reading, S.K. Saxena's general account and Alessandro Bertinetto's comparison of Kant and Hegel on the sublime, which argues that Hegel applied sublimity to art, in contradistinction to Kant, but criticized sublimity as 'bad infinity' and the lowest level of art, on account of the contradiction between its form and content.

9 I mark the standard pagination of the German edition of Hegel's *Aesthetics* by 'H.'

10 For those who read Polish, a commentary on Adorno's proximity to Kantian sublimity in *Aesthetic Theory* is promised in Rafal Czekaj's essay; for English-speakers with access to *SATS: Nordic Journal of Philosophy*, there is an article on Adorno and the sublime by Espen Hammer.

11 Certainly, Derrida and Lyotard both wrote frequently on issues of language, as well as psychoanalysis, prior to their work on sublimity, but Lyotard's *Lessons on the Analytic of the Sublime* pays relatively little attention either to psychoanalysis or language, while Derrida's 'Parergon' pays some attention to these issues, particularly psychoanalysis, as it is published in a text partially on Freud and it contains a Freudian subtext in its frequent suggestions that the Kantian sublime is really all about the phallus, masturbation and castration. Žižek's accounts of sublimity are very much concerned with Lacanian psychoanalysis and thus, also concerned with structuralist linguistics.

12 As we have seen, the *Philosopher's Index* lists 517 references to Kant and beauty or the beautiful and about 300 references to Kant and the sublime; the comparable figures for Hegel are just 94 on beauty and 17

on the sublime. In JSTOR, the proportions are closer: there are 10,570 references to Kant and beauty, 7,555 to Hegel and beauty, 5,008 to Kant and sublime, and 3,607 to Hegel and sublime.

13. Kirwan, by contrast, argues that '[t]here is little in Lyotard's sense of the aesthetic that is not in Heidegger or in his account of the relationship between the sublime and art that is not in Adorno' (Kirwan 2005: 143). But Derrida is likely the more proximate influence, despite their differences on the moral reading of sublimity, and Adorno, in contrast to Lyotard, emphasizes the moral elements of Kantian sublimity.

14. Alan Schrift, email exchange with author, 28 April, 2011.

15. In a 1996 interview, Derrida is clear on this point: '*Oui, mes livres sont politiques*'. 'Yes, my books are political'. Entretien avec Didier Eribon, *Le nouvel observateur* (1633), 1996: 84–6.

16. For Kirwan, Lyotard's work is insignificant, except in its popularity and influence, and '[i]t is this popularity that is significant to the history of the sublime' (Kirwan 2005: 143).

17. Four of the six works in which Guyer's name is mentioned are *by* Guyer, and most of the works citing Derrida and the sublime do not actually focus on Derrida and the sublime (some concentrate on Lyotard and the sublime). Derrida is not well-known for his work on sublimity, despite his influence on French postmodernists.

18. This is not to say that Derrida did not elsewhere address the questions of the limit and representation that he associated with the sublime, and that formed his primary subject matter throughout his career. For instance, in *Specters of Marx*, it is difficult not to think that he is talking about the sublime when he describes the problems of the uncanny and of self-deconstructing representations, which cannot be said to be either in or outside of the head (Derrida, *Specters of Marx*: 171–3).

19. Žižek continually shifts back and forth between forms of 'representation' and 'presentation', where both translate *Vorstellung*.

20. Lacan associates sublimity and sublimation without identifying them (Lacan: 161).

21. Here and in a response to critics, Žižek argues that there are three forms of the Real, the real, the imaginary and the symbolic, all of which reflects itself in each form (Žižek 2001b: 97).

22. In *The Spirit of Terrorism*, Jean Baudrillard argues similarly that 'the distinction between Western good and terrorism is the product of a mutually reinforcing binary opposition' in which each idea depends on its other for its existence (Shaw: 141).

Bibliography

Addison, Joseph, *The Works of Joseph Addison: Complete in Three Volumes Embracing the Whole of the "Spectator," &c.* (New York: Harper & Bros., 1837), vol. 1, 1–314; vol. 2, 315–635.
Adorno, Theodor, *Gesammelte Schriften* (GS), hrsg. von Rolf Tiedemann unter Mitwirkung von Gretel Adorno, Susan Buck-Morss und Klaus Schultz. Bde. 1–20 (in 23 Bdn. geb.). Revidierte und erweiterte elektronische Ausg. auf CD-ROM (Berlin: Digitale Bibliothek 97, 2003).
——, *Ästhetische Theorie* (AT), bd. 7.
——, *Dialektik der Aufklärung*, bd. 3.
——, *Dissonanzen. Einleitung in die Musiksoziologie: Kritik des Musikanten*, bd. 14.
——, *Kierkegaard: Konstruktion des Ästhetischen*, bd. 16.
——, *Kriterien der neuen Musik*, bd. 2.
——, *Negative Dialektik*, bd. 6.
Allison, Henry, *Kant's Theory of Taste: A Reading of the Critique of Aesthetic Judgment* (New York: Cambridge University Press, 2001).
Ameriks, Karl, 'On Paul Guyer's *Kant and the Experience of Freedom*', *Philosophy and Phenomenological Research*, 55/2 (June 1995), 361–7.
——, 'A defence of the objectivity and conceptuality of Kantian taste', IX. International Kant Kongress, Berlin, March 2000.
Anahory, Ana, '*Leituras do sublime: Lyotard e Derrida*', *Philosophica: Revista do Departamento de Filosofia da Faculdade de Letras de Lisboa*, 19–20 (April–November 2002), 131–54.
Aristotle, *The Basic Works of Aristotle*, ed. Richard McKeon (New York: Random House, 1941); *Rhetoric*, trans. W. Rhys Roberts, pp. 1325–1454.
——, *On the Art of Poetry*, Horace: *On the Art of Poetry*, Longinus: *On the Sublime*, *Classical Literary Criticism*, trans. T. S. Dorsch (Baltimore, MD: Penguin, 1965).
——, *Ethics*, ed. Hugh Tredennick, trans. J. A. K. Thomson (London: Penguin, 1976).
——, *Nicomachean Ethics*, trans. J. A. K. Thomson and Hugh Tredennick (New York: Penguin, 2004).

Baker, Eric, 'Fables of the sublime: Kant, Schiller, Kleist', *MLN*, 113/3 (April 1998), 524–36.

Banham, Gary, *Kant and the Ends of Aesthetics* (London: MacMillan, 2000).

Barchana-Lorand, Dorit, 'Sublime curiosity: Edmund Burke's physiological explanation', *Iyyun* 51 (October 2002), 359–74.

Baumgarten, Alexander, *Aesthetica* (Hildesheim: G. Olms, 1961 (reproduction of Frankfurt, 1750–8 edition)).

Bäumler, Alfred, *Kants Kritik der Urteilskraft. Ihre Geschichte und Systematik*, Band I (Halle: Niemeyer, 1923).

Beck, Lewis White, *Early German Philosophy: Kant and his Predecessors* (Bristol: Thoemmes Press, 1996).

Beidler, Paul G., 'The postmodern sublime: Kant and Tony Smith's anecdote of the cube', *Journal of Aesthetics and Art Criticism*, 53/2 (1995), 177–86.

Beiser, Frederick C., *Diotima's Children: German aesthetic rationalism from Leibniz to Lessing* (New York: Oxford University Press, 2009).

Bertinetto, Alessandro, '*Negative Darstellung: Das Erhabene bei Kant und Hegel*', in Karl Ameriks (ed.), *Internationales Jahrbuch des Deutschen Idealismus/International Yearbook of German Idealism: Bd. 4, 2006: Ästhetik und Philosophie der Kunst/Aesthetics and Philosophy of Art*, (Berlin: Walter de Gruyter, 2007).

de Bolla, Peter, *The Discourse of the Sublime* (Oxford: Blackwell, 1989).

Bosanquet, Bernard, *A History of Aesthetic* (New York: MacMillan & Co., 1892).

Brandt, Reinhard, '*Beobachtungen zum Erhabenen bei Kant und Hegel*', in Christel Fricke (hrsg.), *Das Recht der Vernunft: Kant und Hegel über Denken, Erkennen und Handeln*, (Stuttgart: Frommann-Holzboog, 1995).

Brett, R. L., *The Third Earl of Shaftesbury: A Study in Eighteenth-Century Literary Theory* (London: Hutchinson's University Library, 1951).

Budd, Malcolm, *The Aesthetic Appreciation of Nature: Essays on the Aesthetics of Nature* (Oxford: Clarendon Press, 1992).

Burke, Edmund, *Reflections on the Revolution in France*, ed. J. G. A. Pocock ([1790] Indianapolis: Hackett Publishing, 1987).

——, *A Philosophical Inquiry into the Origin of Our Ideas of the Beautiful and Sublime*, ed. Adam Phillips. (New York: Oxford University Press, 1998).

——, *A Philosophical Inquiry into the Origin of Our Ideas of the Beautiful and Sublime*, with an introduction by David Womersley. (London: Penguin Classics, 2004).

——, *A Philosophical Inquiry into the Sublime and Beautiful* ([1790] London: Routledge, 2008).
Charlton, William, 'Moral beauty and overniceness', *British Journal of Aesthetics*, 20 (1980), 291–304.
——, 'Horror in literature', *Dialectics and Humanism*, 15 (winter–spring 1988), 219–31.
Cheetham, Mark, *Kant, Art and History: Moments of Discipline* (Cambridge: Cambridge University Press, 2001).
Clewis, Robert, *The Kantian Sublime and the Revelation of Freedom* (Cambridge: Cambridge University Press, 2009).
Cohen, Ted, 'Why beauty is a symbol of morality', in Ted Cohen and Paul Guyer, *Essays in Kant's Aesthetics*, pp. 221–36.
—— and Paul Guyer (eds and intro.), *Essays in Kant's Aesthetics* (Chicago: The University of Chicago Press, 1982).
Cohn, Jan and Thomas H. Miles, 'The sublime: in alchemy, aesthetics and psychoanalysis', *Modern Philology*, 74/3 (February 1977), 289–304.
Cooper, Anthony Ashley, third earl of Shaftesbury (1671–1713), *Characteristics of Men, Manners, Opinions, and Times* ([1711] Westmead: Gregg International Publishers, 1968): vol. 1, *A Letter concerning Enthusiasm; Sensus Communis: An Essay on the Freedom of Wit and Humour; Soliloquy, or Advice to an Author*; vol. 2, *An Inquiry concerning Virtue and Merit; The Moralists: a Philosophical Rhapsody*; vol. 3, *Miscellaneous Reflections on the said Treatises, and other Critical Subjects; A Notion of the Historical Draught, or Tablature of the Judgment of Hercules*.
Crawford, Donald W., 'The place of the sublime in Kant's aesthetic theory', in Richard Kennington (ed.), *The Philosophy of Immanuel Kant* (Washington, D.C.: The Catholic University of America Press, 1985), pp. 161–84.
Crowther, Paul, *The Kantian Sublime: From Morality to Art* (New York: Oxford University Press, 1989).
Cutrofello, Andrew, *Continental Philosophy: A Contemporary Introduction* (New York: Routledge, 2005).
Czekaj, Rafal, 'The spirit of art and the unfulfilable promise: looking for positive conclusions of Adorno's aesthetic theory' (in Polish), *Sztuka Filozof*, 28 (2006), 151–63.
Dahlstrom, Daniel, 'Moses Mendelssohn', Edward N. Zalta (ed.), *Stanford Encyclopedia of Philosophy*, (winter 2006), http://plato.stanford.edu/archives/win2006/entries/mendelssohn/.
Derrida, Jacques, *La Vérité en Peinture* (Paris: Flammarion, 1978).

——, *The Truth in Painting*, trans. Geoff Bennington and Ian McLeod (Chicago: The University of Chicago Press, 1987) (1987a).

——, *The Postcard: From Socrates to Freud and Beyond*, trans. Alan Bass (Chicago: University of Chicago Press, 1987).

——, *Specters of Marx*, trans. Peggy Kamuf (New York: Routledge, 1994).

——, entretien avec Didier Eribon, *Le nouvel observateur*, 1633 (1996), 84–6; collected as 'Heidegger: l'enfer des philosophes', in Jacques Derrida, *Points de Suspension: Entretiens* (Paris: Editions Gallilée, 1992), pp. 193–202, and in Jacques Derrida, *Points de Suspension: Entretiens*, ed. Elisabeth Weber, trans. Peggy Kamuf et al. (Palo Alto, CA: Stanford University Press, 1995), pp. 181–90.

Diffey, T. J., review of Eva Schaper, *Studies in Kant's Aesthetics*, *The Philosophical Quarterly*, 30/121 (October 1980), 356–7.

Donougho, Martin, 'On the Hegelian sublime: Paul de Man's judgment call', *Philosophy and Rhetoric*, 34/1 (2001), 1–20.

Elam, Diane, 'Sublime repetition', review of *The Sublime Object of Ideology*, *Surfaces*, 1/14 (1991), 4–10.

Ferguson, Frances, *Solitude and the Sublime* (New York: Routledge, 1992).

Friedlander, Eli, 'Kant and the critique of false sublimity', *Iyyun*, 48 (1999), 69–91.

Gasché, Rodolphe, 'On mere sight: a reply to Paul de Man', in Hugh Silverman and Gary Aylesworth (eds), *The Textual Sublime: Deconstruction and its Differences* (Albany, New York: SUNY Press, 1990), pp. 109–16.

Gerard, Alexander, *An Essay on Taste with Three Dissertations on the Same Subject by Mr. De Voltaire, Mr. D'Alembert, F.R.S., Mr. De Montesquieu* (2nd edn, London: 1764).

——, *An Essay on Genius* (New York: Garland, 1970).

Goodreau, John R., *The Role of the Sublime in Kant's Moral Metaphysics*, 1998: http://books.google.com/books?id=0rSCH-cTiRAC&printsec=frontcover&dq=THE+ROLE+OF+THE+SUBLIME+IN+KANT%27S+MORAL+METAPHYSICS&lr=#v=onepage&q&f=false.

Gracyk, Theodore A., 'Kant's shifting debt to British aesthetics', *British Journal of Aesthetics*, 26/3 (summer 1986), 204–17 (Gracyk 1986a).

——, 'Sublimity, ugliness and formlessness in Kant's aesthetic theory', *Journal of Aesthetics and Art Criticism*, 45 (1986), 49–56 (Gracyk 1986b).

Grean, Stanley, *Shaftesbury's Philosophy of Religion and Ethics: A Study in Enthusiasm* (Athens, OH: Ohio State University Press, 1967).

Greenman, Craig, 'The weaker soldier: an aesthetic approach to the problem of suicide' (Ph.D. dissertation, Loyola University, Chicago, 2002).

Guevara, Daniel, *Kant's Theory of Moral Motivation* (Boulder, CO: Westview Press, 2000).

Guyer, Paul, *Kant and the Claims of Taste* (1st edn, Cambridge, MA: Harvard University Press, 1979; 2nd edn, Cambridge: Cambridge University Press, 1997).

——, 'Kant's Distinction between the Beautiful and the Sublime'. *Review of Metaphysics* 35 (1982), 753–84.

——, *Kant and the Experience of Freedom: Essays on Aesthetics and Morality* (Cambridge: Cambridge University Press, 1993).

——, review of John H. Zammito, *The Genesis of Kant's Critique of Judgment*, *The Philosophical Review*, 103/2 (April 1994), 369–73.

——, 'Beauty, sublimity, and expression: reply to Wicks and Cantrick', *Journal of Aesthetics and Art Criticism*, 53/2 (1995), 194–5.

—— (ed.), *The Cambridge Companion to Kant* (New York: Cambridge University Press, 1992).

Hammer, Espen, 'The touch of art: Adorno and the sublime', *SATS: Nordic Journal of Philosophy*, 1/2 (2000), 91–105.

Hammermeister, Kai, *The German Aesthetic Tradition* (Cambridge: Cambridge University Press, 2002).

Hegel, G. W. F., *Phenomenology of Spirit*, trans. A. V. Miller with analysis of the text and foreword by J. N. Findlay (Oxford: Clarendon Press, 1977).

——*Ästhetik*, 4te Auflage, bd. 1, hrsg. von Friedrich Bassenge (Westberlin: Verlag das Europäische Buch, 1985).

——, *Aesthetics: Lectures on Fine Art*, vol. 1, trans. T. M. Knox (New York: Oxford University Press, 1998).

——, *Gesammelte Werke*, hrsg. im Auftrag der Deutschen Forschungsgemeinschaft (Hamburg: Felix Meiner Verlag, 1968–2010); *Phänomenologie des Geistes*, bd. 9, hrsg. von W. Bonsiepen und R. Heede.

Helfer, Martha B., *The Retreat of Representation: The Concept of Darstellung in German Critical Discourse* (Albany: SUNY Press, 1996).

Henrich, Dieter, 'Beauty and freedom: Schiller's struggle with Kant's aesthetics', in Cohen and Guyer (eds), *Essays in Kant's Aesthetics*, pp. 237–60.

Hepburn, Ronald W., 'The concept of the sublime', *Dialectics and Humanism*, 15 (1988), 137–55.

Herder, Johann Gottfried, *Werke*, vol. 8 (Frankfurt am Main: Deutscher Klassiker Verlag, 1998).

Hinnant, Charles H., 'Schiller and the political sublime: two perspectives', *Criticism*, 44/2 (spring 2002), 121–38.

Home, Henry, Lord Kames, *Elements of Criticism*, 2 vols, ed. Peter Jones (6th edn, Indianapolis: Liberty Fund, 2005).

Hügelmann, Karl, 'Ein Brief über Kant', *Altpreußische Monatsschrift*, 16 (1879), 607–12, reprinted in Malter, *Immanuel Kant in Rede und Gespräch*.

Huhn, Thomas, review of Jean-François Lyotard, *Lessons on the Analytic of the Sublime*, *Journal of Aesthetics and Art Criticism*, 53/1 (winter 1995), 89–91.

Hund, William, 'Kant and A. Lazaroff on the sublime', *Kant-Studien*, 73/1 (January 1982), 351–9.

Hutcheson, Francis, *An Essay on the Nature and Conduct of the Passions and Affections with Illustrations on the Moral Sense*, intro. Paul McReynolds ([1742] 3rd edn, Gainesville, Florida: Scholars Facsimiles and Reprints, 1969).

——, *An Inquiry into the Original of our Ideas of Beauty and Virtue in Two Treatises*, ed. and intro. Wolfgang Leidhold (Indianapolis: Liberty Fund, 2004).

Kant, Immanuel, *Religion within the boundaries of mere reason* (1793), trans. George di Giovanni, in *Immanuel Kant: Religion and Rational Theology*, trans. and eds Allen Wood and George di Giovanni, pp. 39–215.

——, *Logik: Ein Handbuch zu Vorlesungen*, hrsg. Gottlob Benjamin Jäsche (Königsberg, 1800).

——, *Religion within the Limits of Reason Alone*, trans. Theodore M. Greene and Hoyt H. Hudson (New York: Harper, 1960).

——, *Critique of Pure Reason* (CPR), trans. Norman Kemp Smith (New York: St Martin's Press, 1965).

——, *Grounding for the Metaphysics of Morals* (GMM) trans. James W. Ellington (3rd edn, Indianapolis: Hackett, 1992).

——, *Critique of Practical Reason* (CPrR) trans. Lewis White Beck (3rd edn, New York: Library of Liberal Arts, 1993).

——, *Critique of Judgment* (CJ), trans. and intro. Werner S. Pluhar (Indianapolis: Hackett, 1994).

——, *Immanuel Kant: Religion and Rational Theology*, trans. and eds Allen Wood and George di Giovanni (New York: Cambridge University Press, 1996).

——, *Immanuel Kant, Lectures on Ethics*, eds Peter Heath and J. B. Schneewind, trans. Peter Heath, intro. J. B. Schneewind (Cambridge: Cambridge University Press, 1997).

——, *Kant im Kontext Plus: Werke auf CD-ROM*. 2te erw. Aufl. (Berlin: Karsten Worm InfoSoftWare, 1997); (esp. *Vorkritische Schriften 1747–1777, Grundlegung zur Metaphysik der Sitten, Kritik der praktischen Vernunft, Kritik der Urteilskraft, Die Metaphysik der Sitten* (MM), 2te Aufl., 'Beobachtungen über das Gefühl des Schönen und Erhabenen' (OFBS) (scanned from *Akademieausgabe*).

——, *Critique of the Power of Judgment*. trans. and intro. Paul Guyer (Cambridge: Cambridge University Press, 2000).

Kearney, Richard, 'Terror, philosophy and the sublime: some philosophical reflections on 11 September', *Philosophy and Social Criticism*, 29/1 (January 2003). 23–51.

Kind, John Louis, 'Edward Young in Germany', Ph.D. dissertation (New York: Columbia University, 1906).

Kirwan, James, *The Aesthetic in Kant: A Critique* (New York: Continuum, 2004).

——, *Sublimity: The Non-Rational and the Irrational in the History of Aesthetics* (New York: Routledge, 2005).

Kuhns, Richard, 'That Kant did not complete his argument concerning the relation of art to morality and how it might be completed', *Idealistic Studies*, 5 (1975), 190–206.

Kupfer, Joseph H., 'Sublimity in Gauguin as anti-moral', *Pacific Philosophical Quarterly*, 73/1 (1992), 63–72.

Lacan, Jacques, *The Seminar of Jacques Lacan Book VII: The Ethics of Psychoanalysis 1959–1960*, trans. Dennis Porter (New York: W. W. Norton, 1997).

Lazaroff, Allan, 'The Kantian sublime: aesthetic judgment and religious feeling', *Kant-Studien*, 71 (1980), 202–20.

Lindsay, A. D., *Kant* (Oxford: Oxford University Press, 1934).

Longinus, *On the Sublime* (with Greek text), ed. and trans. W. Rhys Roberts (Cambridge: Cambridge University Press, 1907).

——, *On Great Writing (On the Sublime)*, trans. G. M. A. Grube (New York: Bobbs-Merrill, 1957).

——, *On the Sublime* (Greek text), ed. D. A. Russell (Oxford: Clarendon Press, 1964).

Lyotard, Jean-François, *The Postmodern Condition: A Report on Knowledge*, trans. Geoff Bennington and Brian Massumi (Manchester: University of Manchester Press, 1984).

——, *Leçons sur l'Analytique du sublime (Kant, Critique de la faculté de juger, §§23–29)* (Paris: Éditions Galilée, 1991).

——, *Lessons on the Analytic of the Sublime (Kant's 'Critique of Judgment',*

§§23–29), trans. Elizabeth Rottenberg (Stanford: Stanford University Press, 1994).
—— with Jean-Loup Thébaud, *Just Gaming*, trans. Wlad Godzich (Minneapolis: University of Minnesota Press, 1985).
Makkreel, Rudolf, 'Imagination and temporality in Kant's theory of the sublime', *The Journal of Aesthetics and Art Criticism*, 42 (1984), 303–16.
Malter, Rudolf, *Immanuel Kant in Rede und Gespräch* (Hamburg: Felix Meiner, 1990).
de Man, Paul, 'Hegel on the sublime' (1983) in de Man, *Aesthetic Ideology*, pp. 105–18.
——, *Aesthetic Ideology* (Minneapolis: University of Minnesota Press, 1996).
Mendelssohn, Moses, *Philosophical Writings*, trans. and ed. Daniel O. Dahlstrom (Cambridge: Cambridge University Press, 1997).
Monk, Samuel, *The Sublime: A Study of Critical Theories of Eighteenth Century England* (Ann Arbor, MI: University of Michigan Press, 1935).
Moore, Jared S., 'The sublime and other subordinate esthetic concepts', *Journal of Philosophy*, 45 (January 1948), 42–7.
Nahm, M. C., 'Sublimity and the moral law in Kant's philosophy', *Kant-Studien*, 48 (1956), 502–24.
——, 'Kant: productive imagination and the creation of another nature', abstract, American Philosophical Association, Eastern Division Paper, *Journal of Philosophy*, 67/20 (1970), 816–17.
Nancy, Jean-Luc, 'The sublime offering', in Jeffrey Librett (ed.), *Of The Sublime: Presence in Question* (Albany: SUNY Press, 1993), pp. 25–54.
Neill, Elizabeth, 'Hume's moral sublime', *British Journal of Aesthetics*, 37/3 (1997), 246–58.
Nuyen, A. T., 'The sublimity of evil', *International Journal for the Philosophy of Religion*, 41/3 (1997), 135–47.
Pacholec, Matthew, 'Time and the sublime self', *Journal of Consciousness Studies*, 6/4 (April 1999), 70–84.
Pillow, Kirk, 'Form and content in Kant's *Kritik der Urteilskraft*: situating beauty and the sublime in the work of art', *Journal of the History of Philosophy*, 32/3 (1994), 443–59.
——, *Sublime Understanding: Aesthetic Reflection in Kant and Hegel* (Cambridge: MIT Press, 2000).
Recki, Birgit, *Ästhetik der Sitten: Die Affinität von ästhetischem Gefühl und praktischen Vernunft bei Kant* (Frankfurt am Main: Vittorio Klostermann, 2001).
Ross, Alison, 'The art of the sublime: Lyotard and the politics of the avant-garde', *Philosophy Today*, 49/1 (spring 2005), 33–45.

Rotenstreich, Nathan, 'Sublimity and terror', *Idealistic Studies*, 3 (1973), 238–51.
Rueger, Alexander and Sahan Evren, 'The role of symbolic presentation in Kant's theory of taste', *British Journal of Aesthetics*, 45/3 (2005), 229–47.
Rush, Fred, review of Henry E. Allison, *Kant's Theory of Taste*, *The Journal of Aesthetics and Art Criticism*, 60/4 (fall 2002), 353–4.
Saxena, S. K., 'Hegel on the sublime', *Religious Studies*, 10 (June 1974), 153–74.
Schiller, Friedrich, 'On the sublime: toward the further development of some Kantian ideas' (1793) (*Vom Erhabenen (Zur weitern Ausführung einiger Kantischen Ideen)*, in *Sämtliche Werke*, bd. V: *Philosophische Schriften/Vermischte Schriften* (München: Winkler-Verlag, 1968), pp. 166–89).
——, 'On the sublime' (1801, composed between 1794 and 1796) (*Über das Erhabene*, in *Werke*, bd. V, pp. 215–30).
Schmidt, James, review: *Immanuel Kant: Text and Context*, *Eighteenth-Century Studies*, 37/1 (fall 2003), 147–61.
Schopenhauer, Arthur, *The World as Will and Representation*, trans. E. F. J. Payne (New York: Dover, 1969).
Shaw, Philip, *The Sublime* (New York: Routledge, 2006).
Silverman, Hugh J. (ed.), *Lyotard: Philosophy, Politics, and the Sublime* (New York: Routledge, 2002).
Sulzer, J. G., *Allgemeine Theorie der schönen Künste* ([1771–4] Hildesheim: G. Olms, 1967)
Teale, A. E., *Kantian Ethics* (London: Oxford University Press, 1951).
Tonelli, Giorgio, 'Crusius, Christian August', in Paul Edwards (ed.), *Encyclopaedia of Philosophy*, vol. 1 (New York: MacMillan, 1967), pp. 269–70.
Trifonova, Temenuga, 'The question of the appendix: the Kantian and the inhuman (postmodern) sublime', *International Studies in Philosophy*, 35/2 (2003), 51–92.
Weiskel, Thomas, *The Romantic Sublime: Studies in the Structure and Psychology of Transcendence* (Baltimore: Johns Hopkins University Press, 1976).
Wenzel, Christian Helmut, *An Introduction to Kant's Aesthetics: Core Concepts and Problems* (Cambridge: Wiley-Blackwell, 2005).
Wicks, Robert, review of John H. Zammito, *The Genesis of Kant's Critique of Judgment*, *Journal of Aesthetics and Art Criticism*, 51/4 (autumn 1993), 643–4.

——, 'Kant on fine art', *Journal of Aesthetics and Art Criticism*, 53/2 (1995), 189–93.

Will, Frederick, 'Cognition through beauty in Moses Mendelssohn's early aesthetics', *Journal of Aesthetics and Art Criticism*, 14/1 (September 1955), 97–105.

Wilson, Jeffrey, 'Incommensurable, supersensible, sublime', *American Catholic Philosophical Quarterly*, 75/2 (spring 2001), 221–41.

Wood, Theodore E. B., *The Word 'Sublime' and its Context 1650–1760* (The Hague: Mouton, 1972).

Young, Edward, *Conjectures on Original Composition in a Letter to the Author of Sir Charles Grandison* (Leeds: Scolar Press, 1966).

——, *The Complete Works: Poetry and Prose*, 2 vols, ed. James Nichols (Hildesheim: Georg Olms, 1968).

Zammito, John H., *The Genesis of Kant's Critique of Judgment* (Chicago: The University of Chicago Press, 1992).

Žižek, Slavoj, *The Sublime Object of Ideology* (New York: Verso, 1989).

——, 'Laugh yourself to death: the new wave of Holocaust comedies', Lunds Universität, 15 December 1999.

——, *The Žižek Reader*, ed. Elizabeth Wright and Edmund Wright (Oxford: Blackwell, 1999).

——, *The Fragile Absolute, or why is the Christian Legacy Worth Fighting for?* (New York: Verso, 2001) (2001a).

——, review: 'The rhetorics of power', *Diacritics*, 31/1 (spring 2001), 91–104 (2001b).

——, *Welcome to the Desert of the Real: Five Essays on September 11 and Related Dates* (New York: Verso, 2002).

——, *How to Read Lacan* (New York: W. W. Norton, 2007).

——, 'Fear thy neighbor as thyself', University of New Mexico, 30 November 2007.

Zuckert, Rachel, 'Awe or envy: Herder contra Kant on the sublime', *The Journal of Aesthetics and Art Criticism*, 61/3 (summer 2003), 217–32.

Index

Addison, Joseph xii, 4, 12–13, 15–20, 23–4, 27, 29, 41, 46, 173, 192n4, 201
Adorno, Theodor W. viii, xiii, 145–6, 158–62, 172, 186–7, 199n10, 200n13, 201, 203, 205
affect(s)/affections 5–7, 11, 18, 20–2, 24–6, 28, 35, 37–8, 41–2, 44–7, 63, 69, 87–9, 91, 116, 125, 149, 170, 177, 206
Allison, Henry 22, 45, 52, 54, 69, 93–6, 99–101, 118, 120–1, 123–6, 139–40, 193–4nn2–3, 197n2, 198n9, 201, 209
Ameriks, Karl 195n12, 201–2
Anahory, Ana 176, 201
Aristotle xi, 4–6, 18, 25, 41–3, 84, 88, 191n2, 199n6, 201
attunement (*Stimmung*) xvi, 20, 47, 56, 66, 70–2, 74, 80, 83, 86, 96, 99, 105, 114, 118, 120–1, 131–2, 135–6, 138–9, 149, 187

Baker, Eric 147, 198n3, 199n5, 202
Banham, Gary 94, 106, 195n7, 202
Barchana-Lorand, Dorit 202
Batteux, Charles 44
Baudrillard, Jean 200n22
Baumgarten, Alexander xii, 9, 12, 14–15, 34, 36–44, 47, 192n4, 199n6
Bäumler, Alfred 15, 39–40, 192n3, 202

beautiful/beauty viii, x–xi, 4, 8, 13–17, 20–2, 25–32, 34–7, 39–40, 42–3, 51–6, 65, 68–70, 73–95, 98, 107, 110–13, 115, 118, 120, 122–3, 129–30, 133, 135, 139–40, 143–50, 155–7, 160–1, 163–5, 168–71, 175–6, 186, 188, 193–4nn1–2, 195n12, 195–6n20, 197n22, 197n1, 198n8, 198n1, 198n3, 199n4, 199n12, 200, 202–3, 205–6, 208, 210
Beck, Lewis White 13, 202, 206
Beidler, Paul G. 52, 100, 202
Beiser, Frederick C. 192n4, 202
Bertinetto, Alessandro 199n8, 202
de Bolla, Peter 162, 202
Bosanquet, Bernard 202
Brandt, Reinhard 202
Brett, R. L. 19, 202
Budd, Malcolm 130, 196, 202
Burke, Edmund 12–16, 19, 20, 22, 26–33, 35–8, 44, 145, 150, 155, 164, 172, 183, 192n3, 192n5, 193n5, 193n2, 202

Charlton, William 52, 203
Cheetham, Mark 203
Clewis, Robert 56, 94, 106, 121–2, 136, 203
cognition (*Erkenntnis*) 34, 39, 64–5, 67, 70, 74, 77, 79–80, 83–5, 96, 100, 104, 110, 112, 119, 130–1, 134–5, 210

Cohen, Ted 56, 94, 106, 121–2, 136, 203
Cohn, Jan 191n2, 203
Colossal, the 164, 166
Cooper, Anthony Ashley (Third Earl of Shaftesbury) xii, 4, 12–13, 15–16, 19–23, 27, 44, 202–4
Crawford, Donald W. 52, 69, 193n2, 203
Crowther, Paul 13, 29, 52, 55, 93–4, 96, 99–101, 106, 108–9, 173, 197nn2–3, 198n6, 203
Cutrofello, Andrew vii, 58, 203
Czekaj, Rafal 199n10, 203

Dahlstrom, Daniel 44, 203, 208
Derrida, Jacques xi, xiii, 144, 146, 157–8, 162–74, 176–7, 181–2, 187–9, 199n11, 200n13, 200n15, 200nn17–18, 201, 203–4
determinability/determination (*Bestimmbarkeit, bestimmen, Bestimmung*) xiv, 21, 23, 37–8, 51–2, 56–73, 75, 77–9, 81–2, 86–7, 90, 95, 97–8, 100–4, 106–7, 109–12, 114, 116–17, 119, 122, 124–6, 128–30, 134, 136–40, 150, 152–4, 159, 162, 168–9, 172, 179, 182–3, 195n6, 196, 198n13
Diffey, T. J. 198n2, 204
Donougho, Martin 155, 204
Dubos, Jean 44

Elam, Diane 177, 204
elevation/elevate(s) (as meaning of sublime) ix, xiv–xv, 4–10, 16, 22, 24–5, 27, 31, 41, 46, 72, 91, 98–9, 105, 121, 123, 126, 131–2, 134, 138, 149, 157, 184–5
enthusiasm 5–6, 8, 16, 22, 24, 37–38, 116, 177, 203–4
Evren, Sahan 209

fanaticism (*Schwärmerei*) 8, 16, 22, 32, 38, 57, 115–16, 177
fear 5, 17, 21, 28, 30, 41, 44, 46, 70, 82, 102, 107, 110, 115, 131–2, 134, 169, 175, 186, 210
Ferguson, Frances 204
Friedlander, Eli 204

Gardner, Erik vii
Gasché, Rodolphe 162, 164, 204
Gerard, Alexander 12, 15–16, 204
Goodreau, John R. 204
Gracyk, Theodore 37, 52, 72, 204
Grean, Stanley 19, 204
Greenman, Craig vii, 198n10, 204
Guevara, Daniel 205
Guyer, Paul x, xiv, 7, 17, 22, 25, 29–30, 41, 52, 57, 73–8, 88–9, 94, 106, 108–11, 143–4, 164, 172, 193–4n1–n2, 195n10, 195n17, 197n22, 197–8nn5–6, 200n17, 201, 203, 205, 207

Hammer, Espen 199n10, 205
Hammermeister, Kai 39–40, 44, 205
Hegel, Georg Wilhelm Friedrich viii, x–xi, 144–7, 154–60, 162–5, 171, 177–82, 186–7, 199nn7–9, 199–200n12, 202, 204–5, 208–9
height (as meaning of sublime) 4–5, 7–8, 16, 25
Helfer, Martha B. 197n24, 205
Henrich, Dieter 205
Hepburn, Ronald W. 205
Herder, Johann Gottfried von 15, 28, 38, 98, 145–7, 150–5, 186, 192n3, 199nn6–7, 205, 210
Hinnant, Charles H. 147, 205
Home, Henry (Lord Kames) 15–16, 20, 24–7, 38, 40–1, 206
horror (horrible, horrific, abhorrence) 21, 28–9, 31–2, 41, 44, 83, 121, 131, 192n5, 203

INDEX

Hügelmann, Karl 192n2, 206
Huhn, Thomas 206
Hund, William 164, 206
Hutcheson, Frances xii, 12–13, 15–16, 20–4, 27, 206

imagination (*Einbildungskraft*) xv, 5, 7–11, 14, 16–22, 24, 26, 29, 35, 37, 46–7, 70, 72, 74–5, 77–82, 84–6, 103, 108–9, 114–18, 121, 123, 128–35, 137, 146, 152–4, 156, 161, 171, 174, 180, 195n10, 198n7, 208
inclination(s) 8–9, 11, 19–20, 25, 37, 54, 59, 63, 65, 69–71, 82, 86–8, 91, 96, 98, 100–3, 105, 114–17, 124, 128–9, 139, 152, 155, 169–71, 175, 183, 197n22

judg(e)ment (*Urteil/Urteilskraft*) viii, x, xi, 4, 6, 9, 11–12, 14, 21, 27, 34–6, 38, 40, 44–5, 47, 51, 53–8, 65–71, 74–6, 78–87, 91, 95–7, 101, 106–9, 111, 113–14, 118–20, 122–3, 126, 128–9, 132, 134–40, 147–8, 150, 152, 162–3, 165, 168–71, 175–6, 186, 192n2, 193–4n2, 195n10, 195n17, 195–6n20, 197n22, 198n9, 201, 203–7, 209–10
  aesthetic 14, 27, 35–6, 47, 53–7, 67, 69, 75–6, 78–9, 81, 84–5, 95–6, 107, 113–14, 118, 120, 123, 140, 150, 152, 165, 170, 192n2, 193n2, 195–6n20, 201, 207
  determinative 58, 66, 68–9
  reflective xi, 51, 53–6, 58, 65, 67–71, 74, 79, 97, 136, 138, 150, 162, 193n2

Kant, Immanuel v, vii–xvi, 1, 3–30, 32–45, 47, 49, 51–140, 143–80, 182–3, 186–90, 191n1, 191nn1–2, 192nn1–3, 192n5, 192nn1–3, 193n5, 193–4n2, 194nn4–5, 195n12, 195n16, 195nn18–19, 195–6n20, 197nn22–3, 197n3, 198n8, 198n11, 199n4, 199nn6–7, 199n8, 199–200nn10–13, 201–10
  Anthropology from a Pragmatic Point of View (*Anthropologie in pragmatischer Absicht*) 15–16
  Critique of Judgment (CJ, third *Critique*, *Critique of the Power of Judgment* (Guyer translation), *Kritik der Urteilskraft*) viii, x–xi, xv, 4, 12, 14, 22, 26–9, 32, 34–7, 39–40, 53–8, 64–71, 73–5, 77–93, 96–101, 103–19, 123, 129, 131–8, 147, 152–4, 163, 166–7, 169, 170–2, 77, 186, 191n1, 192n2, 193n5, 193–4n2, 195n6, 195n10, 195n18, 196n20, 197n23, 198n7, 198n14, 205–7, 209–10
  Critique of Practical Reason (CPrR, second *Critique*, *Kritik der praktischen Vernunft*) viii, 16, 23, 71–2, 97, 101, 108, 114, 134–5, 206
  Critique of Pure Reason (CPR, first *Critique*, *Kritik der reinen Vernunft*) viii, 14, 39, 63, 85, 135, 195n19, 206
  Grounding for the Metaphysics of Morals (GMM, *Grundlegung zur Metaphysik der Sitten*) viii–ix, 16, 58–63, 68–71, 87–9, 97–9, 101–11, 114, 120, 123–9, 131, 134, 137, 149, 152, 194n4, 206
  Metaphysics of Morals (MM, *Die Metaphysik der Sitten*) viii, ix, 15, 16, 42, 55, 58, 97–9, 194n4, 206–7

Observations on the Feeling of the Beautiful and Sublime (OFBS, *Beobachtungen über das Gefühl des Schönen und Erhabenen*) viii, x, 4, 16, 28, 42, 98, 150, 194n2, 202, 207
Kearney, Richard 52, 195n7, 207
Kind, John Louis 207
Kirwan, James x, xi, 5, 16, 52, 74, 88, 94, 96, 106, 114, 143–4, 155, 173, 187, 192n1, 192n5, 200n13, 200n16, 207
Kuhns, Richard 52, 112, 207
Kupfer, Joseph H. 52, 207

Lacan, Jacques xv, 158, 162, 177, 179–82, 184, 187, 199n11, 200n20, 207, 210
Lazaroff Allan, 164, 206–7
Lindsay A. D., 207
Longinus v, viii, ix–x, xii, 3–13, 16, 18–19, 24–5, 27, 41–3, 46, 144, 164, 173, 191n2–n3, 201, 207
Lyotard, Jean–François xi–xii, 32, 44, 52, 74, 78, 93–5, 146, 162–4, 172–7, 182–4, 187–8, 195n8, 197n2, 199n11, 200n13, 200nn16–17, 201, 206–9

Makkreel, Rudolf 52, 130, 164, 198n11, 208
Malter, Rudolf 192n2, 206, 208
de Man, Paul 155, 162, 164, 173, 199n8, 204, 208
Mendelssohn, Moses xii, 4, 12–13, 28, 34, 36–8, 40–1, 44–7, 193n5, 203, 208, 210
Miles, Thomas H. 191n2, 203
Monk, Samuel 5, 191n2, 208
Moore, Jared S. 78, 143–4, 208
moral feeling xiii, 15–16, 23, 32, 52, 64, 68, 72–3, 77, 86–7, 93–6, 98, 101, 104, 106–14, 120, 123, 126, 129, 152, 173, 197n4, 198n9

Nahm, M. C. 16, 52, 208
Nancy, Jean–Luc 146, 162, 164, 208
nature xv, 4, 8–11, 14, 18, 20–1, 23–9, 31, 34, 37, 41, 46, 53–4, 56–64, 66–9, 71–2, 75, 77, 80–6, 89–92, 95–7, 99, 102–5, 107–8, 110–13, 115, 117–22, 124–7, 131–40, 145–54, 156, 158–63, 165, 168–9, 171–2, 174, 176, 191n2, 193n5, 194n2, 195–6n20, 199n5, 202, 206, 208
Neill, Elizabeth 52, 208
Newman, Barnett 146, 162–3
Nuyen, A. T. 52, 74, 195n7, 208

Pacholec, Matthew 174, 208
pain 16, 18–22, 24–5, 27–9, 35, 46, 71, 100, 119, 123, 129, 132, 192n5, 196n20
passions 5–6, 8–10, 17, 19, 21–2, 24, 26, 28–9, 31, 37, 46–7, 116, 175, 206
Pillow, Kirk 52, 94, 96, 106, 130, 173, 193n1, 208
pleasure (and displeasure) 7, 10–11, 16–25, 27–9, 34–5, 46–7, 56, 74, 76–7, 79–83, 86–9, 91–2, 96–7, 105–6, 108–10, 112–15, 117–18, 123, 129, 149, 151–4, 156, 169–71, 174–5, 180, 192n5, 196n20, 197n22, 198n6

reason (*Vernunft*) viii, xi, 5–11, 14, 16–21, 23–4, 26, 28, 34, 36, 38, 41, 43–5, 53–4, 57–70, 72, 74–5, 77, 79–83, 86–90, 92, 94, 96–8, 100, 103–6, 108–9, 111–19, 121, 123–5, 127–9, 131, 135–40, 146, 148–9, 152–5, 161, 164–6, 170–71, 174, 176–7, 180, 183, 192n1, 195n15, 195n19, 196n21, 197n22, 198n7, 199n4, 206
Recki, Birgit 52, 69, 94, 106, 195n7, 208

representation (*Vorstellung*) xiv, 5–6, 9, 27, 35–6, 38–9, 56, 60–1, 64, 70, 79–80, 83–5, 87, 89, 92, 101–2, 109, 111, 115–16, 118, 124, 129, 131, 135–7, 146, 152, 155–7, 164–7, 170, 176, 178, 182, 184–5, 195–6nn19–20, 197n24, 200n18, 205, 209
respect (*Achtung*) xiii, 25, 30, 32, 52, 54, 56, 63–5, 67, 70–3, 77, 81–2, 86–7, 91–4, 96, 98–111, 113–16, 126, 129, 135–40, 150, 161, 165, 173, 175–6, 186, 197nn2–3
Ross, Alison 176, 208
Rotenstreich, Nathan 208
Rueger, Alexander 209
Rush, Fred 93, 209

Saxena, S. K. 199n8, 209
Schiller, Friedrich 53, 145–51, 158, 173, 179, 187, 198–9nn3–5, 202, 205, 209
Schmidt, James 40, 209
Schopenhauer, Arthur 78, 209
sensibility (*Sinnlichkeit*) 5, 8, 10, 21, 26, 37, 39, 46, 62, 67–8, 80–1, 83, 89, 92, 100, 104, 111, 115–19, 121, 128–30, 134–6, 146, 170–1, 174, 199n4
Shaw, Philip 5, 9–10, 18, 20, 26–7, 29–32, 146, 162, 164, 173, 175–80, 182, 184, 192n5, 200n22, 209
Silverman, Hugh J. 176, 204, 209
sublime
 dynamical, 4, 10, 19, 36, 47, 51, 55–6, 79–80, 93, 130–4, 136–7, 151–2, 159, 198n11
 mathematical, 4, 19, 36, 47, 51, 55–6, 71, 79–80, 93, 104, 130, 132–7, 152, 159, 166–7, 187, 192n1
Sulzer, J. G. 29, 37, 209

Teale, A. E. 209
terror 19, 24, 27–32, 113, 131–2, 146–7, 175–6, 187–9, 200n22, 207–8
Tonelli, Giorgio 37, 193n2, 209
Trifonova, Temenuga 174, 209

understanding (*Verstand*) 5, 14, 16–19, 35, 38–9, 47, 55, 60, 62–3, 66–7, 74–5, 79, 83, 85–7, 111, 116, 118, 120, 123, 126, 128, 133, 137, 192n1, 195n19, 199n4, 208

violence 5, 10, 22, 41, 44, 71, 74, 80–2, 92, 96, 105, 115, 117, 121–2, 130–2, 134, 136, 147, 159, 170–1, 174, 176, 185, 199n5

Weiskel, Thomas 8, 209
Wenzel, Christian Helmut 192n2, 209
Wicks, Robert 52, 74, 193n1, 205, 209
Will, Frederick 210
will, the (*Wille*) 59–65, 69–70, 77–8, 85–7, 92, 101–3, 105–6, 109–11, 114, 119, 124–7, 132, 147, 154, 182–3
Willkür 64–5, 132, 183
 translated as 'Power of Choice' or 'Faculty of Choice' 37, 64–5, 116
Williams, Howard vii
Wilson, Jeffrey 69, 88, 195n7, 210
Wood, Theodore E. B. 4–5, 191nn2–3, 196n21, 210

Young, Edward 12, 15–16, 20, 23–4, 27, 38, 192n4, 207, 210

Zammito, John H. 13–14, 16, 28, 36–9, 44, 52, 57, 73, 88, 94,

97–8, 192n3, 192n1, 192n3,
193–4n2, 195n7, 195n9, 197n1,
197n4, 205, 209–10
Žižek, Slavoj 32, 44, 74, 146, 155,
158, 162–4, 173, 177–88,
199n11, 200n19, 200n21,
210
Zuckert, Rachel 27, 29, 52,
104–5, 130, 151, 153–4, 162–3,
210